A GARLAND OF SILVER

A GARLAND OF SILVER

A JUBILEE ANTHOLOGY
– IN HONOUR OF ARCHBISHOP MARIO CONTI –

edited by
TONY SCHMITZ

with a preface by
HIS EXCELLENCY ARCHBISHOP PABLO PUENTE

THE OGILVIE PRESS

Copyright © Ogilvie Institute

First published Great Britain in 2002 by
THE OGILVIE PRESS
16 Huntly Street
Aberdeen AB10 1SH

www.ogilvie.ac.uk

British Library Cataloguing-in-Publication Data
A CIP catalogue record for this book is available from the British Library

ISBN 0954259505

CONTENTS

PREFACE

His Excellency Archbishop Pablo Puente,
Apostolic Nuncio

It is with much pleasure that I have accepted the request to provide a short preface for Archbishop Conti's Silver Jubilee Festschrift.

My first meeting with Archbishop Mario Conti was in November 1997 when I was invited to attend the Bishops' Conference of Scotland. I had a little earlier been appointed as Apostolic Nuncio to Great Britain, and this was my first opportunity to meet with the Scottish Bishops.

My first impression of Archbishop Conti, and one that has remained with me, is of a man of exceptional openness, sincerity, humility and deep apostolic zeal. He has many qualities that have endeared him to so many people: qualities among which are his warm nature, his goodness and intelligence, his unwavering commitment to the people entrusted to his care, and his dedication to furthering ecumenical dialogue.

It was therefore with great pleasure that, in January 2002, I informed him of his new appointment by the Holy Father: that of Archbishop of Glasgow, an office which had been vacant since the death of Cardinal Thomas Winning in June 2002.

Archbishop Conti has an exceptional personality and the Holy Father has full confidence in his abilities to lead the Archdiocese of Glasgow. I am sure that he will continue to further the spiritual and pastoral well being of his people, and to continue to speak out for those who have no voice, the underprivileged and the defenceless.

On his Twenty-fifth Anniversary of episcopate, I offer my heartfelt prayers and best wishes to him for a long, happy and fruitful pastoral ministry.

+ Pablo Puente

Archbishop Pablo Puente
Apostolic Nuncio

EDITOR'S INTRODUCTION

This volume, as both the title and subtitle indicate, is a collection of essays offered as a tribute to mark the twenty-fifth anniversary of the episcopal ordination of its recipient. The book was conceived when the jubilarian was Bishop of the Diocese of Aberdeen. In the interval between the commissioning of the essays and their publication and presentation Bishop Mario was translated to the Archbishopric of Glasgow.

The lot of a *Festschrift* editor is often considered a vexatious one demanding unusual patience. That has not obtained in this instance. My burden has been light and the yoke did not chafe. Our nine months of gestation have in fact been virtually trouble-free. That this was so is thanks to a number of people. At the outset of the project I sought the counsel of a small but select editorial committee. Dr Leslie Macfarlane, doyen of medievalists in Scotland, agreed to serve on our committee, as did Canon Peter Moran, the Aberdeen Diocesan Administrator, and also Rev Stuart Chalmers and Mrs Eileen Grant, who gave unstintingly of her time both to secretarial support and to the copy-editing of the texts as they came in from the contributors. I thank them all for their advice and their work.

But it was above all the prompt and unfailingly gracious response from each of the essayists that has made editing this collection such a pleasure. Each remembers Archbishop Mario with affection and each was ready to find time, in a busy life, to pen an essay to a tight deadline on the subject proposed. The writers are all expert in their subjects which are reflective of the wide-ranging areas in which Archbishop Mario has taken an interest and has made a significant contribution during his twenty-five years as bishop. It scarcely needs to be added that the limitations of a collection such as this allow us to cover only a dozen or so of these interests and involvements. Thus it is to be regretted, for example, that more could not be included on the visual arts or sacred music. To all of the essayists I am profoundly grateful for their alacrity and kindly cooperation. I would also wish to thank the well-known Aberdeen artist Pauline Jacobsen who designed and lettered the front cover of the volume.

All *Festschriften* – whether they are written in honour of a retiring professor or to mark the silver jubilee of a bishop who has served so well his diocese and the universal Church and also the civic society in which he lived – require some form of subvention to be enabled to see the light of publication. This one could not have been published without the generous support of the following friends and benefactors: the Honourable Mrs Susan Buchan; Lt Col & Mrs Robert Campbell; Dowager Countess Cawdor; Messrs Craigens of Aberdeen; Mr & Mrs Gerry Cunningham; Sir Archie and Lady Amelia Dunbar; the Honourable Mr & Mrs Hugo Fraser; Mr & Mrs Michael Fraser; the Edinburgh Morayshire Club; Mr & Mrs Rick Hoskins; Messrs Hayes & Finch; Sir Harold and Lady Hood; Lady Innes of Edingight; Monsignor Robert McDonald; Sheriff Principal John Maguire; Mr Christopher Methven; Mr & Mrs David Moss; Messrs T & R O'Brien of Glasgow; the Earl of Perth; Pluscarden Abbey; Messrs Ritsons of Elgin; Mrs Gail Schmitz; the Bank of Scotland; the Scottish Friends of the Foyers of Charity; and Mr & Mrs Tony Ward.

Finally I should like to thank warmly the Right Reverend Hugh Gilbert OSB, Abbot of Pluscarden Abbey, which was often acknowledged by Archbishop Mario as the contemplative heart of the diocese. Besides writing the fine short essay on the jubilarian's episcopal motto, it was Abbot Hugh who had the original idea that such a tribute as this should be gathered and presented.

TONY SCHMITZ

SEPTEMBER 2002

Tony Schmitz is Director of the Ogilvie Institute, Aberdeen. He was recently ordained Permanent Deacon.

Most Rev. Mario J. Conti
A Biographical Note

Canon Peter A. Moran

Mario Giuseppe (or Joseph) Conti was born in Elgin, cathedral city of the ancient diocese of Moray, on 20th March 1934, the first of two children of Louis Conti and Giuseppina Quintilia Panicali. His parents ran a café in the town, where his father's brother was a carpenter. (Mario's grandparents had come to Britain from Barga, in Tuscany, where the Caproni cousins still live.) The young Mario attended the Mercy Sisters' school (Saint Marie's) in Abbey Street, Elgin, adjacent to the ancient Greyfriars monastery, restored some forty years earlier by the Crichton-Stuarts; and the Springfield school. At the age of twelve he entered Blairs College, just west of Aberdeen, the Junior Seminary for Scotland which traced its line directly to the remote school founded at Scalan in Glenlivet in 1714.

Hardly had he left home when his father died unexpectedly. In later years Mario was to recall with gratitude the understanding and support he received from the seminary staff, particularly from Father John A. Sheridan ("the Baxter" to his pupils). His mother sold up the Elgin business and, with her daughter Stella, moved to Solihull, Birmingham, where three other Panicali sisters were already living. Thus, when the young seminarian went home for summer holidays (the only holidays at home allowed in those days) those months were spent in Birmingham.

Apart from the secondary school subjects studied at Blairs College, where the curriculum at that time was decidedly classical (and where a group of Cambridge University graduates were prominent among the all-priest staff), Mario Conti showed a distinct aptitude for the visual arts and also became a competent violinist.

In 1952, after six years at Blairs, he was assigned to the Pontifical Scots College in Rome, where he and four other "Blairentians" met two further recruits who had come from Catholic day schools in the West of Scotland. The seven entrants began a three-year course for the Licentiate in Philosophy. The lectures (and the oral examinations) at the Pontifical Gregorian University were conducted entirely in Latin, as was daily Mass in those pre-Second Vatican Council days, but life at a more informal level within the Scots College itself was conducted in a mixture of Scots and English.

This college life ran for two years and nine months before the students had their first holiday back in Britain: term-time was spent in the Via Quattro Fontane on the slopes of the Quirinal Hill, while in the summer holiday months the college community moved to the summer house among the vineyards near the village of Marino, between Castelgandolfo, with its Papal villa, and Frascati, with its memories of Cardinal Henry Benedict Stuart, younger brother of Bonnie Prince Charlie. Even during term-time it was not all study. During the autumn term the students prepared a modified version of a different Gilbert and Sullivan operetta each year and gave several performances during the Christmas holidays for guests from English-speaking colleges and embassies. The artist in Mario Conti was called on to design and paint the stage sets – though he also appeared among the actors.

Surrounded as he was, however, by the churches, the museums and the *palazzi* of medieval and Renaissance Rome, to say nothing of the classical remains in the *Forum Romanum* and elsewhere, Mario found his interest in art and heritage nourished and developed at every turn and he became very knowledgeable, especially about painting and architecture.

The following four years (with one further holiday at home) led to the Licentiate in Theology, but also to the Sub-diaconate, the Diaconate and, on 26th October 1958, while he was still an undergraduate, ordination as a priest.

His first, and only, appointment as an assistant was at the Cathedral in Aberdeen with Canon John Lewis McWilliam who would go on to serve eighteen years under his former apprentice and die in harness at the age of ninety. Then, in 1962, when his contemporaries in the larger dioceses were still lowly "junior curates", Father Mario Conti was made Parish Priest not just of Wick but of the entire county of Caithness. It was, and remains, an isolated posting, remote in summer and sometimes entirely cut off in winter. There he ministered to fisherfolk on the East coast and also to the new arrivals who swelled the population of Thurso as they came to work in the atomic energy station at Dounreay on the North coast. He oversaw the transfer of the priest's residence to Thurso and installed the Sisters of La Sainte Union in the presbytery at Wick. He made friendly contacts with other churches and was active in the community.

But his competence and his pastoral diligence did not go unnoticed. Fifteen years later he was called to London in connection with the choice of a successor when Bishop Foylan died, and to his own surprise found himself appointed, a month short of his forty-third birthday, as bishop of his native diocese, and came to live in the city of Aberdeen. He was to serve there for almost twenty-five years, longer than any of his post-Reformation predecessors except Bishop George Bennett (1918-1946).

As bishop of a diocese spread over an enormous section of Scotland, from coast to Cairngorms to the Northern Isles, Bishop Mario displayed the energy and commitment necessary for constant long-distance visitation of his diocese. He also tackled with vigour the problem of considerable reduction in clergy numbers, by skilfully "juggling" priests, borrowing from other dioceses and inviting a steady stream of Jesuits to come north, plus a Carmelite presence in the Chaplaincy to Aberdeen University. He introduced with enthusiasm the Permanent Diaconate, leaving behind on his translation to Glasgow, twelve Permanent Deacons, with more in the pipeline. He has long been a doughty fighter for Catholic Religious Education provision in non-denominational schools, a provision which he saw as vital in an area that has very few Catholic primary schools and no Catholic secondary schools.

Bishop Mario was acutely aware of the importance of cultivating friendly contacts with the secular world, both locally and nationally. He has been at the forefront of developing ecumenical relations and instituting new ecumenical structures and instruments: he was the first President of ACTS (Action of Churches Together in Scotland) and has been co-chairman of the Joint Committee of the Catholic Church and the World Council of Churches, travelling to the recent World Council of Churches assembly in Harare in 1998. He has never been afraid to speak up on behalf of the underprivileged in our society and in defence of the most vulnerable in our midst, writing frequently to the press, especially on pro-life issues or on bioethics, an area on which he is particularly well-informed, having served on the National Joint Committee on Bioethics since its inception. This Committee is the first instance of a joint initiative of the three Bishops' Conferences of Scotland, Ireland and England and Wales.

Known throughout Scotland for his enthusiasm for cultural heritage Bishop Mario never lost his interest in this field and cultivated it with vigour, as a member of the Pontifical Commission for Cultural Heritage (*per i beni culturalii*) and as President of the Scottish Catholic Heritage Commission. One of his most satisfying moments must have been when a project very close to his heart, the Blairs Museum, was opened in May, 2000. He has always been a stalwart and well-informed defender of historic diocesan sites and buildings. He has also maintained an awareness of, and pride in, his Italian ancestry and connections, especially with the *Comune* of Barga in Tuscany; and on the diocesan pilgrimage to Rome during the Millennium year he delighted pilgrims with his knowledge and love of the art treasures in Roman churches.

In recognition of his many achievements and enthusiasms, Bishop Mario has received several academic and similar awards: *Commendatore* in 1981; an honorary doctorate from Aberdeen University in 1989; a Fellowship of the Royal Society of Edinburgh; and many others. As a tribute for his Silver Jubilee and in recognition of his years of work and prominence in the city, the University of Aberdeen this year awarded him an Honorary Chair in Divinity, in Catholic Studies. Aberdeen's loss is undoubtedly Glasgow's gain.

Canon Peter A. Moran is Parish Priest in Inverurie and is currently Diocesan Administrator pending the appointment of a new bishop. He studied in Rome at the same time as Archbishop Mario and was his companion on their daily walks to the Gregorian University.

SINCERO CORDE SERVIRE
ORIGINS AND MEANINGS OF A MOTTO

ABBOT HUGH GILBERT O.S.B.

"It was the motto of a bishop eminent for his piety and good works in King Charles II's reign, *Inservi Deo et laetari,* Serve God and be cheerful." So wrote Joseph Addison early in the eighteenth century. The not dissimilar *Sincero corde servire,* "To serve with a sincere heart", has been since 1977 the motto of another bishop "eminent for his piety and good works", Mario Conti, now Archbishop of Glasgow and this year celebrating the silver jubilee of his episcopal ordination. Phrases often have more history and resonance than first appears, and this brief essay hopes to pay tribute to our jubilarian by exploring a little of his motto's background and meaning.

The phrase itself is drawn from the Roman Missal. It is not directly biblical (though comprised of strongly biblical words), nor, following a word search, does it appear to exist, as such, in any other Latin Christian source. Specifically, it consists of the concluding three words of what is now the Collect or Opening Prayer of the Twenty-ninth Sunday of Ordinary Time (*Tempus per annum*):[1]

> Omnipotens sempiterne Deus,
> Fac nos tibi semper et devotam tibi gerere voluntatem,
> Et maiestati tuae *sincero corde servire.*

> Almighty, eternal God,
> Make us always both to have a will devoted to you,

---

[1] *Missale Romanum* (1975), p.368

And to serve your majesty with a sincere heart.[2]

Like many another collect, this one is lapidary,
balanced and focussed upon essentials. It ranks, however,
among the more austere, and could be overlooked. That,
though, would be to miss some things of value, and not
least the final phrase: *sincero corde servire*.

First, a word of history. This prayer is, as mentioned,
one of the thirty-four provided for the Sundays and weeks
of Ordinary Time in the Missal of Paul VI. Almost all of
these prayers, however, have roots in the early formative
period of the Roman liturgy, usually dated from the late
fourth to seventh centuries of the Christian era, and this
prayer is no exception. It is first found in the so-called
Gelasian or Old Gelasian Sacramentary, a book for the
use of celebrants, generally regarded as a reliable witness
to the liturgy as celebrated in the parish churches of Rome
in the seventh century. Much of the material in it will
already have been traditional, and our own prayer has
been ascribed to the late sixth century.[3] Beyond that,
precision eludes us, and no author can be named.

---

[2]The ICEL translation runs as follows: "Almighty and ever-living
God, our source of power and inspiration, give us strength and joy in
serving you as followers of Christ." This may be politely described as
embarrassing. The rendering in *The Divine Office*, where this prayer is
also used, is preferable: "Almighty, ever-living God, make us ever
obey you willingly and promptly. Teach us how to serve you with
sincere and upright hearts in every sphere of life."
[3] By A. Chavasse. Cf. G. Moore, *Vatican II and the Collects for Ordinary
Time. A study in the Roman Missal (1975)*, (San Francisco: International
Scholars Publications, 1998), p.295.

Of the three places in which this prayer features in the Gelasian, it is probably the first that is most significant:[4] viz, as an opening prayer for the Mass of the Fifth Sunday *post clausum Paschae*, i.e. after the Easter Octave. It is also as an Eastertide collect – for the Sunday after the Ascension – that our prayer appears in the *Gregorian* Sacramentaries, those books which reflect the Roman liturgy of the same period as celebrated by the bishop of the City, the Pope himself, and were, with the Gelasian, to have such a future north of the Alps.[5] Early in the ninth century, it was incorporated by St Benedict of Aniane into his supplement to the *Hadrianum* Gregorian, again as a prayer for the Sunday after the Ascension, and from then on would float serenely along the mainstream of medieval and post-medieval euchology. Thus it appears in thirteenth century missals of the Curial tradition, in the first printed Roman Missal of 1474,[6] and in the Missal of St Pius V from 1570 onwards.[7] As a matter of Scottish interest, it also features in the so-called Arbuthnott missal of 1491[8] – an indication that this prayer would have been

---

[4] Nn. 561, 1210, 1264 in the edition of L.C. Mohlberg, L. Eizenhöfer, P. Siffrin, *Liber sacramentorum Romanae Ecclesiae ordinis anni circuli* (Rome, 1960)

[5] For full references to the prayer's appearances in the medieval sacramentaries, cf. E. Moeller, J.M. Clement, B. Coppieters 't Wallent (eds), *Corpus Orationum*, T. VI (Turnhout, 1995), pp.62-63.

[6] *Missalis Romani Editio Princeps, Mediolani Anno 1474 Prelis Mandata,* curantibus A. Ward & C. Johnson (Rome, 1996), n.1184.

[7] *Missale Romanum, Editio Princeps (1570),* a cura di Manlio Sodi & Achille Maria Triacca (Vatican City, 1998), n.1733. Cf. also C. Johnson & A. Ward (eds), *Missale Romanum anno 1962 promulgatum, reimpressio introductione aucta* (Rome,1994), n.1292.

[8] A.P. Forbes (ed.), *Liber Ecclesiae beati Terrenani de Arbuthnott, missale secundum usum Ecclesiae sancti Andreae in Scotia,* p.194.

in regular use, on its allotted Sunday, throughout the medieval dioceses of Scotland.

The 1970 Missal of Paul VI brought with it a revised *Collectarium*, or collection of opening prayers. The Sunday after the Ascension, now become the Seventh Sunday of Easter, was equipped with a prayer of great beauty and appositeness found in the Verona Sacramentary for the Ascension itself.[9] Our prayer, in turn, became one of five from the former Sundays after Easter to be transferred to the Sundays of Ordinary Time.[10] It is also one of nine taken from the Eastertide Masses of the Gelasian Sacramentary and now gracing the "Ordinary" Sundays of the year.[11]

What of the content of the prayer? As mentioned above, it is austere even for a collect. It opens with the standard and simple formula of address to God: *Omnipotens sempiterne Deus*, and proceeds abruptly, without any expanding subordinate clause, to the business of petition. Nor is the petition itself followed by any "purpose clause". The full weight of the prayer, therefore, falls upon the petition, which is twofold:

> fac nos tibi semper
>> et devotam gerere voluntatem
>> et maiestati tuae *sincero corde servire.*

This is Latin praying of great elegance and eloquence. The petition opens with two monosyllables, *fac nos*, then gathers momentum with *tibi* and *semper* and continues with

[9]L.C. Mohlberg, L. Eizenhöfer, P. Siffrin (eds.), *Sacramentarium Veronense* (Rome, 1956), n.169.
[10]The other instances are the prayers for Sundays 10, 14, 15 and 21.
[11]The prayers for Sundays 6, 10, 11, 12, 14, 15, 21, 23 and 29.

the tri-syllables of *devotam* and *gerere* to crescendo with *voluntatem* and *maiestati*. *Sincero corde servire* thus functions with its pattern of 3-2-3 as a gentle *rallentando*.[12]

At the level of meaning, the two elements of petition are parallel one to another: the bearing towards God of a devoted (i.e. dedicated or committed) will and the service of his majesty springing from a sincere heart. Yet, at the same time, we can see a certain movement from within to without: from the dedicated will sincere service will follow, as a natural and practical expression. The prayer embraces both the inner and the outer. Both, however, are fully the gift, the doing, of God himself: *fac nos*. No Pelagianism here! Both, too, are *always* (*semper*) desirable.

What we seem to have here is a quiet transposition to the whole Christian people of the exhortation to slaves that comes towards the end of the Letter to the Ephesians:

> Slaves (*servi*), obey your masters with fear and trembling, in singleness of heart (*insimplicitate cordis*), as you obey Christ; not only while being watched, and in order to please them, but as slaves of Christ, doing the will of God from the heart(*facientes voluntatem Dei ex animo*). Render service with enthusiasm (*cum bono voluntate servientes*), as to the Lord and not to men, knowing that whatever good any one does, he will receive again the same from the Lord, whether he is a slave or free. (Eph.6:5-8)

The parallels of thought and vocabulary are surely striking.

And what of the final three words? They are, perhaps, the most appealing to modern ears. Clearly, priority goes

---

[12] The phrase also obeys the rhetorical device of the *cursus*, in this case the *cursus velox*.

to the last, the verb, *servire, sincero corde* functioning as qualifier. Yet, in "service" we have a word so familiar that we can easily delude ourselves into thinking we know what it means, especially as our current instincts are always to interpret it "horizontally", in terms of serving one another. A first clue to its meaning here lies in its object: *maiestati tuae.* This is a service, then, directed towards God, and specifically towards his *maiestas,* majesty. In the Christian Latin of the period to which this prayer originally belongs, *maiestas* evoked particularly the glory (Greek *doxa,* Hebrew *kabod*), power and name of God.[13] It is not too fanciful to see here an implicit allusion to Isaiah's Temple vision of God's glory and the service of the Seraphim.[14] What is more, *servire* itself, in the context of a prayer such as this, has a primarily religious and thus derivatively liturgical sense. A glance at a concordance of liturgical Latin reveals that, in the great majority of cases, *servire* has God himself as its immediate object, and when not, then it is frequently God's "altars" (*alteribus tuis*) or "mysteries" (*mysteriis tuis*) which are the focus of our serving.[15] "In classical Latin, the verb *servire* is applied to the actions of worshippers who offer service to the gods",[16] and the Christians, who had "turned to God from idols, to serve (*servire*) a living and true God"(1 Thess.1:9), were not ashamed to follow this usage. In the phrase before us, then, the sincere service envisaged and for which the prayer is asking is above all that service which the petitioners themselves are in the very act of beginning:

[13] Cf. G. Moore, *op. cit.*, p.299, and footnote 16.
[14] Cf. B. Botte and C. Mohrmann, *L'Ordinaire de la Messe: texte critique, traduction et études* (Paris, 1953), pp.112-113.
[15] Cf. J. Deshusses & B. Darragon, *Concordances et tableaux pour l'étude des grands sacramentaires* (Fribourg, 1982-83), T. III, 4 pp.222-224.
[16] G. Moore, *op. cit.*, p.212f.

divine worship. This interpretation is, in turn, corroborated by the qualifying *sincero corde*. *Sincerus* – famously derived from *sine cera*, "without wax", thus of one strong material throughout – "denotes that disposition of mind and heart which is willingly open and wholeheartedly devoted to what is justifying in the sight of God. It, too, is especially linked with worship".[17] Nor is there need to say that the undivided heart – *cor* – is precisely the place whence worship in spirit and truth can be made. Commenting on James 1:27, "religion that is pure …", Ps-Hilary glosses "pure" (*munda*) with *sincero corde*,[18] and St Bede will speak of those who "serve the Lord in unity and chastity and celebrate his feast with a sincere heart (*sincero corde celebrarent*)."[19] These are small signposts, but they point in similar directions: the service for which this prayer asks is that of a pure and wholehearted *worship* of God, especially within the liturgical functions themselves.

Biblical parallels are not far to seek:

> But the hour is coming, and is now here, when the true worshippers will worship the Father in spirit and in truth, for the Father seeks such as these to worship him. God is spirit, and those who worship him must worship in spirit and in truth. (Jn.4:23-24)

Sincero corde servire, then, within this original context, primarily means to *worship* with a sincere heart: to worship the Father in spirit and in truth, to keep the Christian

---

[17] *Idem*, p. 299.

[18] Ps-Hilary of Arles, *Tractatus in septem epistulas catholicas* (CCSL 108B), *In epist. Iacobi*, 1. 314.

[19] Bede the Venerable, *In Ezram et Neemiam* (CCSL 119A), II, 11. 674-676.

pasch (this is originally a paschaltide prayer!) with sincerity and truth. This, of course, has a wider field than liturgical celebrations; rather, these latter function as "source and summit" of an attitude and activity characterising the whole Christian life.

Servire, however, has other connotations too, and they include that of the fulfilment of one's *ordo* or office within the body of the Church.[20] Here another perspective opens. A clear example of this usage is found in a Good Friday prayer from the same Gelasian Sacramentary (also maintained in the Missal of Paul VI):[21]

Omnipotens sempiterne Deus,
cuius spiritu totum corpus ecclesiae sanctificatur et regitur,
exaudi nos pro universes ordinibus supplicantes,
ut gratiae tuae munere ab omnibus fideliter serviatur.

Almighty, eternal God,
by whose Spirit the whole body of the Church is sanctified and ruled,
hear us praying for every order [within it],
so that by the gift of your grace, it may be served faithfully by all.

Here the service, sustained by divine grace, has the Church as its object and consists precisely in the accomplishment of the duties flowing from one's *ordo*, or allotted function, within the body of the Church. Romans 12:3ff; 1 Corinthians 12:4ff; Ephesians 4:7ff provide the theological background. It might seem a little forced to

---

[20] G. Moore, *op. cit.*, p.212.
[21] *Liber sacramentorum* etc. (fn. 4 above), n.405.

apply this connotation to our own prayer, yet it can function as a pointer to a further layer of meaning. The concept of fulfilling one's *ordo* (or, as the Second Vatican Council would say, *munus*) on behalf of the whole Body is, radically, a Pauline one, and our phrase's own combination of "service" and "sincerity" inevitably conjures up the image of Paul the Apostle, who saw himself so clearly as the servant/slave (*doulos, servus*) of Christ or God (Rom.1:1; Gal.1:10; Phil.1:1; Tit.1:1), and on two crucial occasions in 2 Corinthians, claimed sincerity (Greek *eilikrineia*) as an authenticating mark of his ministry. While *sincero corde servire* is not an immediately biblical phrase, it expresses a distinctly Pauline ambition

> Indeed this is our boast, the testimony of our conscience: we have behaved in the world with frankness and godly sincerity [literally: the sincerity of God], not by earthly wisdom but by the grace of God — and all the more towards you. (2 Cor.1:12)

> For we are not pedlars of God's word like so many; but in Christ we speak as persons of sincerity, as persons sent from God and standing in his presence. (2 Cor.2:17)

As Ceslas Spicq comments, "there is no higher way of describing the apostolic faithfulness, which can be referred to Mt.5:37 ('Let your yes be yes, your no, no'); but more precisely, the contrast with falsifications indicates that Paul neither adds to nor subtracts from the message received from the Lord. He transmits it whole, without adding heterogeneous elements, without mixing in his own personal ideas. He only gives voice to what he has heard from the Master and his first apostles. That is why he is trustworthy."[22]

More generally, "NT *eilikrineia* is 'perfect purity' and describes the mind, heart, one's conduct. Better yet, it describes Christian existence in its relation to God and to people. It is not so much the absence of duplicity or hypocrisy as a fundamental integrity and transparency; it can be compared to innocence, the candour of children, to whom the kingdom of heaven belongs."[23]

Sincero corde servire, then, on this reading, asks for a commitment to one's ecclesial responsibilities unmixed with secondary considerations, integral, transparent, after the image and likeness of that great servant of Christ and the Church, St Paul. Nor is it hard, especially for anyone who presides at liturgical celebrations, to integrate this meaning with that outlined above. A bishop, for example, is surely most fulfilling his *ordo* and most effectively serving the Church precisely when engaged in the liturgical worship of the divine majesty. He is at his most "apostolic" when most "angelic", closest to Paul when closest to the Seraphim of the *Sanctus*.

Finally, one can hardly overlook the "heart". *Sincere servire* would not have the depth of *sincero corde servire*. The whole "inner man" is being summoned to involvement in worship and ecclesial service: affectivity and love, mind and will. It is out of this "centre", this "pure heart" (Mt.5:8), which refuses to "serve" two masters (cf Mt.6:24; Lk.16:13), that the "almighty and eternal God" will make (*fac*) true service spring.

---

[22] C. Spicq, *Theological Lexicon of the New Testament* (Peabody, 1994), Vol.I, p.423.
[23] *Ibid.*

Clearly, any phrase such as *sincero corde servire*, once taken from its context, takes on a life of its own. This is natural and right. The prayer and experience of the motto-bearer himself may well uncover further meanings within it, some perhaps inalienably personal. What has been offered here is simply an interpretation in context, that is, in the original context of an ancient prayer of the Latin liturgical tradition, that great part of our Catholic heritage. A paraphrase of this interpretation might go as follows: to serve God by worshipping him, celebrating the liturgy, and accomplishing one's mission within the Church with a heart and from a depth that is pure and whole. Such a reading, we like to think, cannot be far from the heart and mind of our distinguished jubilarian.

Abbot Hugh Gilbert O.S.B. studied history at King's College, University of London. In 1974 he entered the Benedictine monastery of Pluscarden where he was solemnly professed in 1979 and ordained priest in 1982. In 1992, he was elected as their second Abbot. He has a particular interest in the liturgy and, as Abbot of Pluscarden, has nurtured the rich beauty of the Church's liturgical heritage.

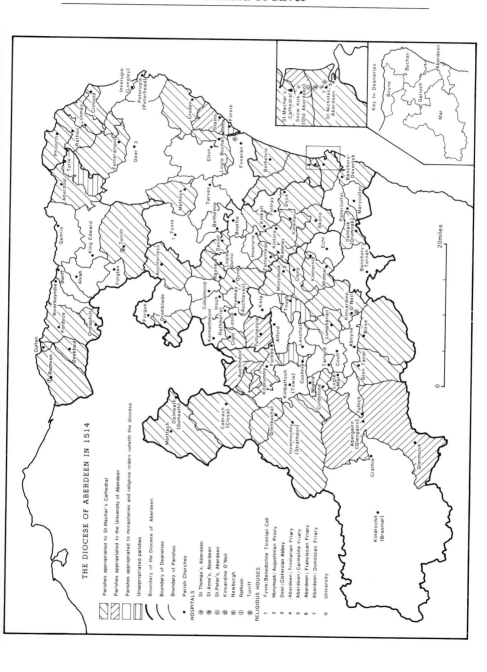

THE DIOCESE OF ABERDEEN IN 1514

Parishes appropriated to St.Machar's Cathedral

Parishes appropriated to the University of Aberdeen

Parishes appropriated to monasteries and religious orders outwith the diocese

Unappropriated parishes

Boundary of the Diocese of Aberdeen

Boundary of Deaneries

Boundary of Parishes

• Parish Churches

HOSPITALS

ⓐ St Thomas's, Aberdeen
ⓑ St Anne's, Aberdeen
ⓒ St Peter's, Aberdeen
ⓓ Kincardine O'Neil
ⓔ Newburgh
ⓕ Rathven
ⓖ Turriff

RELIGIOUS HOUSES

1 Fyvie:Benedictine Tironian Cell
2 Monymusk:Augustinian Priory
3 Deer:Cistercian Abbey
4 Aberdeen:Trinitarian Friary
5 Aberdeen:Carmelite Friary
6 Aberdeen:Franciscan Friary
7 Aberdeen:Dominican Friary
U University

Key to Deaneries

20 miles

The Medieval Diocese of Aberdeen
1131 - 1560

Dr Leslie Macfarlane

Although literary evidence is now widely available to show that Celtic missionaries were Christianising the area between the rivers Spey and Dee by the end of the sixth century, the diocese of Aberdeen was not formally established until 1131, when the centre of the ancient See was moved from Mortlach to Old Aberdeen following the papal reforms of Gregory VII and the subsequent reorganisation of the Scottish Church by David I. Charters then begin to show the extent of royal and other gifts of land and rents to be held by the Cathedral as free alms in perpetuity, in addition to which papal and royal letters in the twelfth and early thirteenth century confirm the Cathedral's earliest privileges: fishing and milling rights, and its exemptions from tolls and taxes. A separate series of episcopal registers also now begins to be compiled which delineate the organisation of the diocese and the duties and stipends of its canons and parish clergy. In short, what we are beginning to see with all this burgeoning of Cathedral records from 1131 onwards is the gradual absorption of the diocese of Aberdeen into the legal and administrative structure of the Western Church as a whole, of which the Scottish Church was now firmly an integral part. The boundaries of the diocese, too, now become definable. As shown in the accompanying map of the diocese, they follow the coast northwards from Old Aberdeen as far round as Rathven, then turn southwards across the Cabrach and the Ladder Hills to Braemar in the west, then eastwards through the forest of Birse to Banchory Devenick, returning northwards again to Old Aberdeen by way of the royal burgh of Aberdeen, but excluding the parish of Nigg. Thus, by 1240, the medieval diocese included the whole modern county of Aberdeenshire less Strathbogie, plus twelve parishes in Banffshire and three in Kincardine: in all some eighty five parishes grouped within the five deaneries of Aberdeen, Mar, Buchan, Boyne and Garioch; while the fact that these boundaries bore little resemblance to those of the Scoto-Norman sheriffdom would seem to indicate that the diocese preceded it in time, and that its shape owed more to the development of the old Celtic church and its monasteries within the Mormaer province, rather than to the political and administrative structures of the Scoto-Normans in the eleventh and twelfth centuries. It owed its shape, perhaps most of all, to the basic geological structure of the area, with its great watershed created by the northeast thrust of the Grampians, and its long and devious river courses.

The existing Cathedral in Old Aberdeen, however, is not the one built by Bishop Nechtan and his successors in the twelfth century. All that remains of that building is a small flat stone abacus which once adorned the top of one of the slender columns dividing its Norman nave from its aisles. But if we look at similar contemporaneous churches then being built throughout twelfth century Scotland, like Monymusk or Leuchars, we can reasonably deduce that this first Cathedral was a modest sized building of sandstone with strong exterior walls, rounded windows, a simple but impressive west entrance without a narthex or covered portico, and a light interior culminating in the chancel, possibly with a semicircular apse at the east end. Given the expansion of Cathedral business throughout the thirteenth century, however, which witnessed the introduction of a Cathedral Chapter consisting of some thirteen prebendary canons living in the Chanonry, it is clear that this first Cathedral became too small to accommodate all its activities; for it is evident that it now required a Chapter House where the canons could meet weekly to discuss diocesan affairs, a library for its clergy, and a court where disputes in ecclesiastical law could be heard.

In consequence, at some stage in the 1280s, the then bishop of the diocese, Henry Cheyne, decided that the time had come to build a new and bigger Cathedral. This was clearly going to be a difficult operation since it had to be on the same site, and he simply could not demolish the old Cathedral when it was in daily use. Accordingly he screened off the old nave which was to be kept in use, demolished only the east end of the building and began to build what he intended to be a large and beautiful choir which would form the central crossing of his new Cathedral. He had no sooner positioned the two massive columns which were to form the western pillars of this crossing however, when Edward I invaded Scotland and Bishop Cheyne found himself compromised and forced to accept fealty of the English king, as a result of which Robert I exiled him and the work ground to a halt. Letters in the Vatican Archives show that Bishop Cheyne's successor, Alexander Kininmund I appealed to Pope Clement VI in 1344 to allow him to raise funds to continue the building, but this was a period of severe political disorder when English ships anchored off Aberdeen and the City was burnt and looted, so little could have been done to encourage progress for some years. How much of the new nave had been marked out by this time we have no means of knowing. But we have clear evidence that the work was able to be taken firmly in hand, some eleven years later when Alexander Kininmund II became Bishop of Aberdeen in 1355, for it was he who demolished what he could of the old Cathedral while still allowing it to remain operable, and then spaced out and began to build the massive cylindrical columns of the present nave, marked out and partially built the Cathedral's external walls, and then went on to construct the two fortress like towers at the west end; and all this during his episcopate between 1355-1380.

With the return of James I from his captivity in England in 1424, a period of comparative peace followed in the North East, which allowed successive bishops of Aberdeen to press ahead and try to complete the Cathedral. And here the work of Henry Lichton, its bishop from 1422 to 1440 was decisive. It was he who completed the nave and the aisles up to the roof, who completed the western front between Alexander Kininmund's towers, built the north transept (where he was buried), and began the central tower over the crossing. His successor Ingram de Lindsay roofed the nave of the Cathedral between 1441 and 1458, paved the floor with flagstones, fitted the doors, glazed the windows, decorated the interior walls and brought the building into use. The choir and central tower were then roofed, and the building of the south transept begun. His successor Thomas Spens (1458-80) furnished the choir with its stalls, but it was left to Bishop Elphinstone to build a beautiful steeple over the central tower, to lead the roof of the nave, to continue the south transept, and to plan an enlarged choir and Lady Chapel to the east of the central crossing. His successor Gavin Dunbar added the

twin spires at the Cathedral's west end to give balance to
Elphinstone's central spire, he furnished the nave with a
handsome ceiling, completed the south transept (where he
was buried), and began to extend the Lady Chapel to the
east, in order to give the building, by about 1532, the
cruciform structure which Henry Cheyne has planned in
the 1280s but which in fact was never completed. So at
last, after a prolonged disastrous war with the English,
raids and sporadic attacks, and many other set backs, the
building was almost complete. It had taken two hundred
and fifty years, but it was undoubtedly one of Scotland's
finest Cathedrals, reflecting all that was best in the
Aberdeen character and its craftsmanship: a mostly granite
structure, somewhat architecturally conservative with its
Romanesque west front, massive cylindrical interior
columns, and rounded clerestory windows above the
aisles, but strongly compact and able to resist the harsh
winter storms which so often assailed the North East.

Let us now turn to those monks and priests who
served the diocese of Aberdeen before and during this
period. If we examine the legends of those Celtic and
British saints associated with Deeside and Donside in
Dark Age Scotland, it is clear that monks like Machar,
Devenick, Drostan and Moluag were literate, widely
travelled – some having already been on pilgrimage to
Rome – and that besides preaching the Gospel they
looked after the sick, comforted the dying, and introduced
the Christian form of burial to the native Picts. Moreover,
given that similar Culdee communities elsewhere in
Scotland, like Kinrimund at St Andrews, took in orphans
and young persons dedicated to the religious life, it is
more than likely that the monks had already established a
school at St Machar's by the tenth century, if not long
before, for the instruction of the young, as well as a

hospice for guests and for the sick. Theirs was a hard life of total commitment. It was they who not only laid the foundations of the Christian faith in our area, but also the beginnings of community care, both in New and Old Aberdeen, and our debt to them is incalculable.

The Gregorian reformation of the secular clergy in eleventh century Europe, however, together with the reforms initiated by St Margaret and her royal sons, had brought to an end the predominantly monastic and Culdeian structure of the Scottish Church, and from the early twelfth century onwards, as we have already briefly indicated, the Scottish Church entered the administrative framework of the Western Church with its firm provincial, diocesan and parochial structures and its adherence to a universal canon law. Its bishops were, as always, responsible for the moral and spiritual welfare of the whole diocese, but since, with the rest of the Scottish bishops, they were now among the king's chief counsellors, and therefore often required to be with the king, it was soon evident that they would need a small team of clergy at St Machar's Cathedral to conduct the affairs of the diocese in their absence. By 1157 Bishop Edward had received authority from the English Pope Adrian IV to institute canons at the Cathedral, and by the 1230s they are a recognisable team with specific duties: the dean, to take the bishop's place at the weekly meetings of the Chapter where diocesan problems were discussed; the precentor or chanter who was responsible for the liturgy at the Cathedral – to look after the choir, arrange the music for the services and to take charge of the "sang" school; the treasurer, whose duty it was to oversee the lighting and heating of the Cathedral, to be responsible for all the furnishings and vestments, and to maintain a constant supply of oil and wine for the daily services; the chancellor, who looked after the bishop's and the Chapter's correspondence with popes, kings and others, besides being responsible for the Cathedral grammar school; the archdeacon who watched over the problems and difficulties of all the parish priests throughout the diocese, and who spent much of his time crossing and crisscrossing the whole area and reporting back to the Chapter at regular intervals; and the official of the diocese, the bishop's chief legal officer, who held court in the north west tower of the Cathedral four or five days a week throughout the year to hear and settle disputes concerning marriage, legitimation, testamentary debts, property, contracts, moral misdemeanours, and much other business which would now be heard in burgh and sheriff courts and the Court of Session.

By the 1230s, too, additional canons were required to oversee the management and the finances of the bishop's and the Chapter lands, namely those lands which had been gifted to St Machar's since the eleventh century. Just how extensive these were can be gleaned from one of the Cathedral's earliest charters which lists the benefactions made by Malcolm III, David I and Malcolm IV as "the whole vill of Old Aberdeen, half the waters of the River Don, Sclattie, Goval, Murcar, Kinmundy, the tenth of the royal tax on ships coming into Aberdeen, of the corn there, the king's tenth of the burgh of Aberdeen itself, a tenth of the royal dues between the Dee and the Spey, the vills of Clatt, Tullynessle and Rayne and the church of Daviot". When one examines the ninety-five charter entries which follow, and takes into account the fact that all these lands, fishings and other rights were leased out or feufermed, we begin to see how steadily the Cathedral grew in wealth, and why it eventually needed not only the twenty-eight canons it had by 1445, but also a whole team of procurators, lawyers, surveyors, bailies and clerks to keep an eye on its income, collect its rents and watch for dilapidations of its property. By 1511 the rentals alone on the bishop's and Chapter's lands amounted to £682.17s.8d., so that by the Reformation in 1560, the Cathedral's income in cash and kind must have amounted to well over £1000 per annum, a very large sum indeed in those days.

What did the Church do with all this money? First there was the upkeep of the twenty vicars choral, the chaplains and the choir boys, who sang the Divine Office daily in the Cathedral on behalf of the whole community. Next came the care of widows, orphans, the destitute and the sick, a constant obligation the Church was pledged to maintain; then there were the educational needs of the diocese, chiefly the maintenance of the boys and young men aspiring to the priesthood, and those being trained at the Cathedral grammar school. There was also the cost of law suits, mostly over disputes concerning Church lands; there was papal taxation, and of course, the upkeep of the Cathedral fabric and the heavy cost of its building programme. Whether the Cathedral Chapter was wise to have burdened itself with all this pressing expenditure is simply an academic question; they were a part of an ecclesiastical system common throughout the western Church, which in itself merely reflected the social and economic pattern of feudal Europe in the later Middle Ages. And one has to remember that it also provided employment and inspiration to generations of stonecutters and masons, joiners, stained glass craftsmen and artists of all kinds, and that the majority of people saw the beautiful Cathedral which their generosity had created, as a valid and worthy expression of their faith and devotion.

But before we leave this medieval clerical enclave centred around St Machar's, with its canons, vicars choral, choir boys, grammar school boys and chaplains, all living in the Chanonry and going about their daily tasks, we ought to pause for a moment and think of the bishops of Aberdeen who lived among them; for it is clear from those registers which have survived that these were the men who really changed the character of Old Aberdeen itself. From the late thirteenth century onwards they were almost without exception university graduates. And although, whether they liked it or not, much of their time was spent on the king's business, either in Council or on Parliamentary Committees, or as ambassadors to foreign countries, few of them ever forgot their obligations to their diocese, or the social conscience required of them. As early as the 1170s we find Bishop Matthew founding St Peter's Hospital on the Spital, from which it derives its name today; Hugh de Benham in the 1270s encouraged the Earl of Buchan to found an almshouse at Turriff; and Bishop Gavin Dunbar founded an old folk's home for twelve old men just outside the west end of St Machar's Cathedral in 1532. These bishops also cultivated good relations with the royal burgh of Aberdeen, giving over a portion of their fishing rights of the Dee to them, supporting the costs of the building of their parish church of St Nicholas, and one of them, Bishop Elphinstone, built the handsome stone bridge over the Dee for them which is still much in use today. But the greatest change they brought about was in Old Aberdeen. For quite apart from their continued support in building the two successive cathedrals here, one of them, William Elphinstone, won over James IV to create Old Aberdeen into a burgh of barony in 1489, which gave its inhabitants the right to hold a weekly market on Mondays under their own Mercat Cross, besides two major fairs a year, and most important of all, authority to elect their own magistrates and other officials needed to control the affairs of the burgh, thus no longer making Old Aberdeen economically and politically dependent on the royal burgh of Aberdeen – an identity they were to preserve for the next four hundred years. Then in 1495 Elphinstone gave his most lasting gift to his newly founded Burgh by creating in its midst Scotland's third University, an event which not only profoundly changed the social and economic life of Old Aberdeen, but which also transformed it into the intellectual centre of the North.

Dunbar's true greatness did not fully emerge until he was provided to the see of Aberdeen on 5 November 1518. The uncertainty of the times following the disaster of Flodden, combined with the indifferent health of Bishop Alexander Gordon during his years in office from 1515 to 1518, meant that the diocese had been virtually leaderless since the death of William Elphinstone in 1514. It was Dunbar's achievement to provide the needed leadership. Besides completing the south transept of St Machar's, his cathedral, he extended its choir eastwards, added twin spires at its west end, and created a unique heraldic ceiling for its nave. He enlarged the body of his vicars choral and presented them with a beautiful *epistolare*; he also built or extended an existing residence for them near by. All this has to be viewed within the context of his liturgical reforms, which, being based on Bishop Elphinstone's Aberdeen Breviary of 1510, were devised to bring added meaning and dignity to the singing of the Divine Office in his cathedral. As chancellor of the University of Aberdeen, Dunbar immediately set about completing those of its buildings left unfinished by its founder, resuscitating the administration of its funds, and enforcing those of its bulls and charters which had become ineffective by having them reconfirmed by the crown and the papacy. By 1529 he had seen to the completion, opening, and maintenance of the Bridge of Dee and in that year, remembering his family roots, he endowed two chaplaincies at Elgin Cathedral in Moray. In the prologue of his almshouse charter he stated that "whatever was left from the fruits of his church, after satisfying its necessities, a prelate was bound to devote to the poor and disadvantaged". Those who knew him all record that as Bishop of Aberdeen, and indeed throughout his career, Dunbar saw this responsibility as his own.

As for William Stewart's work as bishop of Aberdeen, the same integrity and careful attention to detail may equally be discerned throughout the twelve difficult years of his episcopate. He firmly resisted heresy in his diocese, and is recorded as attending the condemnation of heretics in 1534 and 1540. His constitutions of 1537 and 1540 for his cathedral clergy reinforced those meticulously laid down by Bishop William Elphinstone in 1506. He was a friend to the Franciscans of Aberdeen, but for reasons of jurisdiction his relations with the Benedictines and Augustinians in his diocese were often troubled. As chancellor of the University of Aberdeen, Stewart completed the building programme at King's College planned by his predecessors, and added its library, sacristy, and jewel house; he was a generous benefactor to its chapel, and actively encouraged the advancement of humanist studies within the university.

In 1547, once installed as bishop, William Gordon soon found himself confronting the spread of heretical doctrine as well as such matters of ecclesiastical discipline as the lack of adequate clerical training. As the heavily scriptural and theological content of the fifty surviving books of his own personal library makes evident, he must have been fully aware of the importance of these issues, and as a first measure, on 9 July 1547, he commissioned a canon of his cathedral, the theologian John Watson, to refute error and preach the gospel annually throughout the churches of the diocese; and he himself attended the provincial council convened in 1549 to undertake the reform of the Scottish church.

In 1559 his cathedral chapter warned Bishop Gordon that heresy was growing, that it was losing control of its income through his excessive leasing of its lands. All these issues, however, were swept away by the Reformation Parliament, meeting in July and August 1560, which abolished papal authority throughout the realm, forbade the celebration of the Mass, approved the Scots Confession of Faith, and recognized the sole competence of a reformed ministry. The return from France of the Catholic Queen Mary in August 1561, her grant of protection in 1562 to the University of Aberdeen, of which Gordon was chancellor, together with the support on which he could expect to rely from his nephew George Gordon, fourth Earl of Huntly, may have persuaded him and many in his conservative diocese that they could lie low until the protestant programme had shown itself to be unworkable. But events were to prove otherwise. Queen Mary was forced to abdicate in 1567 in favour of her infant son James VI, and the regency passed to her protestant half brother, the Earl of Moray. Those secular clergy (including its teachers in the three universities) who would not subscribe to the Scots Confession of Faith, were relieved of their ministry, which passed to those who were willing to serve in a newly reformed church. Gordon's failure to effect any lasting reform in his diocese, however, has to be seen in its wider context: the crown's capture of the right to nominate to high ecclesiastical office, mostly for its own political and fiscal advantage, and the strong links of kinship in Scottish society, visible in Gordon's own promotion. He died in his palace in the Chanonry, Old Aberdeen, on 6 Aug 1577, and was buried in his cathedral church of St Machar.

To end this brief account of the medieval diocese of Aberdeen in the midst of its sober pre-Reformation difficulties, however, would be disproportionate to the equally well recorded fidelity, loyalty and devotion of its bishops, clergy and laity to the Holy See during this period. But our purpose, now, rather, is to place its past history within the context of its present standing before the challenges which face it today. For the past twenty-five years, Bishop Mario Conti as he then was, ruled the diocese of Aberdeen with complete devotion, love and equity, facing up courageously to the immense problems of a secular world, just as did his medieval predecessors in the See like William Elphinstone and Gavin Dunbar. Like them, open and untiring, he watched over and educated his clergy, instructed and edified the faithful, and beautified the house of God. We are confident that with God's help, he will continue to do so in Glasgow as its present archbishop.

The Bishops of Aberdeen 1131 – 1577

Nechtan 1131-1147	Gilbert de Stirling 1228-1239
Edward 1147-1171	Ralph de Lamley 1239-1247
Matthew 1172-1199	Peter de Ramey 1247-1256
John 1199-1207	Richard de Pottun 1256-1272
Adam de Kalder 1207-1228	Hugh de Benham 1272-1282

Henry de Chene 1282-1328
Alexander de Kininmund 1329-1344
William de Deyn 1344-1350
John de Rate 1350-1355
Alexander de Kininmund II 1355-1380
Adam de Tyninghame 1380-1389
Gilbert de Greenlaw 1390-1421

Henry de Lichton 1422-1440
Ingram de Lindsay 1441-1458
Thomas Spens 1458-1480
Robert Blackadder 1480-1488
William Elphinstone 1488-1514
Alexander Gordon 1515-1518
Gavin Dunbar 1518-1532
William Stewart 1532-1545
William Gordon 1545-1577

In 1560 the Estates of Parliament passed an Act forbidding the celebration of Mass and abrogating the authority of the papacy over the Scottish Church.

REFERENCES

Registrum Episcopatus Aberdonensis 2 vols., ed. C. Innes (Edinburgh 1845).

Fasti Ecclesiae Scoticanae Medii Aevi, ed. D.E.R. Watt (St Andrews 1969).

L.J. Macfarlane, *St Machar's Cathedral, Aberdeen and its Medieval Records* (Aberdeen 1987).

R.G. Cant, *The Building of St Machar's Cathedral, Aberdeen* (Aberdeen 1976).

I.B. Cowan, "The Church in the Dioceses of Aberdeen", in *The Medieval Church in Scotland*, ed. J. Kirk (Edinburgh 1995).

L.J. Macfarlane, *William Elphinstone and the Kingdom of Scotland, 1431-1514* (Aberdeen 1995).

A.D.M. Barrell, *Medieval Scotland* (Cambridge 2000).

Dr Leslie Macfarlane BA, PhD, D Litt (Aberdeen and Edinburgh), LLD, FRHS, FSA, is an Honorary Reader in Medieval History at the University of Aberdeen. He is the author of *A Guide to the Vatican Archives*; *A Guide to King's College, University of Aberdeen*; *William Elphinstone and the Kingdom of Scotland 1431-1514*; and of numerous articles on Scottish medieval history in learned journals.

On Proclaiming the Gospel of Life

Professor J. J. Scarisbrick

Perhaps, after all, there are some big events in history which are inevitable. Was not Hitler's Nazism, like the ancient gods, doomed in the long run? Was not the Russian Communist empire destined to implode? Was it not inevitable that the Atlantic slave trade would eventually be repudiated by the civilised world? Are not today's protests against human rights abuses, exploitation of women, violation of the environment – at least to some extent – expressions of the human spirit's unquenchable thirst for justice?

What is deeply Godless, false, destructive of the natural order, debasing, in a word, what is truly evil, cannot avoid ultimate self-destruction. The Gates of Hell cannot hold out against truth and justice. That is why we can know that the pro-life cause must ultimately prevail. The mass destruction, trivialisation and manipulation of human life which we are now witnessing in today's world – millions of human lives deliberately extinguished every year by surgical and chemical abortion, hundreds of thousands of human beings manufactured in IVF laboratories and less than five per cent emerging as live births (the rest being thrown away, perishing in the womb, stored in deep freezers or used in destructive experimentation) – are without parallel in our history and must sooner or later be repudiated. Children produced by IVF can have at least five "parents": the commissioning couple, the gamete donors, the surrogate mother. Lesbian couples can bear children without any direct male contribution. Male homosexual couples can have offspring using hired wombs of surrogate mothers. Male pregnancy is now a real possibility. Human cloning is already upon us and will produce a new kind of human being – one generated asexually and without any parents in the traditional sense. Therapeutic cloning (already declared lawful by the British Parliament) involves the manufacture of human beings who are jerked into life by an electric shock passed through an ovum which has had its nucleus replaced. That new human being is then stripped of its stem cells and killed. So Parliament, which in 1990 approved the use of human beings produced by IVF in destructive research, has taken a further step down a forbidden road by allowing cloned human beings to be created in order to be cannibalised.

All cloning, therapeutic and reproductive, exploits human life as it has never been exploited before. It completes the "commodification" of human life begun by the "family planners" and assisted conception industry. Parents can achieve the ultimate designer-baby by ordering gametes to their specification over the Internet. A deaf lesbian couple recently insisted on being guaranteed a child as disabled as they were by using the sperm of a male who had a family history of genetic deafness. A couple whose child is discovered at birth to be "substandard", i.e. a special-needs child, may sue doctors for "negligence" in allowing him/her to be born. Surrogate mothers effectively provide a rent-a-womb service. Reproductive cloning will probably be first allowed to enable grieving parents to replace a lost child. The hard case will carry the day. But, since children are already being produced by IVF to provide material for repairing damaged siblings, it will not be long before clones will be used as a source of replacement hearts or livers or whatever for them. A new serfdom – blasphemy hitherto undreamt of – awaits. Meanwhile the euthanasia lobby presses on inexorably.

Though truth and justice prevail they do so despite human error and the fact that self-seeking and hypocrisy often makes common cause with them, sometimes almost stifling them, as bindweed does to summer flowers. Cynical *Realpolitik* as well as sincere idealism brought the Allies to victory in 1945, for example. Wilberforce was greatly aided by evidence that the Atlantic slave trade was a graveyard rather than (as previously claimed) the nursery of British sailors. Some latter-day feminism can be shockingly egocentric. Moreover have we not been warned that, even as the Kingdom approaches, we will have to survive a final conflict between Good and Evil, which will see the Church torn by apostasy and infidelity? We must expect trial and tribulation, bewildering setbacks, enemies from within as well as without. The ways of the Lord of History are not our ways.

For a pro-lifer, one of the more bewildering things has been the poverty of our opponents' arguments. Defending the indefensible inevitably breeds evasion, incoherence, muddleheadedness. Given that our society has been deeply afflicted by utilitarian habits of thought and the latter's denial of moral absolutes, the chances of engaging it in rigorous discourse was never good and, thanks to prevailing materialism and hedonism, have become steadily worse. But nothing could have prepared us for the low level of moral reasoning which we have encountered.

In 1967, while the future Abortion Act was being discussed in Parliament, the only serious contribution to the debate on the moral status of the unborn child was that he/she was a "dependent" being. This is true (despite the fact that in some respects the child is the dominant partner in the mother/child partnership) but irrelevant – because dependence implies duties towards the dependant, not rights over him/her. It could equally justify infanticide. Much play was made then and since with the "back-street" argument. "Keep it [abortion] safe, keep it legal" was the cry. Recently this has been refined to run thus: "no one likes abortion but women have always been able to get it and probably always will be, whatever politicians or churchmen say; so let us face facts and at least keep the damage to a minimum by legalising it". If this is acceptable we should go on to say that, because there have always been rape, murder and paedophilia, and (alas) probably always will be, let us set up clinics where these can be performed under medical supervision. Such a line of thought is immediately seen to be absurd. If (say) old people are being mugged in the back streets it is no solution to provide clinics in front streets when they can be mugged in hygienic conditions.

A variant on the back-street argument has been that abortion is often the lesser of two evils. Leave aside the difficulty in accepting that motherhood can ever be described as an evil, even a lesser one; and leave aside the crucial principle that we may choose the lesser of two evils only if there is absolutely no third choice (which there is in every crisis pregnancy, namely, to strive to turn what initially seemed to be a disaster into something wonderful, joyful, life-enhancing). Those who dare to say that abortion is the lesser wrong are making a wholly unfounded judgement – a mere guess. They are claiming to know the unknowable, to foresee what cannot be foreseen (certainly not in its entirety) and then to weigh against each other things for which there is no unit of measurement. As a piece of moral reasoning, their verdict is worthless.

An American academic has recently argued – to the acclaim of the pro-abortion lobby – that, since no one can be forced to be a Good Samaritan, no woman can be forced to sustain a life which happens to have attached itself to her – contrary to her wishes and intention.[24] But the difficulty with this line of thought lies precisely in that "happens". A woman does not just "happen" to find herself pregnant. And is there not a conflict between this view of the unborn child as an alien intruder and the familiar slogan about the child being merely part of the mother (which he clearly is not)?

The momentous Warnock Report of 1984, which paved the way for the legislation of 1990 permitting manufacture of human beings in IVF laboratories, boasted in its foreword of its commitment to rigorous moral reasoning. Clearly the central issue in the debate about the new biotechnology was the moral status of the human embryo. If human life at the embryonic stage is indeed human, it must be given full protection; if it is not, screening and throwing away of "defective" specimens, freezing of "spares" or use of them in destructive research would be permissible. The Report recognised the centrality of the question but then did a remarkable thing. It said that, since there were conflicting views about whether the human embryo was truly human, the committee had "gone straight" to discussing how it

---

[24] E. McDonagh, *Breaking the Abortion Deadlock* (New York and Oxford: Oxford University Press, 1996), esp. pp.6ff.

should be treated.[25] What audacious evasion! How can we know how to treat any thing until we know what it is?

In 1967 the then Archbishop of Canterbury persuaded the House of Lords that there had to be an Abortion Act because doctors were living in intolerable uncertainty about what was lawful and what was not. No one asked why the law should therefore be loosened to allow almost complete freedom of supply. In 1990 the then Archbishop of York argued that it was misguided to ask when human life begins because becoming human is a process, like becoming middle-aged, with no exact beginning. His views influenced many peers, but are specious. Processes can have exact starting-points. A tennis match, for example, is a process, but it begins at the moment when the umpire calls "play". Human life is a process but has a precise beginning (conception/fertilisation). So, for that matter, is being an archbishop.

The Warnock committee concluded that the first fourteen days of human life was, so to speak, an open season, during which anything could go. Thereafter we could be sure that a real human life was in existence, so nothing would go. Strangely no one was able to explain clearly why day fourteen had such momentous significance. There was talk about that being the time when the "primitive streak" appeared (few had heard about this event before and fewer had accorded it much importance) and after which identical twinning could not occur. But no one was able to explain why that fact was significant. If twinning is genetically determined, as it seems to be, two separate lives have been present since fertilisation. That being so, day fourteen simply becomes

---

[25] *Report of the Committee of Inquiry into Human Fertilisation and Embryology* (HMSO, 1984), paragraph 11.9.

the point at which we today, in our still very incomplete understanding of the astonishing "explosion" of activity following conception, can know that twinning no longer becomes apparent. Day fourteen has never been particularly important to any twin – or God. Australia was the largest island in the world even before the Europeans discovered it. Yet more strangely, having declared that human life becomes inviolable at fourteen days, Lady Warnock herself voted for abortion - up to birth, in some cases.

While our Parliament was recently debating the human cloning issue, official doctrine was that only reproductive or "birth" cloning, i.e. producing born clones, was true cloning. Therapeutic or research cloning, which simply took stem cells from embryos cloned from adults, was not. This is absurd. Cloning is achieved by "cell-nuclear replacement" and this technique is used for both birth and therapeutic cloning. The difference lies in the outcome, not the procedure. Therapeutic cloning is deliberately intended to result in destruction of new human beings after they have been stripped of their stem cells. Birth cloning would result in copies of existing born people being born themselves. The Government's mendacity greatly helped to secure Parliament's consent to yet further trivialisation of human life. MPs and peers believed – or chose to believe – that they were banning cloning when really they were licensing it.

Some years ago a paediatrician was charged with murder of a Down's syndrome baby in Derby City Hospital. The doctor admitted to the police that he had given the child a large overdose of the sedative DF118 to stop him from seeking food. That drug had served no therapeutic purpose. It was intended to procure death. Nevertheless the judge ruled that this was merely a "holding operation", albeit "holding" surely requires that one does nothing decisive and tries to keep all options open. The doctor was acquitted. Had he been found guilty, over thirty other cases of neonatal euthanasia would have been taken into account. The judge's perversity in this case is matched by that of the law lords in the Tony Bland case, who ruled that it was in his best interests to be put to death. But unless they knew what awaited him after death (and they made no claim to such knowledge) how could they make this calculation?

Faced with the urgent need to ensure that abortifacient chemicals and devices should not be subject to the Abortion Act, the medical establishment allied with politicians and the pharmaceutical industry to re-write human biology. Fertilisation and conception, they suddenly claimed, are not the same event, after all. Conception begins several days *after* sperm and ovum fuse (fertilisation). Conception and pregnancy begin at implantation, that is, when the new human being attaches to the mother's womb. So we have all been wrong about all this for centuries.

These remarkable discoveries were further explained thus by an attorney-general in 1983: abortion is miscarriage; "miscarriage" requires "carriage"; "carriage" requires what is carried to be attached to the carrier; therefore abortion cannot occur until implantation; destruction of human life before then is contraception. Never mind that an attorney general certainly carries money in his pocket although it is not attached to him. It is "generally accepted", we were categorically told, that there could be no carriage without attachment. The courts have twice upheld this ruling. The "morning-after pill" and other abortifacients contracept, we are told. They do not abort. Thus the New Biology has triumphed. Rarely has science been so abused to serve political ends.

Some Catholics now openly agree that "it's a woman's right to choose" – or would say "yes" if the child were severely disabled or the result of rape. Others would take the Tony Blair stance: they would not themselves take the abortion route but would not "impose" their views on others by stopping them. As Cardinal Winning famously pointed out, this is moral schizophrenia. The reason for being personally opposed to something gravely wrong – such as torture or paedophilia – is the reason for being publicly opposed to it also. To opt out of public opposition is cowardice. It is even more egregious if, as Mr Blair has done in his parliamentary voting career, one publicly promotes the wrongdoing, by voting for it on every possible occasion.

Some accuse Rome and pro-lifers not merely of being "out of touch" with the modern world but of overstating traditional Catholic teaching on life issues. They claim that the Church has never made up its mind about when human life begins and that its absolute ban on abortion dates only from 1869, when Pius IX re-imposed excommunication for it. They argue that pro-lifers are fundamentalists, extremists, etc. But they are seriously amiss. That every human life is sacrosanct from the moment of fertilisation has been the Church's constant teaching. Some of the Fathers and Scholastics, like St Thomas, misled by ancient science (especially Aristotle's), concluded that God infuses the immortal soul several weeks later. But they insisted that to destroy a life that is going to be ensouled, even if the act is not homicide in the full sense of the word, is gravely sinful. Abortion before ensoulment (animation) was as forbidden as abortion after it. If St Thomas were alive now he would surely be an "immediate" rather than "delayed" animationist, because modern science shows conclusively that human life begins at conception, i.e. fusion of sperm and ovum. But his opposition to abortion would not be increased as a result.

Some theologians have tried to argue that, up to a certain point (and there are different opinions as to when that is), pre-born human beings are human but not yet humanised, not yet persons. Whether these distinctions are valid is doubtful. It is difficult to accept, for example, that a human being could ever be absolutely "non-person". What is not in doubt, however, is that they are irrelevant to the abortion debate. Like that life which is due to be ensouled, the life which is going to become fully human and possessed of personhood – because it already has the radical capacity to do so – has a special place in God's creation and must be protected against an aggressor. Not to allow it to achieve its ordained goal is to do it injustice. Some may object that, since injustice can be done only to human beings, to speak of injustice in this case is to beg the question. The reply to that runs thus: the not-yet-but-soon-to-be-fully human person (assuming that such a being actually exists) must be accorded a privileged place in the human family and can suffer injustice precisely because intended by the Creator to become fully human.

We have heard much "not yet" talk from secular sources: the human embryo is "not yet" really human because "not yet recognisably one"; the pre-born child is "not yet" socialised, "not yet" self-conscious or capable of choosing and deciding and therefore "not yet" possessed of the right to life. All these claims, even if true, are of *no* consequence. Since these human beings are capable of achieving all those things and will do so if not prevented by an outsider, to prevent them is to do them grave harm, i.e. injustice – as grave as denying their right to life after they have achieved it. It is as wrong to cut off an infant's foot as it is to cut of an adult's; and it is no defence to say that the infant was not yet capable of walking. Even if we accept that there are humans who are not yet fully human, abortion remains prohibited. The "not yet" argument does not work.

In Catholic circles it has been replaced by an equally seductive one – one which talks about the "seamless garment" of moral issues. What that seamless garment is may not always be very clear, but those who appeal to it seem to mean that we must reverence all Creation and all living things, and that, unless we are preserving rainforests and wildlife, feeding the hungry worldwide, fighting global warming, poverty and discrimination everywhere, campaigning for disarmament and world peace and so on, we are not truly pro-life. They accuse self-styled "pro-lifers" of being obsessed with a single issue to the point of hypocrisy, or at least of having failed to see the whole picture.

Yes indeed, there is a seamless garment of moral issues. Pro-lifers are outraged by the sight of victims of flood, famine, plague or war, and deplore arms races, genocide, the growing gap between rich and poor nations, reckless disregard for the environment and the ravages of the drug culture, etc. But we cannot fight on all fronts at once. To be "pro-life" has from the first had a precise meaning, namely, commitment to proclaiming the unique worth of human life and the duty of society to reverence it from fertilisation to natural death. Moreover the right to life is the fundamental right. It may not be incumbent on pro-lifers to demand unilateral disarmament. It is incumbent on those who speak out against a future nuclear holocaust to speak out also against the actual holocaust of the unborn. It is not incumbent on pro-lifers to campaign against fox-hunting or seal-culling. But those who so campaign ought to be yet more committed to protecting the right to life of human beings. There is a hierarchy of causes facing us today. The pro-life cause, in the strict sense of the word, is the supreme moral challenge of our time. As Cardinal Winning remarked, "it is not *a* cause. It is *the* cause."

Pro-lifers say that, far from being blinkered, they are the ones whose eyes are really open. "Seamless garment" talk smacks too often of political correctness. To claim that we must seek total conversion of society before tackling particular issues can easily be an excuse for doing nothing.

The pro-life cause has to be ever finding new ways of breaking through public indifference and ignorance. It must challenge the world – as Pope John Paul II does so powerfully in *Evangelium Vitae*[26] – to face up to the glaring contradiction between its profession of belief in justice and human rights, and its toleration, even active approval, of the denial of basic rights to a whole section of society. How can we denounce racism, sexism and other forms of discrimination but turn a blind eye to ageist and sizeist discrimination against pre-born human life? How can we be so concerned to provide jobs, ramps, parking spaces, etc. for disabled born people while devising ever more efficient ways of detecting and eliminating them before birth? How do we reconcile commitment to a fairer Britain and equal opportunities with abortionism, deep-freezing of human embryos or using them as involuntary subjects of destructive research? The contradictions grow daily.

---

[26] *Evangelium Vitae*, paragraph 18.

We rejoice today in the growing solidarity of the human race, which owes so much to the extraordinary achievements of modern communications. The "global village" is an increasing reality. But, so far, that sense of solidarity extends "horizontally" across the world. Pro-lifers have to challenge their neighbours to think "vertically", too. Further, thanks to the modern media, especially television, disasters and suffering and injustice – wherever they happen – touch us, affront us as they could never do in the past. The abominable violence of 11 September 2001, for example, did more than shock. It bruised humanity. So does the violence of abortionism. It wounds us all, even though many do not realise this, because every abortion is an act of violence against humankind, an affront to the dignity and integrity of a woman and a failure in human relations. A Christian will want to add that every abortion is an affront to God the Creator and His Son, whose Incarnation radically united Him to the human race and gave it new dignity (just as His nine months in Mary's womb gave new dignity to every womb), and an insult to God the Holy Spirit, for whom every human body is intended to be a temple.

New opportunities for promoting the pro-life cause open up almost every day. The world is not threatened with overpopulation, as the doom-and-gloom scaremongers used to predict. Many parts of the world, especially Europe, black Africa and white America now face demographic collapse. In 1967 we were promised that readily available abortion would strengthen marriages and families. But as cohabitation and divorce rates soar and the extra-marital birth-rates rise from five per cent of live births to nearly fifty per cent, such promises now sound hollow. We were promised that every born child would be a wanted child, but child abuse has increased.

We were promised a healthier society, but thirty-five years on, are now beginning to be able to see what we have really done to ourselves.

Post-abortion trauma is now a major women's disease. Grief, guilt and anger leave a trail of sexual dysfunction, broken relationships, loss of self-esteem, alcoholism, drug-taking, nightmares and flashbacks. Over ten per cent of women suffer severe psychological disorders; suicide rates among post-abortion women seem to be much higher than those for women who have borne children. There is now considerable evidence that induced abortion is a significant risk-factor for later breast cancer, especially among women who have had no previous full-term pregnancy – and that thousands of UK women have died and will soon have died of that disease, now the commonest form of cancer and becoming ever more widespread, often (although not necessarily) resulting from abortions procured decades previously. There is also clear evidence of the connection between abortion and other female diseases. In many of our cities sexually transmitted diseases such as chlamydia, human papilloma virus (a major cause of cervical cancer) and bacterial vaginosis, not to mention more familiar complaints, have reached epidemic proportions. It is young women's bodies that are suffering most. The ravages are due to the explosion of promiscuity for which readily available abortion is partly responsible. Furthermore, following abortion, diseases like chlamydia can result in miscarriage and infertility.

Abortion humiliates womanhood and wounds it. It generates shame and distress that can rarely be shared. Other people usually do not want to know, especially if they have been party to the decision-making. The woman cries alone.

Pro-lifers have prophetic roles to play in today's post-Christian society. Certainly there is a place in their programme for direct action: protests, demonstrations, public acts of witness. But these must be done with care and humility. We must expect to be hated but must not hate others or condemn in return. The people who engage in direct pro-life action will always be searching their consciences with the question: "whom am I really serving first, myself or my neighbour?" The Gospel of Life is also a Gospel of Love. That does not affect the duty to speak out against injustice and to defend the weak. It is not easy to decide what the duty was of a German Catholic as he watched trainloads of Jews being carried off to Belsen. Should he have shot the train-driver or lain on the rail tracks? Perhaps – but only if that action would have had a real chance of being effective, i.e. if dozens, perhaps hundreds, had been prepared to so the same? I am bound to try to stop a neighbour strangling a child and will be applauded for doing so, because the neighbour's action is accepted as criminal. But if I try to stop a woman going to an abortion or an abortion doctor from doing his dreadful work I am in a different situation, because what they are doing is lawful and I am likely to damage my cause by seeming to be a fanatic, especially if the woman is already deeply distraught. If I perceive a duty to intervene I have to do so with great sensitivity.

We must challenge our fellow-citizens with the hard truth. There is a place for the shocking picture and brutal statistic. But these have to be used very carefully lest they alienate and embitter the very people we wish to convert. Truth spoken out of turn can be the enemy of conversion. Alas, it is easier to demonise one's opponents than to love them. Abortionists caricature pro-lifers as misogynists and religious bigots. We must not caricature them. Many women go for abortion with heavy hearts, believing it is the only way out of a terrible crisis. They may be the least guilty parties in the whole sad story. They may be unselfishly seeking to spare parents heartbreak, husbands and partners burdens they believe they cannot bear, friends shame. Many doctors and nurses involved in the abortion industry may think that they are being compassionate.

An unwanted, unintended pregnancy, initially at least, can seem like a disaster – even in a happy, stable marriage. Perhaps only those who have "been there" should speak out in public on the issue. Certainly only those who are prepared to roll up their sleeves and help people "not to" should dare say "thou shalt not". It has sometimes been a weakness of the pro-life movement that it seemed so preoccupied with the unborn child as to have forgotten the woman and those around her. Conversely, the great strength of pro-lifers has always been their often heroic efforts in providing the positive alternatives – a comprehensive pregnancy counselling and care programme for any woman, housing, initiatives like Zöe's Place baby hospice, the LIFE Fertility Programme and Cardinal Winning's celebrated venture.

Pro-lifers are pro-woman and pro-child – equally. They have a better way, a more civilised response to unwanted pregnancy, disability and childlessness, and a higher vision of human sexuality than the World offers. Far from wanting to put the clocks back, they are tomorrow's people, radical democrats passionate about human rights, women's dignity and the respect due to both human life and the human body.

The Culture of Death has so corrupted society that the struggle to convert from within, so to speak, has been overtaken by the need to create a pro-life counter-culture without. Pro-lifers must look to the day when an alternative health service – an exemplary pro-life alternative – has been set up offering pro life doctors and nurses a career structure and pro-life patients treatment by people with clean hands. We must launch pro-life research into curing genetic disorders, women's disorders, etc. We look for the day when schools and colleges, firms and businesses are proud to proclaim their pro-life commitment, and politicians, pop stars and football heroes boast of it.

We dream dreams. The Catholic Church is spiritually equipped to make a unique contribution to making them come true, thanks not least to the inspiration which its leaders, like the man whom this volume honours, provide. Furthermore, in much of the Western world, including Scotland, churches, schools and seminaries have been facing closure, and many religious orders are shrinking – even to the point of extinction. All this is heartrending and often requires painful decisions. But it also offers new opportunities: opportunities to turn the fruit of pious generosity of past generations to new uses and to serve the Lord, especially the Gospel of Life, in new ways. As we have been told, God often draws straight with crooked lines.

J. J. Scarisbrick is Emeritus Professor of History at the University of Warwick. After receiving his doctorate at Cambridge, he taught in London, Ghana and the USA, before moving to the Chair of History at Warwick. He is co-founder and National Chairman of the charity LIFE and its associate charities, the LIFE Hospital Trust and Zöe's Place Trust. His wife Nuala is a fellow-trustee of LIFE and has been a pioneer of pro-life activism since the early 1970s.

THE ARTISTIC-CULTURALHERITAGE OF THE CHURCH
AN EVANGELISING HERITAGE

ARCHBISHOP FRANCESCO MARCHISANO

I am truly honoured to be able to make this small contribution on the wonderful occasion for which this volume is being published: the twenty-fifth episcopal anniversary of His Grace Archbishop Mario Conti, Archbishop of Glasgow, for whom I cherish sentiments of deep friendship and esteem for the interest he has always had for the Cultural Heritage of the Church - so much so that the Holy Father has nominated him Member of the Pontifical Commission for the Cultural Heritage of the Church over which I preside. I have been able to attest personally to his interest on the occasions when he participated in the Plenary Assemblies of our Pontifical Commission, and when I was in Aberdeen for the inauguration of the Blairs Museum that collects memorabilia of the life of the Catholic Church in Scotland prior to the Reformation. At the latter ceremony Catholics and Protestants alike were able to admire Msgr. Conti's dedication and organisational abilities.

It is for this reason that I wish to offer in my contribution a brief overview of what this enormous and splendid historical heritage of religious art, created by the faithful in the course of the two millennia of the life of the Church, has meant both for the Church and civil society.

We should ask ourselves first of all: why has the Church used art so abundantly for her evangelising mission? And then pose ourselves another question: are the motivations that have led the Church throughout the centuries to see in art – in its threefold expression of painting, sculpture, and architecture – a very efficient means of evangelisation, still valid today and can they still be a source of inspiration in our every- day life? In fact, the artistic dimension that the Church has widely adopted in proclaiming her message and preaching the word of God, constitutes an element that is an integral part of the life of the Church. John Paul II reiterated this basic view in his *Letter to Artists*, issued on April 22, 1999.

Before dealing directly with this theme, in order to examine the function of the Cultural Heritage of the Church in the context of the Church's evangelising activity, I would like first to present an introductory summary of a more theological nature, to which more concrete considerations and practical observations will be added later on. This is in order to suggest a fundamental reason why the Church has always turned a particularly watchful eye towards the creation, conservation, and enhancement of all the artistic and historical heritage she has produced in the course of two millennia.

Theological Introduction

God wanted to entrust His truth to a history, an experience, and a revelation (let us think of the story contained in the Old and New Testaments), so that man might learn to know Him as well as himself. This compendium of deeds and words is called "divine economy", that is, a providential plan through which God has operated throughout the centuries. Divine economy postulates a chain of events and a previous, as well as connecting, willpower behind these same events. In order to partake in such an economy, that is, in this providential plan of God, one should know events and words: one should make memory – have memory – become memory.

Jesus entrusted to us the words of the Father and he made memorial gestures that have left to us His memory. He often said: "Every time you do this…you will remember". "This will make you remember". The Church is thus the living memorial of the Emmanuel, that is, God among us. But the Church also knows that Jesus has not said or done everything. His economy – in other words, His universal plan of salvation – is still in a process of becoming. The fullness of truth has not yet been reached by man. If the Acts of the Apostles have been already written, the Acts of the Church are still being written.

The gesture of remembering, therefore, on the part of the Church, is not only a "retrospective" gesture, but is, and should be, a gesture of constant understanding of our daily reality, of the living memory of an experience that has always had a mysterious co-protagonist, the Holy Spirit, who places it as a perennial "sacrament" in the midst of history and orients it towards its fulfillment.

The attitude of remembering, of fixing events in memorials, of educating and reading such "memorials", is thus an intrinsic attitude of the Church. If one loses "memory", all understanding of divine economy is paralysed, because "it is this economy that supports theology".

From this derives the Church's efforts to express in every era the economy of God in words and comprehensible signs to the perceiver of the message. From this derives the force of concrete cultural expressions of this message, in the many different places of evangelisation and throughout the epochs of Christian experience: above all, from the first cultural expressions that have maintained intact the "marvel" of the first hour and the force of its origins - the first Greek and Latin inculturation; the first encounter between Christianity and art as reflected in early catacomb paintings; the initial development from a non-Christian to a Christian architectural model; the earliest iconography of the Christian mystery.

But equally important in order to understand divine economy, is the safeguarding of everything that has been produced by the meeting of cultures, sensibilities, and techniques with the Gospel truth and the Christian vision of history.

As in the case when one studies saints and their existence in order that their lives' itineraries may be re-proposed in order to create a paradigm and a "memory", from which it becomes easier to grasp the essence of the complete synthesis realised by Christ, so it is when one studies Christian archaeology, figurative art, architecture, music and popular traditions, and theology in general. Every authentic expression and experience in such areas is safeguarded and conserved by the Church as an expressive "icon" of the known, represented and celebrated mystery.

These are the fundamental reasons why the Church has been anxious not to dissipate her own patrimony of art and history, liturgy and theology, hagiography and legislation, pastoral and pedagogical activity. In everything there is, or there can be, those "*semina verbi*" which cannot be destroyed or dismissed by anyone. Certainly, "supernatural" memory, which is the work of the Holy Spirit, will never decrease. But human activities also that have assisted the history of the Church and are recorded through artistic forms will be protected with responsibility and effort, for their deep significance as well as the ecclesial function which they are called to carry out even today, as I will now explain briefly. First let us ask ourselves: "What is this cultural-artistic-historical patrimony, referred to today as the Cultural Heritage of the Church?"

Then let us reflect upon how we can continue this work of preservation, conservation and promotion of the Cultural Heritage of the Church, in its multi-faceted aspects, in order to discover the deep message it can transmit to us, the teaching that it can offer to that modern day man who approaches it with an open heart in order to grasp its intrinsic value.

What is the Cultural Heritage of the Church?
First of all we must pinpoint what is meant by the "cultural-artistic-historical patrimony of the Church" or the "Cultural Heritage of the Church". This cultural-artistic-historical patrimony of the Church is made up of all those assets and values, material and immaterial, mobile and immobile, tangible and intangible, in which the precious legacy of the local community, or that which is shared between individual communities, becomes embodied in relation to the universal Church. Placed at the service of the Church's mission, which is universal by her very nature, this legacy and this patrimony potentially serve all of humanity.

The artistic-historical patrimony is much more than simply an object with property rights. For the Church, it represents a necessary instrument, which is often indispensable, for the exercise of her evangelising mission.

From here originates the right of the Church (and of institutions and persons, who historically and organically comprise her) to manage a cultural-artistic patrimony; to administer, use, protect, and enhance it since it is essential for the purpose of carrying out her ecclesial task.

The origin of this patrimony has its roots in the exercise of the evangelising and pastoral function of the Church. It is an essential instrument for this function and, thus, it is a condition of religious freedom. It has been added to throughout the centuries, thanks both to the spontaneous generosity of the poor as well as the offerings of individuals better off both economically and culturally. But always, in every case, it has served as a sign and witness of the faith and deep aspirations of individuals as well as of communities to place at the service of the Church and to offer to God, through her, the best they could create.

Here is the origin of a patrimony that, even though religious, has become the expression of the best a culture, a people, a local community can create. Thus, the ecclesiastical cultural-artistic-historical patrimony often represents the highest expression of both human creativity and religious devotion and we can see how artistic and historical value is inseparable from the conviction of faith; that from here originate works that spring from the fruitful encounter between religious and aesthetic inspiration, as one can easily see in three-dimensional works, in music, architecture and literary works. The Church has, in fact, stimulated human creativity in the artistic field, knowing well that it is a primary means of elevating the soul towards the Creator.

What is the purpose of this patrimony?
Now let us ask ourselves: why has the Church used art so abundantly for her mission? As we reflect upon the principal reasons why the Church throughout the centuries has wanted to spread throughout the world such

an enormous amount of artistic works, we can discern some practical consequences that touch us directly even today.

Worship
The Church has created her enormous cultural-artistic-historical patrimony for three principal functions: above all for the *function of worship*. Worship is, in fact, the essence of the religious phenomenon, which, if it has personal and intimate dimensions (let us think of the prayers that we raise to the Lord from the intimacy of our souls), also has necessary communal and public expressions: churches; images; sacred furnishings; sacred books; other religious objects; sculptural, literary and musical works have been made in order to be placed at the service of divine worship. The first purpose for which the Church has used art is always worship.

I will not dwell here on what the Second Vatican Council has said about art and worship. The Conciliar Fathers dealt widely with this issue in the document on Liturgy. The message of the Council to artists is also well known. I will simply mention the famous address that Pope Paul VI delivered to the artists gathered in the Sistine Chapel on May 7, 1964. The beautiful analogy made by Pope Paul of Jacob's dream, in which he had seen a ladder that arose from the earth to touch the sky and on which angels were ascending and descending, has become famous. The immortal Pontiff compared that ladder to art, because art leads God to men and men to God. I have already cited the letter that Pope John Paul II addressed to all artists just three years ago and which summarizes the importance that art has always had for evangelisation.

The first function of art has always been to bring the splendour of beauty to worship so that it can be easier for the faithful to ascend towards God, because God is ultimate beauty and goodness.

Catechesis
The Church has employed art for a second fundamental function: *for a catechetical function.* The preaching of the Gospel has been carried out in an infinite number of works of art. One need only think back to those pictorial works constituting the *"Biblia pauperum"*, which have represented visually all the salient points of Christian doctrine, from the Creation of the world to the Last Judgement. We find in all nations marvellous examples. I would like to cite the Cathedral of San Gimignano in Italy whose walls are decorated with pictorial representations of the Old and New Testaments and whose ceiling is covered with paintings moulded with such lifelike representation that they can be easily read by everyone: I will not refer here to what condemnation has been allotted to those who swear! The examples of churches that have become schools of catechesis in this manner can be cited endlessly and everywhere. I cannot but remember also the Cathedral of Monreale in Sicily, which is covered with over eight thousand square metres of mosaics that narrate the entire Old and New Testaments.

Today, in a society dominated by audiovisual material, when so much attention is devoted to the visual image, one should particularly underline this catechetical function of the artistic and historical patrimony of the Church.

Charity
The third fundamental reason for which the Church has used art is *for the exercise of charity*, which is carried out,

above all, through the various specific charisms of the religious vocation in convents and monasteries that have conducted their charitable and social work in different ways. Let us think of hospitals, for example. I can cite the first hospital in Rome, San Giacomo Hospital, dating from the end of the thirteenth century and planned as a great monumental complex; or the Hospital of Santo Spirito in Rome, built about a century later, whose central building complex resembles a beautiful church nave because it was intended to receive the suffering Christ in the sick. I must mention also the Hospital of the Innocent in Florence with its marvellous works by Luca della Robbia. Prior to the earthquake there a few years ago, I visited the hospital building in Fabriano, built in the late Middle Ages and recently entirely restored, offering another splendid example. In this regard, we should not forget the astonishment of the young Luther who during his trip to Rome reported on the magnificent hospitals he had seen. And one could indeed cite many other examples of such buildings in all parts of the world.

Besides hospitals, let us think of Confraternities, established by the first religious associations of lay people from the beginning of the late Middle Ages. Innumerable are the Confraternities which have created marvellous headquarters from an artistic point of view and have operated in an exemplary way in charitable works. One should also mention the fact that they have gathered archival material of fundamental importance for the knowledge of historical, social and religious events dating back to distant periods.

Finally, let us think of monasteries which from the time of Saint Benedict onwards flourished all over Europe and throughout the world as centres of culture and charity, and which have been responsible for preserving a civilisation that constitutes even today the fundamental cultural stratum of our entire continent - and not only ours!

The immense patrimony that the Church has created in two millennia for these three major functions constitutes a precious patrimony for the whole of humanity. As we know, at least eighty per cent of the artistic-historical patrimony in nations all over the world has been created by the Church. This important contribution is also clearly perceived by international organisations. The Council of Europe, which comprises forty-seven European nations, has organised in recent years three important meetings – in Paris, Strasbourg, and Santiago de Compostela - whereby three Jews, three Muslims, three Catholics (of whom I was one), three Protestants, and three Orthodox, were invited to discuss the contribution of religious denominations in rendering Europe beautiful as well as considering the initiatives underway to protect this precious patrimony. These meetings were characterised by an exemplary spirit of fraternity. From these gatherings a very interesting picture emerged of how religions – and especially the Christian religion - have contributed to the artistic field in Europe. This simple example demonstrates how, even within a civic environment, the consciousness has grown to accept that religions – and particularly Christianity – have indeed created the largest cultural artistic-historical patrimony on our continent.

This fact, together with the works produced throughout the centuries for the three functions mentioned above, constitute the historical memory of a local and national community, of its culture and faith. In order to understand a population, an historical period or the physiognomy, life, and activity of a community, one must have some awareness of this patrimony and of the historical and social function it has exercised in the various periods of its existence.

Relevance for today

This awareness can certainly fill us with admiration regarding what has been produced by our ancestors. But in the heart of each one of us, doubts can arise that we are capable of imitating them today. Historical circumstances different from ours, diverse cultural periods, different political and social perspectives, and so on, can lead us to conclude that we are facing a time in which we cannot continue along the marvellous path traced by those who have preceded us in past centuries. Today our young people live close to computers, the Internet, cell phones, e-mails etc, and perhaps it might seem to them that everything we have cited earlier belongs to the distant past! The Cultural Heritage of the Church would therefore be a witness of a past that is not really relevant to our every day life.

Before giving an answer to this important problem, I would like to narrate the tale of an episode in Florence back in the autumn of 1977. I was invited to dinner by the Archbishop – at that time His Eminence Cardinal Benelli – and was seated next to Professor Bargellini who was well known as the city mayor as well as for his extraordinary literary and artistic knowledge.

While we were dining I addressed to him this question: "Why is it, dear Professor, that such an enormous flourishing of art and artists took place right here on Florentine territory during the Renaissance period?" Professor Bargellini replied with a smile: "It's easy to explain why. Two words will suffice – the sins and the wealth of the Florentines." Noticing my surprised silence, Professor Bargellini continued: "At that time the

Florentines were very rich because of the many commercial and financial ties which they had established with all of Europe; and they were also great sinners, as often happens when one is very rich. As they got older and began to think about death, many individuals wanted to appease their consciences and they donated large bequests to the Franciscans and the Dominicans, who ran the two great artistic schools in Florence. This patronage, stimulated by remorse, was at the origin of the great artistic flourishing which we have had."

If this interpretation given to me by Professor Bargellini can be considered true, one could say perhaps that the reason for today's lack of an artistic flourishing similar to those times must lie in the fact that Florentines, but not only Florentines, have become poorer and more saintly!

The Church's patrimony and the theological virtues
Let us return to our real problem. What has led the Church and Christians consistently to use works of art for worship, catechesis and charity?

If we formulate the question along these lines, we can see immediately the assonance with three other words that summarise the essence of Christian life: that is, faith, hope, and charity. If someone asked us to explain in a few words what characterizes our Christian living, we should be able to answer that the essence of a Christian life consists in believing, hoping, and loving.

We have thus discovered the secret of all this work carried out throughout the centuries: worship, catechesis, and charity are the concrete reflection of the three fundamental virtues for every Christian: faith, hope, and charity. Faith was made visible throughout the centuries in great cathedrals just as it was in unadorned church-huts in missionary lands. Hope is found in the innumerable pictorial representations of our entire Christian dogma – from the Creation to the Last Judgement – the profound reason of her existence because through these representations the Christian soul was comforted and assisted in its hope towards an otherworldly reality. Charity was reflected in all those cultural assets briefly described earlier, which were placed at the service of neighbour, above all of the poor, the sick, the abandoned and the least of our brethren.

Thus the message of salvation in Jesus is made visible, becomes concrete as a real force; it becomes attractive to the open soul of a Christian who through these representations may perceive this message with a greater intensity than he might simply through a sermon or a theological lesson. Through a cultural, pictorial representation contemplated and meditated upon one can apprehend not only the Word of God which is being proposed to us, but also its practical application in our every day life. One can then clearly understand that the life of faith, hope and charity – that is the real Christian life – is not simply a far away ideal, perhaps difficult or less relevant to our daily living. Two thousand years of Christianity, reflected in the cultural heritage of the Church as a whole, proclaim that this life of faith, hope, and charity is indeed possible, real and attainable.

Therefore, as we have said earlier, the doubt that could have arisen in our hearts from a purely exterior, aesthetic, and historical contemplation of a patrimony so precious, should subside and lead us to a more radical question: if those who preceded us were capable of doing so much, can we remain content in doing less?

Thus, the Cultural Heritage of the Church – whether it is expressed through architecture, painting, sculpture, archives or libraries – if examined according to its profound significance and value, may well represent the beginning of a path that can lead us a long way, because through these marvellous examples, Christ the Word becomes once more alive, concrete, operative in society and a practical ideal which we must allow to inspire our lives.

.

What we can do today
Let us pose ourselves another question: What can we do today on a practical level to achieve this? In fact, it is useless to propose, and listen to, a lot of beautiful considerations regarding the artistic treasures that surround us, if we do not attempt to realise somehow what each one of us perceives to be profoundly true and in which we can justly glorify.

I believe we can proceed in stages. First of all, on an individual level, we should become more conscious of the religious art-historical patrimony we do have and which surrounds us. How many times have we entered into our own churches without knowing exactly what is inside or have we passed by a monument without asking ourselves what it truly represents, why it is there in that specific place, and so on? Still on a individual level, I would like to extend to you the invitation that I usually address particularly to priests and pastors: why don't you organise a Sunday gathering every two or three years of your own parish community to tour the artistic and historical treasures in your church?

Every Church building, however simple in structure, contains *memorabilia* that can be taken as examples for each one of us. There might be a painting offered as a gift for a grace received, or a chalice donated on a special occasion, or some work of embellishment made in the past with the help of the entire parish community. The building's architectural structure and many other things contained in it can give to the faithful the pleasure of appreciating the historical and religious richness of the Church they are frequenting. I know priests who have put into practice this suggestion, and they have observed a noteworthy renewal of interest, on different levels, within the religious life of their parishioners.

I believe that this sort of effort aimed at a deeper knowledge of the artistic-historical richness of our monuments can be an important contribution towards the elevation of the religious culture of our community. Different initiatives can be developed on a diocesan level.

In every diocese a specific Diocesan Commission for Cultural Heritage should be established to address all those areas comprising this cultural heritage: from sacred art to Church archives, from diocesan and parish libraries to diocesan museums, and sacred music. The Diocesan Commission for Cultural Heritage can stimulate very useful initiatives on both diocesan and parish levels. All those who have a specific and personal interest in the artistic field, can bring their contributions and experience in order to assure the appreciation and enhancement of the religious cultural heritage which characterises their own diocese. I also want to recall here those archival collections in parishes, religious communities, and Confraternities, that serve often as fundamental instruments in understanding the history, culture and religious life of a community, city, and nation.

One should think of ways to train and prepare guides, capable of accompanying visitors to our religious monuments, by enabling them to acquire sufficient knowledge to appreciate not only the artistic value of the monument but above all its religious value, as well as the practical significance it can have in the Christian life of each visitor. Accordingly, I am reminded of the examples I have witnessed of Confraternities that have changed their previous specific pastoral purpose and have become Confraternities for Cultural Heritage. They immediately attracted the enthusiastic approval of many young people who, as volunteers, on Sundays organise visits to the various religious monuments around the city.

In France some years back I found a religious Congregation of Sisters who for over twenty years lacked vocations. They changed the direction of their Congregation and dedicated themselves instead to the guiding of the faithful on visits to the churches in their own diocese. This resulted in the resurgence of a great spiritual fervour in the religious life of the faithful, and in a short time the Sisters experienced a return of vocations to their religious family.

I could suggest a series of conferences on the most significant monuments that distinguish places and institutions in the diocese, to be held on appropriate occasions or during the most convenient historical or liturgical anniversaries.

Or one could publish very simple guidebooks containing salient data on the most important churches and religious monuments that distinguish the local Church community and which could serve as useful guides for families or groups of friends on one-day outings. This would stimulate cultural and religious pilgrimages aimed at the discovery of that which the Church has created throughout the centuries in the area where one lives. These would not be merely tourist ploys but activities that even in the context of their legitimate aspect of entertainment would have a highly cultural and religious aim. I am aware of different dioceses that have followed this simple suggestion and have not only encountered as a result the total approval of the faithful but have obtained noteworthy effects on the spiritual life of those who have taken part in these small Sunday or holiday trips.

I can think of the exemplary activity of specific catechesis for children and young people, which purposefully makes reference to the cultural heritage of the Church by using diocesan collections and museums in such a way that the young people may learn to consider these works not only for their historical and artistic value but also, and above all, for their religious value since it has always been the religious motive that created them.

Before I conclude, I must refer to the work that the Diocesan Commission for Cultural Heritage can carry out with the help of local artists responding to the pressing invitation that the Council addressed to artists with the famous phrase "The Church needs you!" a reminder repeated on numerous occasions by both Pope Paul VI and Pope John Paul II. Regarding this same issue, I could suggest a number of initiatives. I will simply mention here the importance of holding specific seminars on biblical themes which can provide an opportunity for dialogue between theologians, artists, architects and biblical scholars, in order to deepen those doctrinal truths which have always been the source of inspiration for great religious works.

As an example of what can be done, the Pontifical Commission for the Cultural Heritage of the Church created back in 1991 an "Advanced Study Training Programme" for those working for the Cultural Heritage of the Church at the Pontifical Gregorian University in Rome which is open to priests and lay people from different nations. This initiative has set an example that has borne much fruit so far. Within a seven years period a similar Programme was established at the Institut Catholique in Paris, France; five years ago an analogous Programme was created at the Catholic University in Lisbon, Portugal; four years ago an identical curricular initiative was offered at the Catholic University in Milan, Italy; and two years ago a Course began in two Catholic universities in Mexico.

Just last year I was invited by the Catholic University of Monterey, Mexico, to hold a series of conferences on every area covered by the Cultural Heritage of the Church. I dedicated twelve lectures, each at least an hour long, throughout the mornings, and for three consecutive afternoons, during a three hour debate, I answered all the questions that were posed to me from the hundreds of participants representing practically all the dioceses in Mexico.

The list of possible initiatives could continue. But I would like to finish this contribution by referring to some of the activities conducted during the Holy Jubilee Year that came to a close just two years ago. As President of the Artistic-Cultural Commission of the Great Jubilee Year, I witnessed the arrival of more than five hundred different projects connected with the five major sections into which the Commission had divided its work: art, cinema and television, theatre, literature, and music. By proclaiming the Holy Year, the Holy Father had intended, on this occasion of the second millennium of Jesus' birth, for the Church to reflect upon the good work she has carried out throughout the centuries, in order to draw some examples and make some proposals for the future, as well as on that which was not so good, in order to ask forgiveness for anything which had resulted in less than perfect harmony with what the Saviour would have wanted.

As we look back over the bi-millennial history of the Church, we could certainly not omit that which the Church has done in the field of art and culture. The Jubilee Day for Artists celebrated in the month of February 2000, gathered together in St Peter's Basilica more than eight thousand artists from all over the world. They were welcomed with fraternal kindness and intense interest by the Holy Father, who is an artist himself. As we know, in his younger years he was both a poet and playwright.

I would like to conclude my summary with a thought that the Holy Father has shared with me on numerous occasions: "If, when I was Archbishop of Krakow, I could do something good for those 'afar' from the Church it was because I always began with the cultural heritage of the Church which has a language everyone knows, a language all accept, and in this language I was able to begin a dialogue that would not have been possible otherwise".

This is my wish for all those who work with the cultural heritage of the Church: may their knowledge serve not only to open a new dialogue with those "afar" but also to impress in men's hearts a new outlook and a new appreciation for the cultural heritage of the Church they have, so that their Christian, religious and cultural life may be renewed, strengthened and enlightened by all the beauty that surrounds us; may it stimulate a firm and concerted willingness increasingly to enhance the marvellous treasures passed on to us by our ancestors in the faith, for the religious and cultural good of our lands and of our souls.

Archbishop Francesco Marchisano is Titular Bishop of Populonia, Italy. He is President of the Pontifical Commission for the Cultural Heritage of the Church. He is also President of the Pontifical Commission for Sacred Archaeology.

Lifelong Learning and the Church's Vision of Catechesis

Rev. Paul J. Watson

Education and learning for adults has become a major area of interest in recent years both in the Catholic Church and in the wider society. The concepts of lifelong learning, the learning organisation and the learning society so prominent now in government discourse are paralleled in the Church's documents by a new emphasis on the formation and catechesis of adults in the Church with a view to equipping every believer to take part in the Church's mission of evangelisation. In fact, the *General Directory for Catechesis* emphatically speaks of the Adult Baptismal Catechumenate as the model for all catechesis. It is hard to overstate the significance of the major shift in focus that has occurred but it is unclear as to what extent this shift has actually realised its full impact in the thinking and strategic planning of the Church in this new millennium.

I would like to discuss some of the implications of this paradigm shift both in its secular context and in the context of the Church's mission. There are some interesting points of convergence and divergence and I believe that there are some exciting opportunities as well as challenges arising.

I should, first of all, set out my stall. For three years now I have been working full time in an Institute of

Distance Learning,[27] after the model of the Open University. Our programmes are designed to facilitate the "learning" of students in the fields of Catechesis, Religious Education and Theology. They include programmes of formation and training for Catechists, Teachers and Deacons and more widely for adults who want to fulfil a desire to grow in the knowledge and understanding of, and deeper participation in, their Faith. Over the three years I have come to appreciate the potential of Distance Learning as a tool that is particularly fitting for adult learning in the twenty-first century and, more importantly, most fitting for equipping Christians today to engage actively with the mission of the Church. The Institute occupies a centuries-old historic Catholic House with a tradition of spirituality. It is this context that provides an opportunity for reflection on the productive interaction between modern thinking on adult learning and the Church's mission of Catechesis and Evangelisation.

Participation in adult learning

There are three aspects among developments taking place in the secular world of learning and education that are of particular interest to the Church. The first is the new emphasis on adult learning that has become a major government priority in recent years. The second is the broader concept of lifelong learning. And finally, in the light of targets of widening participation in adult learning,

---

[27] Maryvale Institute, Birmingham is a National and International College of Distance Learning. First established in 1980 as a Catechetical Institute in the Archdiocese of Birmingham, Maryvale has developed into the largest theology faculty in Higher Education in Britain as well as numbering thousands of adults on various other courses at non-H.E. level.

there is the issue of overcoming the barriers to learning among current non-participants.

The use of the phrase "adult learning" hides a major shift in thinking about the whole project of education in modern society. Over the last fifty years, since the 1944 Education Act in Britain, the emphasis on the word "adult" and the concept "learning" in the world of education have accumulated a wealth of debate, some major changes in policy at government levels and some interesting analyses and theories about the various changes that are taking place in society as a whole.

After 1944 government priorities were focussed on initial compulsory education and the maintenance of the Higher Education system. There was acknowledgement of the education that was taking place for adults in extra-mural departments of the Universities, in Local Education Authorities and in Workers' Education Associations, and funding was available for these initiatives. However, there was little interest in or acknowledgement of adult education that might be taking place in a variety of other settings. The truth is that governments held that their responsibility was for initial education and that was to serve for the individual's lifespan. The history of the last fifty years has been one of growing focus on adults within the policies and strategies of governments. For a variety of social, economic and political reasons the boundaries of what is meant by "adult", and of what is included in the education in which they participate, have expanded and become permeable. In fact, in the dominant debates today the word "adult" spans the period from the end of initial education to the end of life. Apparently, governments and society as a whole are interested in the education of adults from their leaving school throughout the entirety of their lives.

If we turn now to the descriptor "learning" we find that a remarkable transformation has taken place. This is not simply a change of words but a real paradigm shift. The change of focus from "education" to "learning" reveals a change from an emphasis on the institutional provider of a product (education) to an emphasis on the experience (learning) of the student. It could be described as a transfer of attention from inputs to outputs. From this changed perspective of the learning experience of the student, what is made available to the student is no longer strictly described as "education" but rather as "learning opportunities".

What was it that brought about this radical change in thinking and what are some of the implications? In sociological terms, we might say that the discourses of adult education that had been current up to the 1970s — discourses that established strong boundaries of demarcation in education for adults, typically restricted to three privileged sites (Local Education Authority, Extramural, & Workers' Education Association) — began to be contested and eventually dominated by discourses of lifelong learning. The many and rapid changes taking place in society (demographic, technological, economic and cultural) were creating the demand for a new response in the way that education was construed. The notion of initial education sufficing for life, with the addition of a few select and specified sites providing for some further and higher adult education, was deemed to be no longer an adequate response. At first, the changes taking place elicited the response of seeking to provide recurrent educational opportunities. The dominant issues here were the social issues of access and equity. It was seen that the existing boundaries constructing adult education were inappropriate, far too limited, marginalised far too many adults, and were failing to recognise what was actually happening among adults. The various distinctions (education, training, leisure, formal, informal, non-formal) of earlier discourses made less and less sense and, moreover, were seen as inhibiting adults' access and progression. Thus boundaries became more permeable and expanded. Eventually in the 1980s, lifelong learning discourses shifted in their focus from access and progression to vocational relevance as government interest in economic change and the development of the labour market began to dominate.[28]

While this government interest is driving the lifelong learning agenda, a number of other factors have helped to shape the discourse and establish "lifelong learning" as the accepted response to the changes taking place in society. Such factors include debates surrounding the notion of "androgogy", i.e. is there a specific way of learning proper to adults?,[29] and also the socio-political concepts of "emancipation" which, following the work of Freire,[30] took a more activist approach towards learning as a means of establishing greater social equality among adults. Finally, we should mention the cultural factor of "individualism", the growing emphasis on individuals taking responsibility for the course and direction of their own lives, and on their status as consumers or customers.

---

[28] Edwards, Richard, "The inevitable future? Post-Fordism in work and learning" in Edwards, R., Hanson, A. and Raggatt, P. (eds), *Boundaries of Adult Learning*, (London and New York: Routledge, in association with the Open University, 1993).

[29] Knowles, M., "Androgogy An emerging technology for adult learning" in Tight, M. (ed.), *Adult Learning and Education*, (London: Croom Helm, 1983).

[30] Freire, Paolo, *Pedagogy of the Oppressed*, (Harmondsworth: Penguin, 1978).

Students today are viewed as customers choosing to buy the education services available according to their own perceived needs. It was perhaps this cultural movement of individualism and consumerism that has particularly influenced the shift towards concentration on students' learning experience through their responsible choice of taking hold of learning opportunities. Allen Tough[31] is credited with the insight that the learning of adults is principally self-directed and depends on their own initiative and takes place (often informally) in an extremely broad variety of ways and at a multiplicity of sites.[32]

This leads to the final element of this section. How is participation in adult learning to be widened? In the main, attention has focussed on overcoming the various barriers to participation that research has brought to light as well as the continuing matter of extending and making more permeable the boundaries by which learning activities may be formally or institutionally construed as "adult learning". The first is a matter of situational and dispositional changes taking place within society, within institutions and within individuals, in order to facilitate access to more and wider learning opportunities for more and socially diverse groups of people. The second concerns the ways in which governments and their policies, and institutions and their policies, decide to construe activities as "learning" and choose both to fund and credit those activities.

---

[31] Tough, Alan, "Self-planned learning and major personal change" in Smith, R.M. (ed.), *Adult Learning: Issues and Innovations*, (ERIC Clearing House in Career Education, Northern Illinois University, 1976).
[32] This multiplicity of sites has increased exponentially with the creation of the Internet, whose social and educational benefits as well as evils are only just beginning to be appreciated.

A huge breakthrough took place in the 1970s with the concept of the Open University and its distance learning methodology. Participation in adult learning has grown so markedly that now the Government felt able to set ambitious targets of enabling access for more of the population to lifelong learning. The Open University has made it possible for people who have long since left initial formal education to take up part-time learning in a way that is both flexible and designed to meet the particular needs of adults.

Perhaps the most significant contribution of distance learning is the fact that it provides a multitude of opportunities for self-directed learning. That it is not dependent on face to face contact with a teacher, traditional lecturing, nor confined to specific sites and times places not only the responsibility but also the sense of personal achievement in the hands of the student. For those who operate with the more traditional model of teaching, the distance-learning model would appear to involve the limitation of requiring the quality in the students of high personal motivation.

Let me here draw on personal experience. While there is certainly a strong element of motivation needed to sustain perseverance during the loneliness of the long-distance learner, it is not necessarily the case that the student arrives fully equipped with such motivation. My observation of hundreds of students at Maryvale is that it is the actual learning that takes place, and the way that it takes place that produces on-going and increasing motivation. Students often arrive with a certain amount of fear and trepidation, conscious that they are dipping their toes in uncharted waters, conscious also that it may be years since leaving formal education. A remarkable thing happens during their first forays into systematic study and assignment tasks. Whatever their previous experience, whatever, often negative, mindsets they carry from their experience of initial primary and secondary education, they find that their experience of assisted but self-directed learning is a tremendous stimulus. The moments of discovery, personal insight and reflection, and the process of articulating these in written assignments are not only occasions of learning, but also of real joy. The time of study becomes one of self-realisation and for many a process of healing. Furthermore, in the context of programmes of Catechesis and Theology, the flexible nature of the method of study allows the opportunity for the students to turn their learning experiences immediately into times of prayer. This builds such a positive memory that the desire to go on with further, even lifelong, learning is greatly enhanced. Compare this with the experience of many who have undertaken more traditional models of study, which often seem to produce a sense of having successfully negotiated a hurdle that can now be left behind!

If this will serve as a very brief summary of the current thinking surrounding participation in adult and lifelong learning, I would like to turn now to the Catholic Church's current thinking about its priorities in the areas of Evangelisation, Catechesis and of growing in the Faith.

Adult Learning and the General Directory for Catechesis
There are a number of features of the new *General Directory for Catechesis* that show interesting similarities with the thinking in the secular world of education and learning. In the first place, the *General Directory* is the result of a development that has been taking place since the Second Vatican Council. It is very much a document that has responded to change and has recognised the inadequacies

and limits of previous models. It is essentially a revision of the *General Catechetical Directory* (1971) called for by the Fathers of the Second Vatican Council. What is new is the restructuring of the document in the light of two new principles: an inspired introductory section based on the Parable of the Sower and the addition of a major section on the Pedagogy of the Faith.

Of particular importance in the intervening years between the two directories was the promulgation of the post-synodal Apostolic Exhortation *Evangelii Nuntiandi* (1975) and the presentation to the Church of the *Catechism of the Catholic Church* (1992). The first of these two "milestones" produced a new principle that would form one of the crucial foundations for the new *Directory*. Following the Synod of Bishops of 1974, which considered the theme of Evangelisation, Pope Paul VI's exhortation, *Evangelii Nuntiandi*, enunciated the principle: that catechesis would in future be understood as firmly situated in the essential mission of the Church – the mission of evangelisation! This principle provides a new context and perspective with which to view the whole task of catechesis. Furthermore, it also provides a new and additional aim. In future catechesis will have as part of its objective the formation of men and women who will themselves be evangelisers.

The second "milestone" is the new *Catechism of the Catholic Church*. The Apostolic Constitution *Fidei Depositum*, which presented the new *Catechism*, specifically offered the *Catechism* to the Church as "a sure and authentic reference text for teaching Catholic doctrine" and asked that Pastors and the faithful "use it assiduously in fulfilling their mission of proclaiming the Faith and calling people to the

Gospel life".[33] This request becomes enshrined in the *General Directory for Catechesis* as a second principle: the requirement of the appropriation of the content of the Faith as presented in the *Catechism of the Catholic Church*.

Embracing the first principle of situating catechesis within the essential mission of evangelisation, the *General Directory for Catechesis* outlines the whole project of evangelisation in terms of three key "moments":

- initial or missionary proclamation of the Gospel leading to personal adherence to Jesus Christ
- an adult baptismal catechumenate leading to communion within the full life of the Church and ultimately within the life of the Trinity
- on-going education in the Faith – a process of maturing in holiness and formation as evangelisers

These moments are seen as progressive – in fact lifelong, and also repeatable. Of great significance is the observation, made several times in the document, that the absence, for many in the Church, of the first moment (Initial Proclamation and Conversion) can account for their living on the margins of Christian life. The second moment, most properly described as initiatory catechesis, also evokes the conclusion that there are many in the Church for whom this catechumenate has never been completed.

The *General Directory for Catechesis* has taken up an important concept from the *General Catechetical Directory* of

---

[33] John Paul II, *Fidei Depositum* § 3.

1971 and given it greater emphasis: "Catechesis for adults, since it deals with persons who are capable of an adherence that is fully responsible, must be considered the chief form of catechesis. All the other forms, which are indeed always necessary, are in some way oriented to it".[34] The new *Directory* goes on to say that the adult baptismal catechumenate, with its emphasis on the four elements of the *Catechism* (Faith as it is believed, celebrated, lived, and finally nourished by prayer) must be considered as the paradigm of all catechesis.

In summary, there is no doubt that the *priority of adults* as the principal locus of the catechetical activity of the Church and an inherent commitment also to lifelong learning is firmly in place. In response to this new agenda, we have seen the production, by National Conferences of Bishops, of documents affirming the commitment to adult catechesis.[35]

As I indicated above, the more fundamental change in the educational world has been the shift from education to learning, from the provider to the learner, and the subsequent research on the barriers to participation in learning. Drawing upon the experience of working with adults in a Catholic Distance Learning Institute and also upon the clear indicators in the *General Directory for Catechesis*, I want to argue that there is a very significant Catholic contribution to the debate about adult learning. This is not simply a matter of the Church taking on board

---

[34] *General Directory For Catechesis*, (London: Catholic Truth Society, 1997), §§ 20 & 59.
[35] *The Priority of Adult Formation*, Catholic Bishops' Conference of England and Wales, (London: Catholic Media Trust, 2000) and *Our Hearts Were Burning Within Us*: A Pastoral Plan for Adult Faith Formation in the United States, (Washington D.C.: United States Catholic Conference, 1999).

the developments in thinking about the way adults can learn, but, more fundamentally, it is a way of utilising and interpreting the current model in the light of the uniqueness of what is involved in the processes of Evangelisation and Catechesis.

In the Introduction to the *General Directory*, the Parable of the Sower from the Gospel of Mark serves as scriptural focus and contextualisation for all that follows in the document. (See §§ 14-15). It is worth noting that it has become a characteristic of the magisterial teaching of the Holy Father to begin with a reflection upon a passage of scripture.[36] Such example gives concrete witness to the principle that one of the key sources for catechesis is the Word of God, as interpreted in the Tradition and Magisterium of the Church.

The primary purpose of presenting the Parable of the Sower is to remind pastors and catechists of the necessity of maintaining a consciousness of the "field" in which the seed of the Word of God is sown. The parable is very familiar and draws attention to the condition of the soil into which the seed falls. The symbolism of the parable represents an invitation to consider the variety of conditions in which the gospel will be proclaimed and the various factors that can inhibit the Gospel's fruitfulness.

It is not difficult, with a slight shift of perspective, to see that the Parable of the Sower is fundamentally a teaching about adult learning and the various obstacles to productive participation. It is worth exploring this further,

---

[36] Other examples are *Reconciliatio et Paenitentia* (1984) – the Parable of the Prodigal Son; *Dominum et Vivificantum* (1986) – Jesus' promise of the Holy Spirit; *Christifideles Laici* (1988) – the Parable of the Workers in the Vineyard; *Veritatis Splendor* (1993) – the Rich Young Man.

since the parable can offer some insights into adult learning not found in the secular analyses.

But before investigating this, I want to introduce another element of the contribution of the *General Directory for Catechesis*. When consideration is given to the methodology that is appropriate for adults learning about their faith and the lifelong nature of their learning, the shifted focus on the adult learner is not entirely adequate in the case of Catechesis and Evangelisation. On several occasions, the *Directory* makes it clear that in the business of carrying out its mission, the Church is not the arbitrator either of the content of the Faith or of the methodology by which it accomplishes its task. Ultimately, the mission of the Church is the transmission of Revelation. It is a mandate received from Christ himself and the Church first of all submits to Revelation as a divine gift before faithfully handing it on. Fidelity to Christ is twofold in the sense that the person of Christ not only gave the mandate, but also Christ himself is the fullness of the Revelation that the Church transmits. The implication here is that in the matter of learning the Faith, neither the learner nor the immediate provider (the Church) determines the learning outcome. The outcome, in fact, is not simply learning but also communion – communion with the person of Christ and with his Body, the Church. Revelation, furthermore, is ultimately a work of the Holy Trinity and its ultimate goal is communion within the life of the Trinity through a process of conversion, transformation and maturing. Since God is the source, and the activity of Revelation is the activity of God, it is necessary to take account also of the Divine Pedagogy. This pedagogy is most clearly seen in the words, signs and actions of the person of Jesus Christ and is sacramentally present also in the words, signs and actions of the Church. The pedagogy of God, therefore, requires the response of personal discipleship of Christ and communion with the life of the Church. This life of the Church involves proclaiming, celebrating, living and praying her faith. All of these elements, summarised in the *Catechism of the Catholic Church*, are essential not only to the content of faith but also to the processes, the pedagogy by which faith is transmitted and grows to maturity. At the heart of it all is the work of the Holy Spirit. It is the action of the Holy Spirit that ensures that the outcome of sowing the Word, of Catechesis in the Church, of adult learning in the Church, is a transformed life. In fact, it is eternal life – "... and eternal life is this: to know you the one, true God and Jesus Christ whom you have sent" (John 17.3).

The methods utilised in the pedagogy of the Faith can be as wide and diverse as the situations and needs of the learners. One requirement remains: that the methods follow the principle of "fidelity to God and fidelity to man" (§ 149). This principle ensures that the process of transmission is adequate to the content of the message. Fidelity to God involves all of those factors mentioned above, while fidelity to man invites the use of the rich diversity of methods that draw upon the pedagogical sciences, the sciences of communication and taking account of the variety of circumstances (age and intellectual development of Christians, their ecclesial and spiritual maturity and many other personal circumstances § 148) pertaining to the individual learner.

The Sower and overcoming barriers to participation in Catechesis
Returning now to the Parable of the Sower, I have long believed that there is more to this parable than is typically acknowledged. Its presence at the forefront of the *General*

Directory perhaps invites some further investigation into the fruit that it might be offering. There are a number of reasons, provided by the text itself, that suggest we should pay particular attention to this parable. The parable is recorded by all three Synoptic Gospels and presented as the first of Jesus' parables. It is also one of only two that Jesus actually explains afterwards to his disciples (the other is the related Parable of the Darnel). This would seem to indicate the importance Jesus attached to it. The third, and perhaps clinching, reason is that in Mark's account Jesus answers the disciples' query with the remark "Do you not understand this parable? *Then how will you understand all the parables?*" (Mark 4.13) It would appear that the Parable of the Sower is a key to understanding all of the parables and perhaps all of the teaching and the deeds of Jesus. If this is the case, then we might conclude that the parable has something to say about the processes that take place when the Word of God comes into contact with an individual mind and heart. In fact, it deals quite specifically with what might be described as barriers to learning and growth in faith.

There is one feature of the parable, which, at first sight, may seem to be a source of disappointment. While there is much said about the various soils that fail to produce lasting fruit, the parable seems to omit any obvious teaching about the nature of productive soil. The very thing that we might be expecting seems to be missing. Here we touch upon the main point about Jesus' use of parables. They serve as a kind of conundrum, a problem to be solved. They engage the heart and mind of the hearer, and as they do so, they raise further questions, thus drawing the person in towards receiving further insight and enlightenment concerning the mysteries of God's Kingdom. What is there in the parable that might tell us about the productive soil? It does not take long before the solution jumps out at us. If we look closely at the different kinds of soil, we will notice that there is a progression. They are not all equally unproductive. In fact, each type of soil makes more progress in producing than the previous type. Each type of soil fails, Jesus tells us, for different reasons. We shall gain a great deal of information about the good soil by observing closely the failure of the three types of poor soil.

For me, the Parable of the Sower has become a source of reflection about the process of lifelong learning in the context of evangelisation and catechesis in the Church. I have come to see that the various soils could represent not only different situations in which the seed is sown, but also describe the progression that must occur if the full process of evangelisation, envisaged by the *General Directory for Catechesis* (the three "moments" described earlier), is to take place and reach full maturity. In other words, the parable outlines for us the principal barriers that need to be overcome in the lifelong journey of faith development and learning.

Here, I think, we meet a unique contribution to the secular debates about adult and lifelong learning as we seek to draw upon them in our thinking about evangelisation and catechesis. The barriers highlighted by the parable – the path, the rocky soil and the thorny soil – are determined both by the nature of the seed and by a Christian interpretation of the state of the human mind, the human person and of society as a whole. The nature of the seed, or in other words, the nature of the material content of learning and growth, is that it is divine Revelation, uniquely present in the person of Jesus Christ, and, as already indicated, sacramentally present in the faith, liturgy, life and prayer of the Church. The human condition (made known through Revelation) is that there is a certain antipathy or resistance to God's Revelation brought about by sin and affecting the readiness of the mind and heart to accept and receive. There is, furthermore, a sense in which the human person and society in general are under some form of influence, even captivity, of the evil one. Human reason ought to be enough for us to come to knowledge of God. However, this capacity of human reason has been damaged by sin and needs the further assistance of Revelation. In addition, there are aspects of the mystery of God, his salvation and his ultimate purposes for human beings that are incapable of being known apart from the work of Revelation.

In short, Revelation is needed both because of the fallen condition of the human mind and its reasoning powers and because there are many things that the human mind could not know by its own powers. In the process of appropriating Revelation or learning the Faith (in the fullest sense of the word), there is a unique set of barriers needing to be overcome. We might describe them as spiritual barriers. It is about these that the Parable of the Sower has much light to bestow.

There is not the space to enter into a detailed analysis of the parable here. Suffice it to say that there appear to be two kinds of difficulty with each of the soils described. I prefer to describe these as an external and an internal difficulty. In the case of the path, the external problem is the birds that steal the seed away. However, this is made all the more likely because of the internal problem with the soil. It is hard and therefore the seed rests on the surface and does not sink into the unreceptive soil. The second stage, illustrated by the rocky soil, is quite different but also manifests both external and internal difficulties.

Internally, the soil lacks moisture; the rocks ensure that water soon drains away. The seed does not have enough water for its life and growth. Coupled with that, the scorching sun ensures that any moisture is soon evaporated. Finally, in the third stage, other seeds, contending with the sower's seed, have also arrived in the soil. And the soil is such that it seems to permit the growth of the conflicting seed at the same time as it facilitates the augmentation of the seed of the Word.

As previously suggested, the productive soil is not simply just better soil, but, I submit, soil which is progressively improved through dealing with the problems – I would say, barriers – that typically arise in the process of evangelisation and catechesis. Fortunately, Jesus himself has given us the beginnings of an interpretation and the unity of scripture allows us to draw some further conclusions regarding the nature of the barriers and the solutions to overcoming them.

The birds of the air, we are told, refer to the work of the evil one; the scorching sun to forms of persecution; and the seed producing thorny plants indicates the values of society and the corrupted desires of the heart. The hardness of the path, we might conclude, designates the unconverted mind and heart.

The path reminds us of the spiritual warfare that takes places in all evangelisation and catechesis. There is a battle for the conversion of the human heart towards Christ. When the evangelisers and catechists ignore this warfare against the evil one we should not be surprised when the Word is not received. In this context perhaps we could take more seriously the words of St Paul: "To me … this grace was given, to preach to the Gentiles the inscrutable riches of Christ, and to bring to light what is the plan of the mystery hidden from ages past in God who created all things, so that the manifold wisdom of God might now be made known through the Church *to the principalities and authorities in the heavens*".[37] This act of warfare, declaring against the evil spirits, would seem to be an element of the very first step in the process of evangelisation and catechesis (initial or missionary proclamation) in order to prevent the robbery of the Word before it has a chance bring about the work of conversion and adherence to Christ.

It is worth mentioning at this point an observation I have made over the last three years in the course of induction evenings with new students arriving to start our distance learning programmes. We usually invite the students to share with each other their reasons for enrolling on the course. Almost universally the story has been the same. While the details differ, the stories tell of an awakened faith and the resultant hunger both for further learning and a desire to share with others what they have received. This would seem to confirm that the process of lifelong learning in the Faith is predicated on an initial proclamation and a personal conversion and appropriation of the Gospel. It is these elements that also seem to produce a desire to be evangelisers. In other words, successfully negotiating the barrier of the first soil – the path – is the key to all further learning and growth. While there is clearly a strong element of divine initiative in this process of conversion, it also challenges us, as an Institute, and our dioceses and parishes, to address the issue of initial proclamation and personal conversion if the priority of participation in adult learning in the Church is to be carried forward successfully.

---

[37] Ephesians 3:8-10.

The rocky soil needing moisture surely refers both to the action of the Holy Spirit and the context of the believing, celebrating, living and praying Church. Only when these are present will a person who has been converted really begin to grow. The absence of any one of these elements would inhibit the growth of the Word, and would constitute a significant barrier to the Faith being firmly rooted. We are minded of the *General Directory's* analysis that adult baptismal catechesis has sometimes been incomplete. Further learning in the Faith for adults needs to provide this ecclesial context. In our distance-learning Institute we have opted to build into the programmes short residential periods not least to provide a context of spirituality, liturgy and sharing. Such a context would seem to be an essential element for learning in the field of Catechesis.

The interpretation of the thorny soil should perhaps call to mind the *General Directory's* consideration of today's religious situation and its invitation "to take into account the extent to which Christians 'have been shaped by the climate of secularism and ethical relativism' ".[38] In some ways, we touch here upon the most difficult task. The culture in which we live and which we breathe in daily is all-pervasive. It is not easy to disentangle those elements of it that are destructive of our faith. Could it be that a barrier to learning and catechesis in the Church is the climate of relativism? It is true that many have become confused, by the multiplication of theologies, into believing the truth is in fact relative. In other words, that a genuine and important diversity of reflection on the truth has subtly led to the view that the truth itself can no longer be certain, can no longer be relied upon with

[38] *General Directory for Catechesis*, § 25.

95

confidence. To counteract this the evangeliser, catechist and teacher in the Church must continue to reflect on the Holy Father's words:

> Whatever be the level of his responsibility in the Church, every catechist must constantly endeavour to transmit by his teaching and behaviour the teaching and the life of Jesus. He will not seek to keep directed towards himself and his personal opinions and attitudes the attention and the consent of the mind and heart of the person he is catechising. Above all, he will not try to inculcate his personal opinions as if they expressed Christ's teaching and the lessons of his life. Every catechist should be able to apply to himself, the mysterious words of Jesus: "My teaching is not mine, but his who sent me".[39]

Turning to the perspective of the learner, the Pope speaks of a right:

> ... from the theological point of view every baptised person, precisely by reason of being baptised, has the right to receive from the Church instruction and education enabling him or her to enter on a truly Christian life; and from the viewpoint of human rights, every human being has the right to seek religious truth and adhere to it freely ... .[40]

Conclusion

In his most recent Apostolic Letter, *Novo Millennio Ineunte* (2001), John Paul II speaks of the present opportunity for

---

[39] John Paul II, *Catechesi Tradendae*, § 6.
[40] *Op. cit.* § 14.

the Church of examining how far she has renewed herself, in order to be able to take up her evangelising mission with fresh enthusiasm. The Vatican Council, nearly forty years earlier, introduced the concept of the "inculturation" of the Faith, since "all the riches of the nations have been given to Christ as an inheritance". The work of the Christian community is to discern which riches to take up as compatible with the Faith, and, on the other hand, to seek to purify and transform modes of thought and life which are contrary to the Gospel and the Kingdom of God.

In what is taking place in secular thinking about adult learning and education there are great riches to be absorbed so that new insights and paradigms, as well as creative new methodologies might enhance the mission of transmitting the Faith. At the same time, reflection on the world's wisdom provides the opportunity for a fresh look at the distinctive contribution that can be made by a deeper penetration of the Scriptures and the Church's renewed understanding of the mission mandated by Christ. One apparently successful response to this double challenge is represented by the development of a Catholic College of distance learning. There is cause for great optimism in the Church's work among adults as the challenges are embraced.

Fr Paul J. Watson was ordained priest for the Archdiocese of Birmingham in 1974. After serving in a number of parishes, he studied in Rome for a Licence in Theology (Spirituality). For the next ten years, while serving two parishes as Parish Priest, he developed and taught a number of programmes of parish catechesis, and became an Associate member of the staff of Maryvale Institute, contributing to the development of a Master's Programme in Personal, Moral and spiritual Development, as well as teaching a course in Spirituality and contributing to other courses. He has undertaken further post-graduate studies in Adult Learning and Management of Higher Education Institutions. In 1999 he joined Maryvale fulltime as Director-elect before succeeding as Director in August 2000. He is also a founder member of Bible Alive and a regular contributor to this monthly publication.

THE CHALLENGE OF TEACHING THE CATHOLIC MORALITY OF SEX, MARRIAGE AND THE FAMILY IN THE THIRD MILLENNIUM

ANTHONY FISHER O.P.

INTRODUCTION: SOME CENTRAL CLAIMS OF CATHOLIC MORAL TEACHING ON SEX, MARRIAGE AND THE FAMILY

Though the purpose of the present volume is to celebrate a jubilee and achievements already made in the life of Archbishop Mario Conti, we also rejoice in his new role as Archbishop of Scotland's largest diocese and thus as a leading pastor-teacher of the Catholic flock of Scotland and beyond. As the Church enters the third Millennium of Grace her leaders face many new challenges in the teaching of sexual, marital and family ethics. Many epistemological, anthropological or moral propositions which have been consistently asserted in the Catholic tradition are now or will be increasingly contested. These include the claims:

- that there are *objective philosophical and theological truths* about the nature of the human person, relationships and actions which are *accessible* to faith and reason and which establish the *proper limits* to human will;
- that genital sexual activity, properly understood, expresses a total *self-giving* and *receiving* which is

marital and so should only be celebrated within the context of marriage;

- that the *unitive* and *procreative* dimensions of "the marital act" are intrinsic and *neither aspect should be deliberately excluded* when a couple engage in genital sexual activity; and

- that misuses of sexuality which may be *gravely sinful* include: adultery, fornication, prostitution, rape, incest, same-sex genital activity, masturbation, bestiality, pornography, contraception, sterilisation, abortifacients, some artificial reproductive technologies...

There are many other propositions in Catholic sexual, marital and familial ethics,[41] and even those that I have

---

[41] Some other such propositions might include:

- That *human beings are a unity of physical, emotional, intellectual and spiritual dimensions*, so that like all animals "we are our bodies" but unlike other animals those bodies make concrete our spiritual reality as free, rational, loving beings, images and children of God, siblings of the Son, temples of the Holy Spirit, destined to eternal (bodily) life with the saints;

- That *sexuality is a fundamental* aspect not only of our bodiliness, but of personality, relationships and activity, so that femaleness and maleness are ontologically fundamental in a way that race and tastes, for instance, are not;

- That the male and female ways of being human are *different* but of *equal dignity, complementing* each other and grounding a reciprocity most perfectly expressed in marital communion;

- That marriage is the free commitment of a woman and a man to unite as wife and husband *exclusively* and *for life* for the sake of their *mutual fulfilment*, for *family* life, for the building up of the *community* (both social and ecclesial), and for the *salvation* of all concerned; any choice directly against any of these aspects is an attack on marriage and wrongful;

listed need a lot of elaboration. Several might well be put differently or better – I will come back to this point later. Interestingly, while some of these claims are contested by people within the Catholic Church today as often as by those outside it, most of them would be common ground with other Christian communions and faith traditions. Indeed, the Vatican often finds itself today at international meetings leading an alliance of countries, including several of predominantly non-Christian faiths, against previously Christian countries which have wholesale embraced secular liberalism and post-modernity.[42]

- That married couple have responsibilities to guard their own and each other's vocations, to *love, honour and serve* each other, to be faithful companions for the whole of life, to share decision-making appropriately, to engage in *chaste* sexual acts, and to *procreate responsibly*, using only upright methods of achieving and limiting family;

- That couples should therefore engage in marital intercourse *generously and responsibly*, taking into consideration the times of fertility and their capacity to bring up a(nother) child;

- That parents should *raise their children* justly and lovingly, promoting their growth to physical, intellectual, social, moral and spiritual maturity according to *Christian principles.*

I have argued for all these propositions briefly in Anthony Fisher OP, "Does the Church's teaching on sex make sense?" *Priests and People* 7 (1993): 317-322 and in "Christian ethics, Roman Catholic," *Encyclopaedia of Applied Ethics* (1998), vol 1, 471-492, but I do not pretend that any of them is easily argued for today. See also Germain Grisez *The Way of the Lord Jesus*, vol 2: *Living a Christian life* (Quincy IL: Franciscan, 1993) ch.9; Ronald Lawler, Joseph Boyle and William E. May, *Catholic Sexual Ethics: A Summary, Explanation and Defence* (2nd Ed, Huntington: Our Sunday Visitor, 1995); William E. May, *Marriage: The Rock on which the Family is Built* (San Francisco: Ignatius Press, 1995); Christopher West, *Good News about Sex and Marriage* (Ann Arbor MI: Servant, 2000).

[42] Cf. George Weigel, "Where Marriage is a dirty word", *Wall Street Journal* August 26, 1994, p.A14.

SEX IN SECULAR LIBERALISM AND POST-MODERNITY

Recreational sex: denaturing and consumerising of the body

Elizabeth Knox's superbly crafted novel *The Vintner's Luck*[43] was described in the London *Times* as "an all-too-human chronicle of burning desire, violence, murderousness, bitter jealousy, curiosity, sexual deviation, shame and a fidelity of a sort". It is interesting what we today regard as "all-too-human". The tale pivots on the annual meeting between Sobran Jodeau, a nineteenth century Burgundian vigneron, and Xas, a gorgeous angel. Along the way Knox elaborates the sexual adventures of the central characters: Sobran marries his childhood sweetheart Céleste after impregnating her, but also continues his sexual affair with his best male friend Baptiste, following him to the Napoleonic campaign in Russia. While away they queue, as soldiers do, for prostitutes and Sobran even penetrates a nine-month pregnant one, inducing her labour. After Baptiste's death Sobran returns to his vineyard and has two affairs parallel to his marriage, one with Xas, the angel with the beautiful man's body, and the other with the local countess, Aurora. Céleste gives him many children but has her own affair with his brother Léon, a sado-masochistic ex-seminarian who has his mistresses strangle him while they make love. The angel Xas roams the earth, looking not for souls he might devour so much as bodies of men with whom he might have some romance, and with Sobran's son.

There is much more to this story and much that is admirable. But what struck me on reading it was how seductive it was: how easily the reader is carried along by

---

43 Elizabeth Knox, *The Vintner's Luck* (London: Chatto & Windus, 1999).

the author's affectionate rendering of a tale with so much violence and perversion; how rarely one flinches; how undisturbing it all is. In the post-modern era each person chooses his/her own sexuality or sexualities, more or less at whim. Nothing is natural or unnatural. Sexuality and sexual behaviour are "privatised", chosen according to taste, and interchangeable; life, life-giving and even, as I will suggest, life-taking are likewise matters of taste. Anthropology, physiology, psychology, practical reason are all irrelevant to sexual choice; what matters is freedom and preferences and the fulfilment of those preferences.

If men want to be mothers, if scientists want to clone and dismember human embryos, if people want sex with any and every other human being – or even with non-human beings – why not, as long as there is consent and no one is hurt too much? If people want legal recognition for "same-sex marriages", or to engage in serial polygamy (whether by simply living together or divorcing and remarrying as often as they like), if they elect to be "dinks" with two incomes but no children or "yuppies" with three dogs, two cars and one child, the numbers of the latter carefully contrived through contraception, abortion or sterilisation – who dare say no? If people want to design their children genetically or get rid of any undesirable characteristics before they are born or pay someone else to carry their child for them – what is to stop them? A President may be shamed into admitting that his serial sexual sins are "inappropriate", but in the end he is a symbol more of sexual consumerism than contrition. Liberal autonomy as freedom from *Nature* – from God and His order in the cosmos, from the requirements of practical reason, from any limit to the human will – has also become in the post-modern era freedom from *natures*.[44]

Leading providers of artificial reproductive technologies argue *for* ever further separating impregnation, reproduction, sex, love and commitment from each other.[45] Just as "the contraceptive pill has assisted the development of recreational sex" so IVF will enable such "unorthodox" but advantageous practices as single and lesbian parenting, eugenics and designer babies. A whole panoply of sexual options including "virtual sex" with a computer-generated 3-D image will be the way of the future; natural sex and especially natural conception may come to be seen as altogether too unpredictable. Entrepreneurs of the lucrative IVF industry are always on the lookout for ways to extend their market and thus to break down any lingering taboos against the disintegration of life-making from love-making. Any caution is dismissed as "religious" and therefore not to be taken seriously in a scientific, secular community; any government regulation or professional "interference" is likewise to be deplored.[46] The marriage-based natural family, until now recognised in international and national law,[47] is obsolete. In a recent

---

[44] See Angela Scola, Il disegno di Dio sulla persona, sul matrimonio e sulla famiglia: riflessione sintetica", *Anthropotes* 15(2) (1999), 313-358 on the denial of the *humanum*, interchangeable sexualities and the androgeny of modern life.

[45] Robert Jansen, "Sex, reproduction and impregnation: by 2099 let's not confuse them" *Medical Journal of Australia* 171 (1999): 666-667; Carl E.Wood, "Future change in sexual behaviour?" *Medical Journal of Australia* 171 (1999): 662-664.

[46] Ibid; also Robert Jansen, "Evidence-based ethics and the regulation of reproduction", *Human Reproduction* 12 (1997): 2068-2075.

[47] The *Universal Declaration of Human Rights* (1948), the *International Covenant on Civil and Political Rights* (1966), the *International Covenant on Economic, Social and Cultural Rights* (1966), the *UN Convention on the*

Rights of the Child (1991) all refer to this. Pontifical Council for the Family, *Family, Marriage and De Facto Unions* (2000), n.21, notes the following inclusion in national constitutions: Germany: "Marriage and the family have special protection in the State system" (Art.6); Spain: "The public authorities assure the social, economic and juridical protection of the family" (Art.39); Ireland: "The State recognises the family as the primary and fundamental natural group of society and as a moral institution endowed with inalienable and permanent rights that are prior and superior to all positive law. For this reason, the State is committed to protect the constitution and the authority of the family as the necessary foundation of the society and as indispensable for the well-being of the Nation and the State" (Art.41); Italy: "The Republic recognises the rights of the family as a natural society based on marriage" (Art. 29); Poland: "Marriage, i.e., the union of a man and a woman, as well as the family, fatherhood and motherhood, must find protection and care in the Republic of Poland" (Art. 226); Portugal: "The family, as the fundamental element of society, is entitled to the protection of society and the State and the attainment of all the conditions that will permit the personal realisation of its members" (Art. 67); Argentina: "The law will decree the integral protection of the family" (Art. 14); Brazil: "The family, the basis of society, is the object of special protection by the State" (Art. 226); Chile: "The family is the fundamental nucleus of society. It is the State's duty to give protection to the people and to the family" (Art. 1); People's Republic of China: "The State protects marriage, the family, motherhood and children" (Art. 49); Colombia: "The State recognises, with no discrimination, the primacy of the inalienable rights of the person and protects the family as the basic institution of society" (Art. 5); South Korea: "Marriage and family life are founded on the basis of individual dignity and equality between the sexes; the State will use all the means at its disposal to attain this end" (Art. 36); The Philippines: "The State recognises the Filipino family as the foundation of the Nation. In accord with this, it must promote intensely solidarity, its active promotion, and its complete development. Marriage is an inviolable social institution; it is the foundation of the family and must be protected by the State" (Art. 15); Mexico: "The Law will protect the organisation and the development of the family" (Art. 4); Peru: "The community and the State also protect the family and promote marriage. They recognise

Australian case an IVF practitioner persuaded a Federal Court judge that to restrict IVF to married and de facto married heterosexual couples is "discriminatory".[48] Single women and lesbians should be allowed artificial insemination and/or in vitro fertilisation if they want it; gay men can presumably use a surrogate mother to the same end. Children, like any other good or chattel, are something to which people apparently now have a right irrespective of their marital status or sexuality – as long as they or their government can pay.

The consumer mentality has profoundly affected not only the way sex and the body are viewed in modernity but also (and literally) our conception of children. Ownership, quantity and quality control, "babies-on-demand", the IVF "take home baby rate", patenting human genomes: the language of the free market has colonised the nursery and the womb. We now have only as many children – or, more accurately, as few – as we want, at the most convenient times, carefully spaced and genetically perfect. In the near future we might even design them. Children are one more consumer item to add to the satisfaction of their consumer parents. Hence the ease with which our society on the one hand disposes of so many children by abortion and on the other engages in almost frenzied efforts to create them through artificial reproductive technologies. It is the logic of the market.

A recent example of just how far we have come is the all-too-influential bioethicist Peter Singer, now Princeton University's Professor of Human Values. He has long

---

them as the natural and fundamental institutions of society" (Art. 4); Rwanda: "The family, as the natural basis of the Rwandan people, will be protected by the State" (Art. 24).
[48] *McBain* v *The State of Victoria* (2000) FCA 1009.

been a promoter of abortion, infanticide, euthanasia, animal liberation – you name it – and a very influential promoter at that. In a recent book review[49] Singer begins:

> Not so long ago, any form of sexuality not leading to the conception of children was seen as, at best, wanton lust, or worse, a perversion. One by one, the taboos have fallen. The idea that it could be wrong to use contraception in order to separate sex from reproduction is now merely quaint. If some religions still teach that masturbation is "self-abuse", that just shows how out of touch they have become. Sodomy? That's all part of the joy of sex, recommended for couples seeking erotic variety. In many of the world's great cities, gays and lesbians can be open about their sexual preferences to an extent unimaginable a century ago. You can even do it in the U.S. Armed Forces, as long as you don't talk about it. Oral sex? Some objected to President Clinton's choice of place and partner, and others thought he should have been more honest about what he had done, but no one dared suggest that he was unfit to be President simply because he had taken part in a sexual activity that was, in many jurisdictions, a crime. But not every taboo has crumbled...

The last taboo is bestiality, and Singer thinks there is nothing especially wrong with it as long as the animal is not caused unnecessary suffering. There is nothing special about humans or human sexual acts which make it a

---

[49] Peter Singer, "Heavy Petting", nerve.com, reviewing Midas Dekkers, *Dearest Pet: On Bestiality* (trans. Paul Vincent, London: Verso, 1994); cf Kathryn Lopez, "Peter Singer Strikes Again: This could be your kid's teacher", *National Review* 5 March 2001; Goldberg, "Taking Singer Seriously: Don't do it", *National Review* 14 March 2001.

problem. He deplores the fact that a human male who has sex with a hen may ultimately kill it, but he wonders if it is any "worse than what egg producers do to their hens all the time". In a follow-up interview in my country's leading Sunday newspaper Singer said he saw much to recommend owners enjoying "mutually satisfying" sexual relationships with their household pets![50]

There is much that could be said about such articles and the corruption of a culture, academy and media that would take them seriously enough to give them space. We have now reached the position in Western societies – Scotland included – where *reductio ad absurdam* will not work in sexual ethics: for there is nothing so unnatural, so absurd that some academic will not advocate it and some journalist praise him for his courage, intellectual consistency and, of course, liberalism. Whatever of the modern philosopher's *Star Trek*ish determination to bravely go where no one has ever gone before, it does point up one crucial point: that having for decades now disconnected our conceptions of the human person, sexuality, marriage and family from human nature and practical reason, and the elements of each from each other, we are now hard put to resist anything, no matter how perverse.[51] Sex is now a merely recreational activity; fertility is a matter of consumer choice.

Commitment-free relationships

---

[50] "The beast and the bees", *Weekend Australian* 21 April 2001, R1.
[51] "Our new difficulty is that we start from a fundamental distrust of everything merely *given*, a distrust of all laws and prescriptions, moral or social, that are deduced from a given, comprehensive, universal whole." Hannah Arendt, *The Origins of Totalitarianism* (New York: Harcourt Brace, 1951), p.435.

Despite the *Times*' claims about "a fidelity of a sort", another thoroughly post-modern aspect of *The Vintner's Luck* is the fickleness of many of the relationships. In their studies of contemporary Western culture Alasdair MacIntyre, Christopher Lasch, Robert Bellah, Allan Bloom and Jeffrey Stout all identify a crisis of understanding of freedom and authority.[52] Thus Lasch observes that in America:

> "Freedom of choice" means "keeping your options open"... Identities can be adopted and discarded like a change of costume. Ideally, choices of friends, lovers and careers should all be subject to immediate cancellation: such is the open-ended, experimental conception of the good life upheld by the propaganda of commodities, which surrounds the consumer with images of unlimited possibility.[53]

---

[52] Jeffrey Stout, Alasdair MacIntyre and Stanley Hauerwas, *The Flight from Authority: Religion, Morality and the Quest for Autonomy* (Notre Dame: UP, 1981); Alasdair MacIntyre, *After Virtue* (2nd ed, London: Duckworth, 1984); Christopher Lasch, *The Minimal Self* (London: Norton, 1984); Robert Bellah, *Habits of the Heart* (New York: Harper & Row, 1985); Allan Bloom, *The Closing of the American* Mind (New York: Simon & Schuster, 1987); Jeffrey Stout, *Ethics After Babel: the Language of Morals and their discontents* (Boston: Beacon Press, 1988); *cf* Little, *The Church and the Culture War: Secular Anarchy or Sacred Order* (San Francisco: Ignatius, 1995); Bryce Christensen, *Utopia Against the Family* (San Francisco: Ignatius, 1990); Michael Novak, "Abandoned in a toxic culture", *Crisis* 10 (1992), 16-17.

[53] Lasch, *op.cit.*, p.38. *Veritatis Splendor* (1993), § 10: "Jesus Christ meets the men of every age, including our own, with the same words: 'You will know the truth and the truth will make you free.' (Jn.8:32) These words contain both a fundamental requirement and a warning: the requirement of an honest relationship with regard to truth as a condition for authentic freedom; and a warning to avoid every kind of illusory freedom, every superficial unilateral freedom, every freedom

This consumerist obsession with freedom, and this fear of anything – including commitment or the demands of the common good – restricting freedom, pay out in various ways on marriage and family. Survey after survey the world over show that people are less inclined than they were a generation or two ago to make sexual fidelity, lifelong marriage and parenthood their personal goals. Motherhood is no longer seen as even part-constitutive of womanhood, or fatherhood of masculinity. The proportion of people who regard marriage and children as burdensome and restrictive has more than doubled in a generation. And interestingly the same surveys show that the proportion of people who regard sacrifice as a positive moral virtue has more than halved.[54]

Notions like "self-sacrifice" and "obligation" have fallen out of the vocabulary of modern liberal Western societies, being replaced by the impoverished mindsets of personal "rights", "balancing" and personal fulfilment. In such societies people now live in a moral universe constructed of half-remembered and half-understood words, phrases and ideas. This ethical bric-a-brac is inherited or collected from inconsistent moral systems and jumbled together incoherently. At best a very thin consensus regarding moral side-constraints is achieved between individuals who otherwise relate as friendly strangers or out-and-out rivals. If this is true of "the world", it is also true amongst "religious" people. Vague recollections of stories and commandments, custom and

---

that fails to enter into the whole truth about man and the world." *Cf.* §§ 31-53 more generally on the error of absolutising freedom and treating it as the source of values rather subject to truth.
[54] E.g. Barbara Whitehead, "Dan Quayle was right, *Atlantic Monthly* 271 (4) (April 1993) cited in Little, *op.cit.*, pp.103-5; Mary Eberstadt, "Home-alone America", *Policy Review* 107 (June 2001).

religious vocabulary, are thrown together with bits of secular liberalism, consequentialism, feminism and cultural studies, as well as morsels of social science (especially pop psychology), new age spirituality and ideas from various religions, to produce a "user-friendly" ethic which bears little relation to the Christian tradition of faith and practice.

In most developed nations, the decline in commitment and self-sacrifice has spelt a crisis of vocations to priesthood, religious life, marriage and parenthood. If anything, the "vocations crisis" is worse for marriage and family than for clerical or religious life. Fewer and fewer people are deciding to marry at all; of those who do, most cohabit before marriage despite the evidence that this radically reduces marital "sticking power".[55] Less than half now marry in church. They marry much later. And they are much less likely to stay together: approximately half of new marriages in this country – Catholic ones included – are expected to fail. Most will have only one or two children, and many of those children will grow up in broken families. I will say something later about the cataclysmic social effects for any civilisation that gives up on commitment and self-sacrifice.

Castration of a civilisation
Set as it is in the nineteenth century, Knox's novel unavoidably contains stories of childbirth and of children. Yet the central character's most crucial emotional and sexual relationship, with a fallen angel, is of course sterile. And ours is a culture just like that. We no longer need

---

[55] E.g. Larry Bumpass and James Sweet, *Cohabitation, marriage and union stability: preliminary findings* (Madison Wis: Centre for Demography and Ecology, 1995).

111

children as we did in the past; not do we even take them for granted as part of life. They are, rather, an optional extra. As Bloom says of people today:

> They can be anything they want to be, but they have no particular reason to want to be anything in particular. Not only are they free to decide their place, but they are also free to decide whether to believe in God or be atheists, or leave their options open by being agnostic; whether they will be straight or gay or, again, keep their options open; whether they will marry and whether they will stay married; whether they will have children – and so on endlessly.[56]

Bloom's listing of the free-for-all in beliefs, in sexuality, in marital commitment and in child bearing is no accident: they come as a package in liberal modernity.

Yet it is not quite a free-for-all. Human beings are inveterate finger-pointers. Try as it may to invent a value-free, non-judgemental humanity, liberalism has ended up with its own list of "sins", though it dare not use the category: sins such as smoking, high cholesterol food, gender-exclusive language, other political incorrectness and child-bearing. The notion that multiple child-bearing, even stretched over many years, even by those with plenty of time and money to spend, is somehow irresponsible is conveyed in many ways in modernity. In some Third World countries there has been a propaganda war against child bearing, backed up with various economic rewards and sanctions and sometimes by force. In the West subtler but equally effective techniques are in place: ordinary cars only take two adults and two children now; people look

---

[56] Bloom, *op. cit.* p.87.

strangely at you if you have several children with you in a public place; children are often unwelcome in people's homes, restaurants, even churches; people whisper quietly to the mothers of more than two: "are you Catholic or something?" or "don't you know how to prevent that?"

"Safe sex", in the modern world, is sex with a condom on. And that's not just for HIV-AIDS prevention. It is for baby prevention. The condomisation of sex and the demonisation of children tend to go hand-in-hand. In a "contra-*ceptive*"[57] or "contra-*life*"[58] culture we are socialised not to love our bodies, life and children but rather to fear our fertility, to withhold it even from our spouses, to cauterise it temporarily or permanently. In the process our civilisation is becoming literally sterile.

Culture of death
Back to our post-modern novel *The Vintner's Luck*. As well as sex there is plenty of violence in this story. The gruesomeness of the Eastern front of the Napoleonic campaign is well evoked. Céleste feeds Léon's sado-masochism and kills one of his mistresses, while Léon kills the others. He then commits suicide; Aurora later attempts the same. Xas is wounded by God and the Archangel Michael, and maimed by Lucifer to whom Aurora offers animal sacrifices. Xas eventually euthanases Sobran as his

---

[57] E.g. John Paul II, *Familiaris Consortio* (1981), §6; Pontifical Council for the Family, *The Truth and Meaning of Human Sexuality* (1995), §§92, 136; John Paul II, *Evangelium Vitae* (1995), §15.

[58] Germain Grisez, Joseph Boyle, William E. May and John Finnis, " 'Every marital act ought to be open to new life': towards a clearer understanding", *Thomist* 52 (1988): 365-426; Germain Grisez, *Living a Christian Life* (Quincy IL: Franciscan Press, 1993), ch.8; William E. May, *Catholic Bioethics and the Gift of Human Life* (Huntington IND: Our Sunday Visitor, 2000), ch.4.

last act of love-making. Though the story is set in the nineteenth century the sexual-consumer revolution that it reflects took place in the bloodiest of centuries – a century of unparalleled scale and brutality of violence retold in Jonathan Glover's recent book *Humanity: A Moral History of the Twentieth Century*.[59]

The links between the violence and the sexual licentiousness of the twentieth century were complex and cannot be explored here. One, however, is worth highlighting. At no time in history was there more abortion and less shame about it. The abortion holocaust – involving now hundreds of millions of children and their mothers since the Second World War – would have been unthinkable without the sexual-consumer revolution of the same period. Now that so many women have had abortions, the pressure to "mainstream" this activity and to suppress any dissent, indeed any bad news about this supposed panacea, is relentless.

My thought is that liberalism actually promotes perversion and violence, even if it is within the limits of political harmony. Anarchy in "private life" is tolerated as long as it does not impinge on "public life"; indeed a kind of split moral personality, one for the public realm, one for the private, is at the very heart of liberalism. The rhetoric of "human rights" upon which liberal policies are supposedly founded, is increasingly vacuous and used as a weapon against sexual morality and life. The UN Convention, for instance, once the platform for the highest ideals for human flourishing, has become an organ of Western cultural imperialism and blackmail, as developing nations are required to accept the liberal

---

[59] Jonathan Glover, *Humanity: A Moral History of the Twentieth Century* (London: Jonathan Cape, 1999).

"sexual and reproductive rights" agenda on pain of losing "credibility in the international community"; either contracept and abort your nation's future out of existence or we'll starve you out. The US Supreme Court, supposedly the principal defender of human rights in the leading democracy, has time and again declared that some people – whether slaves in the nineteenth century or the unborn in the twentieth – have no protection of law and may be whimsically subjected to violence, even death. Showing their subjectivist petticoats the judges declared in *Planned Parenthood* v *Casey*: "At the heart of liberty is the right to define one's own concept of existence, of meaning, of the universe and of the mystery of human life."[60] Not only is the relativity of truth an epistemological postulate in modernity, it is a legal and moral dogma: morality is all a matter of opinion, of personal taste; you've got your morals, I've got mine; don't impose yours on me and I'll leave you alone too – end of story.[61]

---

[60] *Planned Parenthood* v *Casey* 505 US 833 (1992); cf. Russell Hittinger, "What really happened in the Casey decision: et tu, Justice Kennedy?" *Crisis* 10(8) September 1992, 16-22; John R. Meyer, "Quid est veritas? Human freedom after Casey", *Faith and Reason*, Summer 1993; Behind the court's rhetoric in this case is an ideology like that of Ronald Dworkin, *Life's Dominion: An Argument about Abortion, Euthanasia, and Individual Freedom* (NY: Knopf, 1993) and T.M. Scanlon, "Partisan for life", *New York Review of Books* 40(13) (July 15 1993), 45-50; cf. Damian P. Fedoryka, " 'Dworking' the abortion issue", *Crisis* 11(1) (December 1993), 50-54. In a series of texts Robert George has powerfully criticised the effects of liberalism on American culture and law: e.g. *Making Men Moral: Civil Liberties and Public Morality* (OUP, 1993) and *Natural Law, Liberalism and Morality: Contemporary Essays* (OUP, 1996).
[61] Allan Bloom, *op. cit.* p.25.

Societies hungry for more...

In the past two decades John Paul II has engaged in a powerful critique of the individualism, moral subjectivism, cultural relativism and values disorientation of modernity. Increasingly he has supporters not just in ecclesiastical circles but amongst secular social commentators. They have begun to detail the range of social problems partly or wholly attributable to the revolution in values which I have just described: spiralling rates of promiscuity, unwanted pregnancy, and abortion; escalating drug abuse, homelessness, mental health problems, behaviour disorders and even suicide amongst the young; widespread disorientation, values bewilderment, an inability to commit; an aging population without an economic base to support it.[62] All these social effects represent thousands of individual tragedies: stories we meet every day in our parishes, welfare agencies and schools, in our own families. Philip Lawler has observed that

> The public consequences of "private" sexual behaviour now threaten to destroy American society. In the past thirty-five years the government has spent four trillion dollars — that is, $4,000,000,000,000 — on a variety of social programmes designed to
> remedy ills which can be attributed, directly or indirectly, to the misuse of human sexuality.[63]

---

[62] Eberstadt, *op.cit.* summarises some of the now considerable literature on the ill-effects of family breakdown on children and adolescents. See also: Maggie Gallagher, "Fatherless boys grow up into dangerous men", *Wall Street Journal*, December 1 1998, A22; David Blankenhorn, *Fatherless America: Confronting Our Most Urgent Social Problem"* (New York: Basic Books, 1995).
[63] Philip F. Lawler, "The price of virtue", *Catholic World Report*, July 1997, 58, cited in West, *op.cit.* 121.

Australian social commentator Anne Manne surveyed a
number of recent writers about what she calls "the
shadowland of moral chaos": the downside of the
contemporary obsession with autonomy which pays out as

> record family breakdown, suicide, rising depression
> among children, drug abuse on an unprecedented
> scale. A world where the explosion of rights talk
> has ushered in what some critics call a "duty-free"
> society ... Travelling upstream from the
> contemporary culture wars on euthanasia, abortion,
> divorce or institutional childcare ... one usually
> comes to a fundamental clash between an ideal of a
> sovereign, autonomous self, which is expressive of
> the individual's rights to freedom, choice and self-
> determination, and an ideal of an obligated self,
> which emphasises interdependence, connectedness
> and limits to freedom, where actions are
> constrained by the consequences for others.[64]

---

[64] Anne Manne, "In Freedom's Shadow", *Australian Review of Books* 4
July 1998. Manne, following philosopher Raimond Gaita (*Good and
Evil: An Absolute Conception*, London: Macmillan, 1991), suggests that
"the vices and virtues of each age are inextricably intertwined. The
virtues of the *ancien régime* – family stability, security, a sense of
community – were not easily separable from its vices – coercion,
stigma and prejudice. The virtues of our age are also tied intimately to
its vices – a tendency for the deepest human relationships to be
commodified and have meaning emptied from them, where people
seek fleeting connection in a society of strangers, where the heart
becomes a lonely hunter. As Eric Hobsbawn observes in *Age of
Extremes*, the weight of the old rules, even unjust ones that bore down
heavily on the human spirit and caused suffering, may be replaced not
by something better but by no rules at all. The natural accompaniment
of such a collapse may also be suffering, although of a different kind,
to do with the absence of meaning, the anxiety and anguish that
comes with postmodernity's unbearable lightness of being."

While the modern emphasis upon autonomy may have been creative in terms of encouraging personal initiative, respect for liberty, and so on, it has also had very real costs: relationships are fractured, the young are disoriented and confused about what is worth valuing and committing to, governments are unable to act against even gross inhumanities like partial-birth abortions, fundamental institutions such as marriage and the family are under stress, and for all their freedom people feel powerless and resentful. Individuals, societies, cultures are hungry for more. We need a reliable moral compass. Our minds and hearts are made for truth. As the Pope opened his latest encyclical on *Faith and Reason*, the two wings on which the human spirit rises to the contemplation of truth: "God has placed in the human heart a desire to know the truth – in a word, to know himself – so that, by knowing and loving God, men and women may also come to the fullness of truth about themselves."[65]

ENGAGING THE CULTURE OF MODERNITY ON SEXUAL, MARITAL AND FAMILY LIFE

The first faltering attempts
The past century has seen a flowering of Catholic thinking on marriage and family life, often at the hands of married lay theologians.[66] The Second Vatican Council celebrated

---

[65] John Paul II, *Fides et Ratio*, (1998), §1.

[66] Of course, Christians have always been marked by their reverence for the human body, sexuality, marriage and family life. From the Scriptures, through Augustine and Aquinas, to Pius XI in *Casti Connubii*, they have esteemed marriage, procreation and child-rearing highly, promoted chastity for people in all states of life, and celebrated the expression of marital love in sexual intercourse; they have opposed practices such as marital and family breakdowns, remarriage

this blossoming, while recognising that the most pressing problems for the Church in the modern world would be in this area.[67] The Council Fathers demonstrated remarkable prescience when in 1965 they identified amongst the emerging threats to marriage and family: divorce, promiscuity, self-obsession, hedonism, contraception, abortion, economic, social and psychological pressures, and concerns about over-population.[68] But rather than simply bleating doom they gave greater impetus to the theology and pastoral care of marriages and families.[69]

---

after divorce, and unchaste or anti-life sexual activity whether within or outside of marriage. On the history of the theology of marriage see: Raymond Dennehy (ed), *Christian Married Love* (San Francisco: Ignatius, 1981); Peter Elliott, *What God Has Joined: The Sacramentality of Marriage* (Sydney: St Paul, 1990); Germain Grisez, "The Christian family as fulfilment of sacramental marriage", *Studies in Christian Ethics* 9(1) (1996), 23-33; Walter Kasper, *Theology of Christian Marriage* (trans. David Smith, London: Burns Oates, 1980); Michael Lawler, *Secular Marriage, Christian Sacrament* (Mystic CN: Twenty-Third, 1985); Theodore Mackin, *The Marital Sacrament* (New York: Paulist, 1989); Edward Schillebeeckx, *Marriage: Secular Reality and Saving Mystery* (trans. N.D. Smith, 2 vols, London: Sheed & Ward, 1965); Angelo Scola, *Il mistero nuziale: L'uomo-donna* (Rome, 1998); Paul Quay, *The Christian Meaning of Human Sexuality* (San Francisco: Ignatius, 1985); Dietrich Von Hildebrand, *Marriage: The Mystery of Faithful Love* (Manchester NH: Sophia, 1984). Examples of recent lay contributors include Grisez, Hittinger, May, Shivanandan, Smith, Von Hildebrand and West whose works are cited here.
[67] *Gaudium et Spes* (1965), §46.
[68] *Ibid*, §47. On contraception and abortion see also: ibid §§27, 50-52; on overpopulation: Pontifical Council for the Family, *Ethical and Pastoral Dimensions of Population Trends* (1994); lecture by Alfonso Card Trujillo, *Demographical Challenges and the Family: From the Myth of Overpopulation to the Globilisation of Solidarity* (John Paul II Institute Melbourne, 20 July 2001).
[69] Second Vatican Council, *Lumen Gentium* (1964), esp. §§11, 35, 41; *Apostolicam Actuositatem* (1965), esp. §*Gaudium et Spes* , esp. §§46-53.

They also called for an urgent renewal of moral theology, so that it would be better grounded in Scripture and Tradition while being open to the best of philosophy and the human sciences.[70]

The first post-conciliar foray into this area was Paul VI's *Humanae Vitae*.[71] The encyclical re-presented traditional Christian thought in the difficult area of birth control and responsible parenthood with a new rhetoric. It presented a beautiful vision of the place of sexuality and fertility in the vocation of marriage. It warned prophetically of the consequences for societies of embracing a contraceptive mentality. But it came, of course, at a particularly difficult time. Despite the Council's insistence on the importance of authority and tradition in Christian life, many took up the Council's views on the dignity of individual conscience and the proper liberties of the person with greater enthusiasm than they did its teaching on moral absolutes, such as the positive norms of respect for sexuality and marriage, and negative precepts against birth control, abortion and divorce.[72]

---

[70] Second Vatican Council, *Dei Verbum* (1964); *Presbyterorum Ordinis* (1965), §19; *Optatam Totius* (1965), §16.

[71] Paul VI, *Humanae Vitae* (1968). *Cf* Avery Dulles, "Humanae Vitae and the crisis of dissent", *Origins* 22 (45) (April 1993); Elizabeth Anscombe, *Contraception and Chastity* (London: CTS, 1979); Germain Grisez, *Contraception and Natural Law* (Milwaukee: Bruce Publishing, 1964); John Ford, Germain Grisez, Joseph Boyle, John Finnis and William May, *The Teaching of Humanae Vitae: A Defence* (San Francisco: Ignatius, 1988); Janet E. Smith (ed) *Why Humanae Vitae was Right: A Reader* (San Francisco: Ignatius, 1993).

[72] G.L. Bray in *New Dictionary of Christian Ethics and Pastoral Theology* (Leicester: Inter-Varsity Press, 1995) makes the point that "Though not intended to be radical, the Second Vatican Council soon became a rallying point for all the most liberal forces inside the Roman Church,

Thus *Humanae Vitae* met with incomprehension and hostility in many quarters, not least the academy. There scholars were attempting to create a new, more permissive morality, more in keeping with the intellectual fashions of the day. The tradition had long recognised the importance of human freedom and conscience; it knew the relevance of context in assessing a moral act; there was a long casuistry of "the lesser evil" and due proportion in self-defence and double effect. Writers such as Peter Knauer, Louis Janssens, Bruno Schüller, Joseph Fuchs, Joseph Fletcher, Charles Curran and Richard McCormick sought to develop these parts of Christian moral thinking by synthesising them either with *subjectivism* – in the case of "situationism" – or with *utilitarianism* – in the case of "proportionalism".[73]

who used its authority to further their own aims. In the process, the real teaching of the Council became obscured and the Roman Curia has since attempted, with varying degrees of success, to move the Church back to a more conservative stance without derogating from the Council's decrees or intentions."

[73] See for example the articles by Knauer, Janssens, Schüller and Fuchs in Charles Curran and Richard McCormick (eds), *Moral Norms and Catholic Tradition* (New York: Paulist, 1979); Curran and McCormick (eds), *Dissent in the Church* (New York: Paulist, 1988) and *Dialogue about Catholic Sexual Teaching* (New York: Paulist, 1993); Charles Curran, *Transition and Tradition in Moral Theology* (Notre Dame: UP, 1979) and *Critical Concerns in Moral Theology* (Notre Dame: UP, 1984); Richard McCormick, *Corrective Vision: Explorations in Moral Theology* (Kansas City: Sheed & Ward, 1994). Taking up the more modern exaltation of freedom and rejection of appeals to nature, authority or any other universals, these writers denied that norms could ever spell out answers to moral questions *in advance*. Instead of the restrictions and fixations of traditional morality, the moral life should be seen as a creative and self-expressive project in which the only "absolute" is freedom, authenticity or benevolently seeking the greatest net good. A mature Christian will consider the well-

With what Servais Pinckaers has described as "an allergy to traditional positions" these writers proposed a new kind of *moral multiculturalism* marked by "a taste for novelty, variety, relativity, adaptation".[74] In time they abandoned the idea that the human body, relationships and actions have any natural or God-given meaning: we make these things mean what we please. The claim that genital intercourse "says" marriage was replaced with "sex says love" and increasingly with "sex says recreation". And the ethical contention that other kinds of genital activity are objectively wrongful was flatly denied: not just contraception and masturbation – the early exceptions to the general rules of chastity and reverence for life – but soon fornication, adultery, homosexual acts, abortion, euthanasia – all were permissible in certain circumstances. Applying the new morality in pastoral care, many a preacher, confessor or counsellor translated "follow an informed conscience" into "do whatever seems most loving to you in the circumstances". "Be true to yourself" became "seek first your own self-fulfilment". And "accept responsibility for your actions" became "consider all the

---

established "rules of thumb" found in the Bible or Church teaching, but must also be willing to set these aside. What matters, in the end, is whether a person is genuinely committed to love of God and neighbour, considers honestly all the pre-moral upsides and downsides of his choices, and then "follows his conscience".

[74] Servais Pinckaers OP, *The Sources of Christian Ethics* (Washington DC: Catholic University of America Press, 1995). Other commentators on recent debates in Catholic moral theology include: J Augustine di Noia OP and Romanus Cessario OP (eds), *Veritatis Splendor and the Renewal of Moral Theology* (Chicago: Midwest theological Forum, 1999). See also Livio Melina, *Sharing in Christ's Virtues: For a Renewal of Moral Theology in the Light of Veritatis Splendor* (Washington DC: Catholic University of America Press, 2001), ch. 1.

goods and bads of what you want to do, and then do whatever seems best on balance".

Not only was this kind of thinking devastating for the moral life of many individuals: it left the Church very ill-prepared to face up to the growing challenges of secular liberalism and post-modernity. Situationism and proportionalism had effectively acquiesced completely to the "me generation" culture. Though philosophically and humanly untenable,[75] these "new moralities" captured most seminaries and theology schools around the world and within a generation were systematically excluding other voices from positions, journals, even seminary booklists. They were only beginning to wane when, in 1993, *Veritatis Splendor* dealt them a lethal blow.[76] The goal

---

[75] Many secular and religious critiques of individualism and utilitarianism apply equally well to situationism and proportionalism, and I need not rehearse those criticisms here. Suffice it to say that we need some objective values and absolute principles if we are: to have a standard of self-criticism of our preferences, feelings, intuitions, past conduct, present proposals; to be prudent and otherwise virtuous in making any situation-or-proportion-specific judgements; to serve the common good, respect people's rights and fulfil their reasonable expectations of us; and to be genuinely *fulfilled* (rather than merely gratified) as human persons.

[76] In *Veritatis Splendor* the Pope observed that certain fundamental truths of Catholic morality were presently at risk of being "distorted or denied" not just by outsiders but from "within the Christian community itself... even in Seminaries and in Faculties of Theology". "It is no longer a matter of limited and occasional dissent, but of an overall and systematic calling into question of traditional moral decline, on the basis of certain anthropological and ethical presuppositions. At the root of these presuppositions is the more or less obvious influence of currents of thought which end by detaching human freedom from its essential and constitutive relationship to truth. Thus the traditional doctrine regarding the natural law, and the universality and the permanent validity of its precepts, is rejected; certain of the Church's moral teachings are found simply

of conscience, John Paul II explained, is not to invent moral reality, but rather to recognise it accurately and respond to it appropriately. Autonomy and sincerity are not enough. Freedom of conscience is never freedom *from* the truth but always and only freedom *in* the truth. While prudence is certainly required in applying norms to specific situations – depending upon opportunity, urgency and competing responsibilities – norms prohibiting gravely and intrinsically evil acts do not allow "creative" breaches consistent with continuing in grace and charity. So no matter how "loving", "benevolent", helpful "on balance" or otherwise well-intentioned, certain kinds of behaviour are actually wrong. The Magisterium serves to highlight those truths which a well-formed conscience would already possess.

Some more promising Catholic responses for the new century
I referred earlier to Anne Manne's frightening description of "the shadowland of moral chaos" in which people float "without a map on a raft of different choices, rudderless and alone in the sea of freedom, in the absence of God or tradition". She asks: "In post-modernity, in this sea of freedom, what islands of obligation, moral constraint and restraint still exist?" Manne is not without her own answers, though I think they are only partial. She argues that there is emerging "a new position on the moral and political map", peopled as much by erstwhile supporters of the new morality as by its traditional opponents. Many of these writers are now proposing the "voluntary

---

unacceptable; and the Magisterium itself is considered capable of intervening in matters of morality only in order to 'exhort consciences' and to 'propose values' in the light of which each individual will independently make his or her decisions and life choices." (§4)

renunciation of a measure of autonomy and the acceptance of limits".[77] Well, that's a start. But where are these limits to come from? And once we know what we cannot do, how will we decide what we should? Rather more will be needed if we are to rebuild the common morality of Church and society.

In the decades after the Second Vatican Council, the Roman bureaucracies published important correctives on various moral questions including those in the area of sexuality and family life,[78] but they considered underlying anthropology and moral methodology only *en passant*. John Paul II has tended to teach at both levels, elaborating a fundamental vision of the human person and his vocation, and some crucial moral principles, before applying them to particular questions.[79] This was especially true of *Veritatis Splendor*. The only ever encyclical on moral theory, it represents the climax of a life-time's engagement with modernity and its many challenges, especially those to marriage and family life. This engagement has included

---

[77] Manne, *op.cit.*

[78] e.g. Congregation of the Doctrine of the Faith, *Declaration on Certain Questions concerning Sexual Ethics* (1976); *On the Pastoral Care of Homosexual Persons* (1986); Pontifical Council for the Family, *Marriage and the Family* (San Francisco: Ignatius, 1989); *The Truth and Meaning of Human Sexuality* (1995); *The Family and Human Rights* (1999); *Family, Marriage and De Facto Unions* (2000). See also Ramon de Haro (ed), *Marriage and the Family in the Documents of the Magisterium* (San Francisco: Ignatius, 1993).

[79] In a recent (22 February 2001) notification regarding the writings of Marciano Vidal, the Congregation for the Doctrine of the Faith said: "With this Notification, the Congregation also wishes to encourage moral theologians to pursue the task of renewing moral theology, in particular through deeper study of fundamental moral theology and through precise use of the theological-moral methodology, in keeping with the teaching of the encyclical *Veritatis Splendor* and with a true sense of their responsibility to the Church."

ground-breaking works such as *Love and Responsibility* before he was Pope and *Familiaris Consortio* soon after, through the long series of catecheses now collected together as *The Theology of the Body*, to his various letters and addresses to families.[80] In addition to his own enormous philosophical, theological and pastoral endeavour, this Pope has also initiated and inspired many others, catalysing the bishops of the world to be engaged in family life and pro-life ministry, convoking the Synod on the Family and many other meetings with families themselves, establishing the Pontifical Council for the Family and the John Paul II Institute for Studies on Marriage and the Family which now has campuses all around the world. I am convinced that in this new century and millennium this work of our present Pope will bear theological and pastoral fruit which we have barely begun to appreciate.[81]

Where next for Catholic moral theology as the Church's leaders and flock confront the challenges of modernity to sexual, married and family life? I want now to explore four especially promising directions which Catholic thought is taking at the moment in this difficult but vital area: where each will lead in the future and whether the four can be synthesised is yet to be seen.

---

[80] John Paul II, *Gravitissimam Sane: Letter to Families* (1994); *The Theology of the Body* (Boston: St Paul, 1997); cf. R.Hogan and J.LeVoir, *Covenant of Love: John Paul II on Sexuality, Marriage and Family in the Modern World* (San Francisco: Ignatius, 1992); Kenneth Schmitz, *At the Centre of the Human Drama* (Washington DC: Catholic University of America, 1993); Mary Prokes, *Towards a Theology of the Body* (Edinburgh: T & T Clark, 1996); Mary Shivandan, *Crossing the Threshold of Love* (Washington DC: Catholic University of America,1999); West, *op.cit.*
[81] On the central significance of this apostolate in the life of John Paul II and its likely enduring significance long after his death, see: George Weigel, *Witness to Hope: The Biography of John Paul II* (New York: Cliff Street Books, 1999).

A more Scriptural moral theology

One of the principal gains of the Second Vatican Council was the greater access it gave Catholics to the Bible. Yet in *Sources of Christian Ethics* Pinckaers points to a great irony: "hardly has Scripture been restored to the Christian faithful than it is taken away from them to become the property of specialists. The current, confusing idea is that one can no longer understand Scripture today without having studied exegesis."[82] Like John Wayne declaring "this town ain't big enough for the two of us", moral theologians are warned off the exegetes' patch while being taunted for not being scriptural enough.[83]

Few moralists are Scripture scholars, and there is rarely available any intelligible consensus of exegetical opinion on the content of particular texts to which non-professionals might refer. Pinckaers' solution is to insist on the priority of a direct reading of the texts over any kind of commentary. This is not to deny the importance of an exact translation, an explanation of terms, some historical and religious background. But at least as important is "an important setting, such as that of private

---

[82] Pinckaers, *op.cit.*

[83] To give two examples: almost immediately after the publication of *Veritatis Splendor*, the first part of which is an inspiring scriptural reflection upon the New Testament story of the rich young man who asked Christ how to live, some of the critics were carping that the Pope had not used the latest Scripture scholarship: e.g. Joseph Selling and Jan Jans (eds), *The Splendor of Accuracy: An Examination of the Assertions Made by "Veritatis Splendor"* (Grand Rapids: Eerdmans, 1995). Likewise exegete Francis Moloney ("Life, healing and the Bible: a Christian challenge", *Pacifica* 8(3) (October 1995), 315-334, recently warned of the risks of ethicists plundering texts from antiquity to find solutions to modern bioethical problems, charging one of the leading Lutheran moral theologians of our age, Dr Daniel Overduin, with text-abuse.

prayer or liturgy": here Pinckaers echoes von Balthazar's call for less of the academy's "theology on our bottoms" and more of the contemplative's "theology on our knees". Reading commentaries is never a substitute for reading texts themselves, and professionals have no monopoly on "authentic" interpretation. Furthermore, the Scriptures are a special case of texts which we believe offer not merely grist for the mills of the cognoscenti, but an inspired word communicating the divine to every reader.[84]To Pinckaers' plea for a "personal, direct reading of Scripture" I would add the importance of the post-biblical Christian tradition, including the Fathers and Scholastics, and the living Magisterium of the Church, as offering some authoritative readings of Scriptural texts.[85]

Around the time of the Council Bernard Häring and others attempted a more Scriptural moral theology,[86] but they soon found its conclusions uncomfortable and so sought other approaches. Others persevered. John Paul II's encyclicals and addresses, and above all his Wednesday catecheses on the theology of the body, marriage, celibacy and birth control, offer us an example of a theology arising from *lectio divina* and offering a spirituality along with a profound anthropology and moral theology. Recently Benedict Ashley has attempted a Scriptural anthropology and moral theology with a strong Thomist flavour. His *Theologies of the Body* and *Living the Truth in Love: A Biblical Introduction to Moral Theology* are remarkably successful attempts to bring together a deeply personal love for the Scriptures and tradition as the sources of any genuine

---

[84] Pinckaers, *op.cit.*
[85] *cf.* Terrence Kennedy, *Doers of the Word, vol.1: Tracing humanity's Ascent to the Living God* (London: St Paul's, 1996).
[86] Compare Bernard Häring, *The Law of Christ* (3 vols. Cork: Mercier, 1961) and *Free and Faithful in Christ* (3 vols. Sydney: St Paul, 1978).

theology, the best of contemporary exegetical commentary, and a scholastic natural law and virtue ethic.[87] In these works Ashley has shown how biblical theology supports the now much-contested claims that the human body, relationships and actions have a natural and God-given meaning, that genital love-making is fitting only to marriage, and that other uses of genital sexual activity are abuses.

The renewal of natural law theory
The Thomist revival promoted by Pope Leo XIII in the late nineteenth century was carried forward into this century by such greats as Dominic Prümmer, Jacques Maritain, Étienne Gilson, Josef Pieper, Henry Veatch and Elizabeth Anscombe.[88] In more recent years they have been joined by Ralph McInerney, Servais Pinckaers, Augustine di Noia, Romanus Cessario and many others,[89]

---

[87] Benedict Ashley OP, *Theologies of the Body: Humanist and Christian* (Braintree: Pope John Paul II Centre, 1985) and *Living the Truth in Love: A Biblical Introduction to Moral Theology* (New York: Alba, 1996).

[88] Dominic Prümmer OP, *Handbook of Moral Theology* (trans. G Shelton,Cork: Mercier, 1956); Jacques Maritain, *The Rights of Man and Natural Law* (Glasgow: University Press, 1944) and *Natural Law: Reflections on Theory and Practice* (ed. William Sweet, South Bend Ind: St Augustine's Press, 2001); Étienne Gilson, *The Christian Philosophy of St Thomas Aquinas* (London: Gollancz,1957); Josef Pieper, *Vom Sinn der Tapferkeit* (19540, *Zucht und Mass* (1954), *Über die Gerechtigkeit (1955)* and *Traktat über die Klugheit (1959);* Henry Veatch, *For An Ontology of Morals* (Evanston: Northwestern UP, 1971); Peter Geach, "Aquinas", in G.E.M. Anscombe & P.T. Geach, *Three Philosophers* (Oxford: Blackwell,1973); Elizabeth Anscombe, *Ethics, Religion and Politics* (Oxford: Blackwell, 1981).

[89] Romanus Cessario OP, *The Moral Virtues and Theological Ethics* (Notre Dame: UP, 1991); J Augustine di Noia OP et al, *The Love That Never Ends* (Huntington: Our Sunday Visitor, 1996); Ralph McInerney, *Aquinas on Human Action: A Theory of Practice* (Washington

not least John Paul II both as philosopher and Pope.[90] Overlapping with this movement, but also responding more directly to developments in modern philosophy, the Second Vatican Council's call to renewal, and the fallout of '68, writers such as Germain Grisez, John Finnis, William E May, Joseph Boyle and Robert George have articulated an important new natural law approach.[91] Their

---

DC: Catholic University of America, 1992), *The Question of Christian Ethics* (Washington DC: Catholic University Press, 1993) and *Ethica Thomistica* (2nd ed, Washington DC: Catholic University of America, 1997); Pinckaers, *op.cit.*

[90] Karol Wojtyla, *The Acting Person* (Dordrecht, 1979). In his series of encyclicals of the past decade, *Veritatis Splendor, Evangelium Vitae* and *Fides et Ratio* John Paul II has addressed the links between what he so tellingly called "the culture of death" and liberal (mis)conceptions of autonomy; the infection of moral theology and catechesis by buffet morality; the various "isms" which pervade contemporary culture not as full-scale theories so much as fragments combined into a kind of moral minestrone; and the false conclusions and harmful behaviour patterns which have followed. *Veritatis Splendor* Part II offers his fullest philosophical critique of the new moralities and some pointers forward.

[91] Amongst Grisez's extensive writings, the most accessible are Germain Grisez & Russell Shaw, *Beyond the New Morality* (3rd ed, Notre Dame: UP, 1988) and *Fulfilment in Christ* (Notre Dame: UP, 1991). His three volumes (so far) of *The Way of the Lord Jesus* (Quincy Il: Franciscan, 1983, 1993, 1997) are a moral-theological *tour de force*. Grisez's philosophical collaborator, John Finnis, successfully reintroduced natural law theory to the world of secular jurisprudence through his book *Natural Law, Natural Rights* (OUP, 1980) and his definitive treatment of Aquinas' political and moral philosophy, *Aquinas – Moral, Political and Legal Theory* (OUP, 1998). See also Germain Grisez, Joseph Boyle, William May and John Finnis, "Practical principles, moral truth, and ultimate ends", *American Journal of Jurisprudence* 32 (1987), 99-151.; Joseph Boyle, "Moral reasoning and moral judgement", *Proceedings of the American Philosophical Association* 58 (1984), 37-49 and "Natural law", in J Komonchak, M Collins and D Lane (eds), *New Dictionary of Theology* (Dublin: Gill & Macmillan, 1987),

methodology is continuous with mainstream Catholic tradition, especially Thomism,[92] but offers some important refinements which have won it a place among the principal contenders not only in Christian ethics but in secular moral and political philosophy. These authors – all married with children – have argued that marriage (and family) are amongst the "basic human goods" or reasons for genuine human action, along with life, health, friendship, creativity, leisure, beauty, knowledge, religion and personal integrity. Equally fundamental and intrinsically good, each should be reverenced in every life; none should ever be directly chosen against;[93] fully realised they constitute genuine happiness or flourishing – that "beatitude" perfected only in heaven. The fundamental

---

702-798; Robert George (ed), *Natural Law Theory: Contemporary Essays* (OUP, 1992) and *Natural Law and Moral Inquiry: Ethics, Metaphysics and Politics in the Work of Germain Grisez* (OUP, 1998); Robert George, *In Defence of Natural Law Theory* (OUP, 2001).

[92] Some Thomists have complained of this new natural law theory that it lacks the elaborated metaphysics, philosophy of God and philosophical psychology of classical natural law theory, and that it denies that there is a unitary end of human choice and a hierarchy among goods. Though clearly most sympathetic to the new natural law approaches, *Veritatis Splendor* does include some comments which might be read as challenges both to the older and to the more recent versions. The encyclical shuns the physicalism, legalism and minimalism sometimes found in older formulations of natural law theory; but it also challenges the new writers to be wary of a theory of intention which might seem to permit acts characterised by the tradition as intrinsically evil and to elaborate a richer anthropology, psychology and theory of virtue. And to both schools it presents a renewed charge to be more obviously scriptural and patristic.

[93] Of course, we may reasonably forego some participation in some good in pursuit of another, or some particular participation in a good in pursuit of another participation in the same good. Not everyone, for instance, is bound to get married or to have a family, though all are bound to reverence and support marriage and family life.

maxim that "the good is to be done and the evil avoided" can thus be specified as a series of moral "first principles" such as preserve and transmit life, develop the riches of the world, cultivate social life, seek truth, contemplate beauty, honour parents, serve God – the very list given in *Veritatis Splendor.*[94]

By reflecting upon these first principles and a series of necessary intermediate principles, these writers have shown how the specific norms which make up the bulk of common morality are derived – both positive norms such as "follow the Golden Rule", "help those in need", "foster

---

[94] *Veritatis Splendor* §51 citing Aquinas, *Summa Theologiae* Ia-IIæ, 94, a.2. In Part II of the encyclical the Pope reasserts the Catholic natural law tradition, i.e. of a morality that is "natural", not in the sense of being "a law of nature" to be read merely from the behaviour of animals or the teleology of organs, but because the natural reflection by which it is discovered and comprehended is "proper to human nature" (§50 citing Congregation for the Doctrine of the Faith, *Donum Vitae* 1987). In his view, "even in the midst of difficulties and uncertainties, every person sincerely open to truth and goodness can, by the light of reason and the hidden action of grace, come to recognise the natural law written in the heart. [Upon such a recognition] every human community and the political community itself are founded." In this way Catholic teaching on matters such as reverence for human life, marriage and the family "has a profound and persuasive echo in the heart of every person – believer and non-believer alike – because it marvellously fulfils all the heart's expectations while infinitely surpassing them" (*Evangelium Vitae* §2). But even these "natural" norms are in constant need of better formulation and appropriate application, and the Church's understanding of them can develop (organically) over time. Faith illuminates the teleology of natural law – for the moral life "consists in the deliberate ordering of human acts *to God*, the supreme good and ultimate end of the human person" – confirms its precepts, and provides a reliable source of moral wisdom where its precepts or their application are unclear (*Veritatis Splendor* Part III; see also *Fides et Ratio*). See also Second Vatican Council, *Dignitatis Humanae* §3; *Gaudium et Spes* §16.

the common good" and "reverence marriage and family life" and negative norms such as "don't harm the innocent", "tell no lies", "do not commit adultery" and "do not contracept". Some negative norms are exceptionless, and this is ultimately the basis of inviolable human rights and moral absolutes.[95] The derivation and permanence of such natural law principles are premised upon a particular theory of practical reason and of philosophical anthropology. But it is ultimately guaranteed by the Word having taken flesh and dwelt amongst us, sharing in the common nature of every human person, coming once-for-all as teacher and saviour, and clarifying and supplementing ordinary human morality with his sublime divine law.[96] For the Christian, therefore, a life based on natural morality will be integrated with that "higher" calling revealed by Christ and with the life of worship, prayer and contemplation.

The new natural law approach offers, I think, the most thoroughgoing exposition of the propositions I outlined at the beginning, such as the objective meaning of human action, the marital significance of sexuality, and the wrongfulness of other uses of genital activity. It also offers an approach which can be communicated to people of other faiths and none. For as I suggested, the propositions

---

[95] See also John Finnis, *Moral Absolutes: Tradition, Revision and Truth* (Catholic University of America, 1991); William E May, *Moral Absolutes: Catholic Tradition, Current Trends, and the Truth* (Milwaukee: Marquette University Press, 1989); *An Introduction to Moral Theology* (Rev. ed, Huntington: OSV, 1994); Mary Midgley, *Can't We Make Moral Judgements?* (Bristol: Bristol Press, 1991).

[96] *Cf.* John Finnis and Anthony Fisher OP, "Theology and the four principles: a Roman Catholic view", in R Gillon (ed), *Principles of Health Care Ethics* (Chichester/New York: John Wiley & Sons, 1993), 31-44.

133

which began my paper are not peculiar to Catholics or even to Christians. Mahatma Gandhi it was who said "There can be no two opinions about the *necessity* of birth control. But *the only method* handed down from ages past is self-control or Brahmacharya. It is an infallible sovereign remedy, doing good to those who practise it."[97] Thus the next generation has the challenge of developing natural law theory further and communicating it accessibly to a world eager for direction on some of these matters.

The recovery of virtue and community

Recent years have seen the revival of "virtue ethics" and "communitarianism" in secular moral philosophy. Despite a long Catholic pedigree, virtue and community had been neglected themes in modern ethical theory – with a few important exceptions.[98] In the late 1980s and 1990s

---

[97] D.G. Tendulkar (ed), *The Collected Works of Mahatma Gandhi* (vol.2; Ministry of information & Broadcasting) cited in A.S. Antonisamy, *Wisdom for All Times: Mahatma Gandhi and Pope Paul VI on Birth Regulation* (Pondicherry: Family Life Service Centre, 1978).

[98] E.g. Peter Geach, *The Virtues* (CUP, 1977); Bernard Williams, *Morality: An Introduction to Ethics* (New York: Harper & Row, 1972); Philippa Foot, *Virtues and Vices* (Oxford: Blackwell, 1981). In *Veritatis Splendor* John Paul II notes that the "conversion of heart" necessary for a reliable conscience requires more than knowledge of moral principles. "What is essential is a sort of "connaturality" between the person and their true good. Such a connaturality is rooted in and develops through the virtuous attitudes of the individual himself: prudence and the other cardinal virtues, and even before these the theological virtues of faith, hope and charity." (§64; see also *Gaudium et Spes* §30). Thus fidelity to the covenant and its commandments is not "blind obedience" but an expression of virtuous compliance and love, of human fraternity and ecclesial communion. In the final part of the encyclical, the Pope recommends the martyrs and the saints as models of Christian *character* and considers the importance of a united

philosophers such as Edmund Pincoffs, Alasdair MacIntyre, Charles Taylor, Martha Nussbaum, Nancy Sherman and Raimond Gaita refocussed attention on questions such as the psychology of moral feeling, commitment and character and the place of tradition and community in constituting the self, values and flourishing[99] – much of which is deeply *simpatico* with the Catholic moral tradition.[100] Virtues constitute the "character" in

Catholic *community* teaching sound Christian morality and supporting each other in the effort not only to understand but to live moral truth.
[99] Edmund Pincoffs, *Quandaries and Virtues* (Lawrence: University of Kansas Press, 1986); Alasdair MacIntyre, *After Virtue*; also *Whose Justice? Which Rationality?* (London: Duckworth, 1988) and *Three Rival Versions of Moral Enquiry: Encyclopaedia, Genealogy and Tradition* (London: Duckworth, 1990); Charles Taylor, *Sources of the Self: The Making of Modern Identity* (CUP, 1989); Martha Nussbaum, *The Fragility of Goodness* (CUP, 1986); Nancy Sherman, *The Fabric of Character* (OUP, 1989); Gaita, *op.cit. cf* Hayden Ramsey, *Beyond Virtue: Integrity and Morality* (London: Macmillan, 1997).
[100] Virtue ethics and communitarianism are now all the rage in secular philosophy departments where utilitarianism once ruled. Not surprisingly some faithful Catholic theologians are now taking up such themes with gusto: e.g. Ashley, Cessario, di Noia, Kennedy, May, Melina and Pinckaers in the works cited. Other examples are surveyed in Joseph Kotva, *The Christian Case for Virtue Ethics* (Washington DC: Georgetown UP, 1996) especially the Protestant virtue ethicists Gilbert Meilaender, *The Theory and Practice of Virtue* (Notre Dame: UP, 1984) and Stanley Hauerwas, *Vision and Virtue: Essays in Christian Ethical Reflection* (Notre Dame: UP, 1981); see also Paul Wadell, *The Primacy of Love* (New York: Paulist, 1992).
Sadly some recent writers seem to be re-dressing individualism and proportionalism in the garb of virtue ethics, and cultural relativism in the garb of communitarianism; the now rather old-fashioned "balancing act" is being equated with *phronesis* and the equally tired denial of objective moral absolutes is being labelled a "virtue-focussed rather than norm-focussed ethic" and "respect for cultural mores". The risk is that, like love, freedom, context and double effect for a previous generation, a new generation will embrace virtue and

"the personal narrative" of every human life.[101] The seven classical virtues (especially *phronesis*) are being explored anew and in greater depth in contemporary moral theory; other virtues, no longer strait-jacketed with the seven are also being rediscovered (e.g. respectfulness, truthfulness, humility, gratitude, modesty, hospitality). It is increasingly recognised that moral formation, counselling and spiritual direction require the cultivation of virtue and the correction of vice – through limitation, habituation, role-modelling, story-telling, and so on). And different roles in life require different virtues: being a spouse, for instance, requires fidelity, a willingness to communicate and to forgive, perseverance, chastity; parenting requires generosity, devotion, patience, hope.

We do not get such virtues by pulling ourselves up by our own bootstraps. Only immersion in a morally sound

---

community talk without the rest of the rich tradition of Catholic moral theology to support it. This may help to explain why *Veritatis Splendor* gives far more attention to the *principles* side of the dialectic between principle and character than to the character side: even if it is only the virtuous person who will know, choose and reveal what is morally good, true *virtues* can only be distinguished from personally or socially approved *vices* by an objective assessment of the kinds of behaviour they encourage. Thus Christian morality must be ready to criticise the pattern of virtues and vices assumed or proposed at any particular time in any particular community with "the norm of truth and the splendour of goodness".

[101] On these accounts virtues are presented as (relatively stable) dispositions or sensibilities which integrate emotions and desires with rational responses to human goods; they socialise people appropriately for a common life with others; they help them not only to act well but to do so more readily and consistently. Vices do the opposite. Both virtues and vices are residues of past good or bad acts and dispositions to engage in similar future acts.

culture will elicit and support good character traits.[102] One of the functions of communities like family and Church is to call people of diverse temper into relationships; here they can draw certain things from the group and they give back in their own way. Affective bonds (of blood, friendship, loyalty, faith, hope, charity), joint projects (such as the upbringing of children and working out salvation together), common role models (such as the grandparents and the Holy Family), shared traditions and practices (such as family meals and acts of worship) – all these knit the members of the group together, shape them with certain virtues, and give them a sense of identity, values and destiny.

With such mutual bonds come mutual expectations. The group has its customs and beliefs. If you are unwilling to be self-sacrificing or you don't like children, marriage isn't for you; if you believe in multiple gods or child sacrifice, you've got the wrong Church. If it's Christianity you want, commit yourself to things like the Decalogue and the Beatitudes, to self-donation as spouse, parent, disciple and martyr.[103] The roles of marriage and family life in cultivating humanity have long been appreciated but may well gain a new impetus in the face of the virtue and community turns in contemporary moral theory. Leon Kass, the recently appointed Chair of the US Presidential

---

[102] The communitarians rightly complain of liberalism, secular or religious, that it fails to take seriously the fact that we are *social* animals, highly interdependent and complementary, and that much of our lives involves shared interests, goals, identities.

[103] The common good of any community requires not just a certain minimum etiquette, but a collective lifestyle founded on a shared vision. One of the functions of documents like Part 3 of the *Catechism of the Catholic Church* (1994) – the moral section – is to "unpack" that vision and life-style in an authoritative way.

Commission on Bioethics, has written of "the household, that nest and nursery of humanity – private, intimate, and vulnerable":

> Though its roots are the needs of bodily life – nurture, protection, reproduction, and then protection and nurture of the young – the household provides for more than the body. A richly woven fabric of nature and convention, it is established by law to nurture our nature. It is sustained by customs that humanise the human animal, engendering love and friendship, speech and education, choice and awareness, and shared beliefs and feelings.[104]

Here Kass echoes the thought developed by John Paul II in *Familiaris Consortio* and elsewhere that marriage and family life not only require certain character traits such as self-sacrifice and fidelity if they are to succeed, but that they in turn *civilise* people in very particular ways – the lack of which helps to explain a great many contemporary social and personal maladies. Study of the internal ends, necessary character traits, customary thought patterns and traditional behaviours of institutions such as marriage and family is another promising direction for Catholic morality in the century ahead.

The specifically Catholic-Christian contribution
In *Ethics After Babel* Jeffrey Stout explores the "nearly complete breakdown of fruitful dialogue between secular

---

[104] Leon Kass, T*owards a More Natural Science: Biology and Human Affairs* (New York: Free Press, 1985), p.273. See also his excellent treatment in "The Wisdom of Repugnance", *The New Republic* 216(22) (2 June 1997).

philosophical thought and the religious traditions", suggesting that this impoverishes both and is the result not only of secular moral philosophers adopting "tropes and fetishes" that virtually preclude such conversation but also of theology failing to offer anything that might make an educated public sit up and listen.

> To gain a hearing in our culture, theology has often assumed a voice not its own and found itself merely repeating the bromides of secular intellectuals in transparently figurative speech... Meanwhile, secular intellectuals have largely stopped paying attention. They don't need to be told, *by theologians*, that Genesis is mythical, that nobody knows much about the historical Jesus, that it's morally imperative to side with the oppressed, or that birth control is morally permissible. The explanation for the eclipse of religious ethics in recent secular moral philosophy may therefore be...that academic theologians have increasingly given the impression of saying nothing atheists don't already know.[105]

Leading Protestant scholars have likewise bemoaned the fact that much of "the new morality" proposed by Christian theologians in the 1970s and 1980s was really the ethics of "the world" dressed up in religious poetry, an ethic of "middle class respectability", "a series of platitudes ranging from the inane to the incoherent", a mixture of the trivial and the sentimental, a picture of God not as a moral law-giver but as a "therapeutic nice-guy" who is uncomfortable with our neat little compromises and double standards. They have called for a radical

---

[105] Stout, *op.cit.*, p.164.

recommitment to the *distinctively Christian* in ethics, to be willing to be "prophetic", "counter-cultural", the advocates of a genuinely *alternative* lifestyle.[106]

John Paul II[107] and others[108] have led the way in developing a distinctively Christian rhetoric with which to

---

[106] Stanley Hauerwas & Alasdair MacIntyre *(eds)*, *Revisions: Changing Perspectives in Moral Philosophy* (Notre Dame: UP, 1983); Stephen Fowl & l.Gregory Jones, *Reading in Communion: Scripture and Ethics in Christian Life* (London: SPCK, 1991); *cf* A.Callinicos, *Against Post Modernism* (London: Routledge & Kegan Paul, 1990); L.Kolakowski, *Modernity on Endless Trial* (Chicago: University of Chicago Press, 1990); David Schindler, *Heart of the World, Centre of the Church: Communio Ecclesiology, Liberalism and Liberation* (Edinburgh: T & T Clark, 1996). See also the extraordinary corpus of Aidan Nichols OP, including: *Catholic Thought Since the Enlightenment: A Survey* (Leominster: Gracewing, 1998) and *Christendom Awake: On Re-energising the Church in Culture* (Edinburgh: T & T Clark, 1999).

[107] This is not the place to analyse the present Pope's enormous contribution to marital and familial morality through the elaboration of his unique philosophical and theological anthropology. Suffice it to say that it reflects his own background as a student not only of Scripture and of Thomism, but also of the existentialist, phenomenological and personalist schools of Continental philosophy and the Carmelite school of spirituality. Reflecting upon the nature of "the acting subject", Wojtyla has been especially attentive to anthropology, sociology, mysticism and aesthetics, and to the psychology of ordinary experience. So as to resist the tendency of such approaches to philosophical idealism, he grounds his "ontological" personalism in Thomistic realism. This personalist strain explains the appearance in *Veritatis Splendor* of some language, possibly unfamiliar to those schooled outside the European Continent – such as the talk of "the acting subject [who] personally assimilates the truth contained in the [natural] law. He appropriates this truth of his being and makes it his own by his acts and the corresponding virtues." (§52)

[108] See for example Karol Wojtyla, *Love and Responsibility* (London: Collins, 1981); Carlos Caffara, *Living in Christ: Fundamental Principles of*

describe the mysteries of the human person, sexual differentiation, marriage and the family, such as "the identity-difference" and "subjectivity-alterity" of the person, the "horizon" and "ground" of beings in Being, "the nuptial significance of body" and its "body language" of sex, the family as "a school of virtue" and "site and vehicle of evangelisation", the "theodrama" of the moral life of each "actor", and so on. By elaborating an anthropology that is unashamedly Christian in its foundations, contemporary in its language, and orthopractical in its conclusions, they have pointed a way forward for those engaged in the Church's internal task of theological understanding and catechesis.

Thus the identity, differences and unity of each human person, and of diverse persons within marriage and family are better understood by reflection upon the unity and diversity of the persons of the *Trinity*. The significance of bodily life is enlarged by reflection upon the Incarnation of God, the Transfiguration of Christ, the resurrection of the body, and the sacramental mediation of divine grace.

Catholic Moral Teaching (San Francisco: Ignatius, 1987); J.F.Crosby, "The personalism of John Paul II as the basis of his approach to the teaching of *Humanae Vitae*", in R.E.Smith (ed), *Trust the Truth: A symposium on the twentieth anniversary of the Encyclical Humanae Vitae* (Braintree MA, 1988), 37-63; Lawrence Porter, "Gender in Theology: The Example of John Paul II's *Mulieris Dignitatem*", *Gregorianum* 77(1) (1996); L.Gardner, *Balthazar: At the End of Modernity* (Edinburgh: T & T Clark, 1999); Melina, *Cristo e il dinamismo dell'agire* (Muria, 2001); Angelo Scola, *Hans Urs von Balthazar: A Theological Style* (Grand Rapids: Eerdmans, 1995) and *Questioni di Antropologia Teologica* (Rome, 1997); David L Schindler (ed), *Catholicism and Secularisation in America* (Notre Dame: Communio Books, 1990); Heinz Schürmann, Joseph Ratzinger and Hans Urs von Balthazar, *Principles of Christian Morality* (San Francisco: Ignatius, 1986); cf Oliver O'Donovan, *Resurrection and Moral Order: An Outline for Evangelical Ethics* (2nd ed., Leicester: Apollo, 1994).

The three traditional *bonae* of marriage can be understood upon the pattern of the relations of God Three-in-One: a love affair with our God (*Sacramentum*) modelled on the Father's own love, a love affair with the spouse (*fides*) modelled on Christ's love for the Church, and a love affair with our children (*proles*) modelled on the love of the One who proceeds from Them both. Likewise the vocation of the family as an *ecclesia domestica* becomes the most concrete human experience and the most powerful retelling of that Trinitarian love, by sharing in "the Christ event" and by receiving the Pentecostal outpouring of the "fruits" or "children" of the Holy Spirit: love, joy, peace, perseverance, kindness, goodness, fidelity, gentleness, chastity.[109]

This project has barely begun and will take decades fully to elaborate; much of it is in a specialised language that requires translation into a more accessible idiom; and it must continue parallel to the more philosophical work necessary if we are to speak in pluralist and increasingly secular societies. But the task of elaborating a sacramental and moral theology of marriage in response to the call of the Second Vatican Council has, after some false starts, at last decisively begun. In its outworking in the years ahead it will bring a new energy to the contest over the central Christian claims elaborated at the start of my paper.

CONCLUSION

Our world is at a crossroads. As John Paul II has so incisively put it, we must choose between "a civilisation of life and love" and a culture of lies and of death. Do we

---

[109] *Gal* 5:22-23; *cf* John Paul II, *Redemptor Hominis* (1979) §70; *Dominum et Vivificantem* (1986) §26.

believe and are we willing to live positive, creative and hopeful propositions about the sacredness, dignity and responsibilities of sexuality, marriage and the family such as those I outlined at the start of my paper – reformulated and developed appropriately with the aid of the best of contemporary moral thinking and, perhaps, with a Scots accent? Or do we prefer to acquiesce in the destruction of the marriage-based family, in consumer sex, wholesale sterilisation, the abandonment of children and the elderly, in values disorientation, and the rest? The development of a new rhetoric of marital and familial morality, premised upon our long and rich tradition and the best of contemporary academic renewal, and expressed in new evangelical and pastoral strategies, is no longer an optional extra: it is literally a matter of life and death for our civilisation and one of the principal vocations of our leaders such as Archbishop Conti. More strength to his arm.

V. Rev. Professor Anthony Fisher OP is Director of the John Paul II Institute for Marriage and the Family in Melbourne, Australia, where he lectures in moral theology and bioethics. He came to this position after doctoral studies in Oxford and six years teaching at the Australian Catholic University. He is a member of the Pontifical Academy for Life. He has published many books and articles. He is also currently Deputy Provincial and Master of Students in the Dominican Order in Australia.

THE ORDER OF MALTA
PAST PRESENT FUTURE?

ARCHBISHOP MAURICE COUVE DE MURVILLE

It is a privilege for me to contribute an essay to the *Festschrift* for Archbishop Mario Conti, a friend of long standing. I am particularly pleased to write on the Order of Malta, which counts the Archbishop among its members. Archbishop Conti was Principal Chaplain of the British Association of the Order from 1995 to 2000 and has greatly contributed to the work of the Association during that time. It is good to add this tribute to the Jubilee Anthology which marks his twenty-five years as Bishop.

The starting point for an understanding of the Order of Malta must be the word *Hospitaller*. It began as the brotherhood that looked after a hostel and hospital for pilgrims to Jerusalem in the second half of the eleventh century[110], a time when an increasing number of pilgrims

---

[110] For the early history of the Hospitallers see Jonathan Riley-Smith, *The Knights of St John in Jerusalem and Cyprus c.1050-1310* (London: Macmillan St Martin's Press, 1967). Alain Beltjens, *Aux Origines de l'Ordre de Malte: De la Fondation de l'Hôpital de Jerusalem à sa Transformation en Ordre Militaire* (Brussels: A. Beltjens, 1995) gives a careful analysis of all the documents concerning the origins of the hospitallers. For an English translation of many of the early texts see E.J. King, *The Rule Statutes and Customs of the Hospitallers 1099-1310* (London: Methuen, 1934. Reprint New York: AMS Press, 1981). Jonathan Riley-Smith, *The Sovereign Military Order of Malta: A Short*

from Europe were visiting the places in Palestine connected with the Old Testament, the life of Christ, and the Early Church. The hospital had been established by the Benedictine monks of the Abbey of St Mary of the Latins, Italian monks from Amalfi. After the conquest of Jerusalem by the First Crusade in 1099, Christian kingdoms and principalities were created in Palestine and Syria, which lasted for some hundred and fifty years. The number of pilgrims increasing even more, hostels and hospitals for them were created along the main European pilgrim routes which led to the Near East.

A Religious Order

In 1113 Pope Pascal II issued a document that can be seen as the foundation document of the Order. The Bull *Pie postulatio voluntatis* was addressed to Gerard as founder and provost of the hospital in Jerusalem and put under his authority not only the communities of brothers and sisters in Jerusalem but also the hospitals and properties in Europe that it mentions by name. Brother Gerard thus found himself at the head of a religious order, which was very different from the abbeys of the time with their practice of the lifelong stability of monks in one place. The Brothers of the Hospital were to combine devotion to a common ideal, lived in community, with the mobility which would allow them to serve wherever they were needed. That can only be described as an twelfth century invention, and it is also found in two other orders founded at the time: the Knights Templars and the English Order of the Gilbertines, founded by St Gilbert of Sempringham.

History (London: British Association, 2001) gives an excellent general introduction with a valuable section on the spiritual life of the Order.

Blessed Gerard was an extraordinary man; his epitaph in Jerusalem contained the phrase:

Pluribus in terris sua sollers brachia tendens
Undique collegit pasceret unde suos

"He stretched forth his arms into many lands so as to obtain what he needed to feed his own." This alludes to Gerard's organisational skill and to what we would call today his international outlook, although national consciousness in our sense was hardly in existence at the time. The Hospitallers began as men and women who were bound to help and to nurse pilgrims, that is, those who were on the move, and the Hospitallers therefore had to be in several places at once to do this. Thus, from the start, they were a religious order composed of hospitallers, who, unlike monks, were able to move from place to place.

A second characteristic of Brother Gerard can be deduced from an expression "Our Lords the Poor", which is first found among the Hospitallers of St John of Jerusalem. Gerard, as the ardent follower of Christ that he was, derived from the Gospel the idea that the values of this world must be reversed by a Christian. The poor are the ones who are closer to God and to the Kingdom of God; the rich and the powerful have the difficult task of using power and wealth without being mastered by them. In a feudal society, where a hierarchy of lordships rose from serf to king, the phrase "Our Lords the poor and the sick" must have sounded very strange. Gerard and his brethren were clearly saying that the sick and the poor must be treated as Lords and served like Lords: nothing was to be too good for them. The hospitals, which the Order later created in many different lands, were marked by a level of health care which was ahead of their time, but the model was set from the start by the Hospital at Jerusalem. It could take up to two thousand patients, male and female. The patients had their own beds when only the greatest in society had individual beds. The diet was lavish: at a time when few people had white bread or a meat diet, the Hospitallers provided both for their patients. The brothers made no distinction between Christians and patients from other faiths: Muslims and Christians were welcomed to the Hospital. When Christian patients arrived, they went to confession and then received Holy Communion; they seem to have been encouraged to go to communion every Sunday. In so many ways, the Brothers of St John, guided by the spirit of their founder, were to remain ahead of their time. Another phrase applied to Brother Gerard in his epitaph encapsulates his religious genius: *Pauperibus servus*, "the servant of the poor". All this is contained in the phrase *obsequium pauperum*, "the service of the poor", which remains the motto of the Order, together with *tuitio fidei*, "the defence of the Faith".

A Military Order
The political situation of the Crusader Kingdoms of the Near East worsened during the twelfth and thirteenth centuries. Muslim Emirates united to fight the invaders from the West, who had only been able to establish themselves in these countries because of the divisions between Arabs. During that difficult period, the Hospitaller Brothers decided that it was their duty not only to accommodate and nurse pilgrims but also to defend them. They thus developed into a Military Order as well as a Hospitaller one. In Palestine, the brothers became knightly brothers with sergeants-at-arms and

mercenaries at their command. Crusader castles were built in Palestine and Syria according to the latest technique of European military architecture. They are magnificent fortresses, of which Krak des Chevaliers in Syria is perhaps the finest example and the most visited by tourists today; but these castles were vulnerable. The resident Christian population in the Holy Land was relatively small, compared to the teeming populations of the Orient. Muslim armies, careless of casualties, were able to prevent Crusader armies from operating in the open field and to rush even the towering defences of Krak des Chevaliers. It was encircled by an Arab army on 3rd March 1271, and mining began under its walls; the south west tower collapsed on 29th March and by 8th April the garrison surrendered. In 1291 Acre fell and the Christians had been driven out of Palestine.

The Hospitaller Knights continued their relief work and their military operation in Cyprus and then, in 1306, conquered the island of Rhodes from the Turks and made it their headquarters, but Rhodes was very near the Turkish mainland and particularly vulnerable. The Knights fought off a Turkish siege in 1480 but forty years later an overwhelming force led by Sultan Suleiman the Magnificent besieged Rhodes for over six months and compelled the knights to surrender. They negotiated an orderly withdrawal, by which they evacuated their forces, their arms and their possessions, sailing off to the western Mediterranean on 1st January 1523. The Knights Hospitaller were then homeless for seven years, after which the Emperor Charles V granted them the island of Malta; from then on they were commonly known as the Knights of Malta.

The Great Siege of 1565

The Order of St John lost no time in settling down in its new home; in fact, aided by the responsions (annual payments) flowing in from all its European commanderies, it immediately built Fort San Elmo, which controlled the entry to the Grand Harbour, and Fort San Angelo on the Grand Harbour itself. The *Conventus*, that is, the Grand Master's headquarters, his household of knights and the community of chaplains who daily celebrated the Divine Office, was located in Fort San Angelo. Malta is in a strategic position and the Order built up its navy and tried to keep the sea lanes of the Mediterranean open for the ships of Christian nations. The Sultan in Constantinople soon found that the Hospitallers were obstructing his lines of communication with the North African Muslim states. Perhaps he regretted having allowed the Knights to leave Rhodes on favourable terms; he certainly decided this time to blot out their power for good. There ensued the famous siege of Malta in 1565, which will always be remembered as one of the greatest feat of arms of Christian Europe. Suleiman the Magnificent, now seventy years old, sent an armada of nearly two hundred ships from Constantinople, carrying an army estimated at forty thousand fighting men. Against them the Grand Master of the Order, Jean Parisot de la Valette, could muster five hundred knights and about nine thousand soldiers, but (unlike the situation which had obtained in Rhodes) he had the whole-hearted support of the native population; many Maltese were killed fighting in support of the knights. The Turks had their difficulties too because of their extended lines of communication and the nature of the terrain. Unlike the verdant island of Rhodes, Malta is a bare rock with very little wood or water; the knights had polluted the few springs and ponds before withdrawing with the local population to the shelter of their fortresses and, as the broiling heat of the Mediterranean summer drew on, dysentery decimated the Turkish soldiers.

By the sixteenth century, cannon dominated siege warfare. The heavy siege cannon of the Turks pounded the walls ceaselessly, sometimes even through the night. When sections of the fortifications collapsed, the knights raked the serried ranks of attacking Janissaries with the shot of their culverins. There was no quarter and the slaughter was terrific. On 23rd June, one month after the arrival of the Turks, Fort San Elmo was captured after every one of its defenders had been killed, except for five Maltese who jumped into the Grand Harbour and swam across to Fort San Angelo to bear the news.

The whole of the Turks' gunfire and the repeated assaults of their foot soldiers were now concentrated on Fort San Angelo; here the indomitable La Valette inspired the defence which could not be broken, even by six weeks of unremitting attacks. On 7th September, Don Garcia de Toledo, the Spanish Viceroy of Sicily, arrived at last with a relief force of some nine thousand and the next day, the Feast of the Nativity of Our Lady, the Turkish army re-embarked and sailed away; it had lost half of its original military force. Of La Valette's original force of five hundred knights, only two hundred and fifty survived and most of these were gravely wounded; the original garrison of nine thousand had only six hundred soldiers still capable of bearing arms. This hard-won victory was hailed throughout Europe; even in Protestant England, Queen Elizabeth ordered that the church bells should be rung in admiration at the courage and tenacity of the distant Hospitaller Knights of St John.

Spiritual Warfare

The story of the siege is an exciting one. It has perhaps been best told by Ernle Bradford, himself a naval officer, in his book *The Great Siege*[111], but one small episode in that epic tale is particularly significant for an understanding of the Order of Malta. The beleaguered defenders had been awaiting the Viceroy and his relief force ever since the Turks had landed on May 19th. On 4th June Grand Master de La Valette had received a message from Don Garcia that he would come with his soldiers by June 20th. The Grand Master refrained from imparting this information to his troops; at first, he did not even tell his council. On the contrary, his constant concern was to make everyone on the Christian side realise that the only hope of success was to depend on God and on the courage of each and every defender. He had said on 31st May: "...we must not look to others for our deliverance. It is only on God and our own swords that we may rely. Yet this is no reason why we should be disheartened. Rather the opposite, for it is better to know the truth of one's situation than to be deceived by false hopes. Our Faith and the Honour of our Order are in our own hands. We shall not fail."[112] How right he was! No help from Sicily materialised by June 20th; in fact, as mentioned above, it did not arrive until September 7th. If a beleaguered garrison had been counting the days, it would have found those weeks endless and demoralising. In the hour of need, the indomitable La Valette gave an example which expresses for future generations the essence of the *tuitio fidei*, "the defence of the faith". In the last resort it is a spiritual

---

[111] Ernle Bradford, *The Great Siege: Malta 1565* (London: Hodder and Stoughton, 1961; Penguin Books, 1964).
[112] *Ibid*, pp.93-94.

warfare on which the knights are engaged and only spiritual weapons can guarantee its success.

However, material weapons continued to be at the fore of the Order's concerns as the seventeenth and eighteenth centuries wore on. In fact, there was distinctly less emphasis on the *obsequium pauperum*, "the service of the poor". The imposing fortifications that encircle the city of Valetta today were built soon after the siege; naval operations against Islam continued, although resources had been considerably reduced by the Reformation and the consequent disappearance of commanderies in the countries of northern Europe. It was during this period that the Order was recognised by some of the countries of Europe as a sovereign entity, with whom they exchanged diplomatic representatives. The closed crown of royalty appeared above the Grand Master's coat-of-arms.

It was also a period when the nobiliary character of the brethren came to the fore. Once the Order had become a military order, it was natural that it should be recruited among the class that provided *milites*, not just foot soldiers but soldiers on horseback, knights. In the thirteenth century, it became a requirement that a candidate should be the son of a knight, which was reasonable, because familiarity with the use of arms required such long training. From the fourteenth century onwards, proofs of noble ancestry became more stringent. This reflected a process which was at work in many European institutions of the time; there was a cult of nobility as something good and proper: something to aspire to.

During the eighteenth century, the style of the Order changed as its members were drawn more and more into the service of secular princes. An example very creditable to the order was Antonio Maria de Bucareli, Marquis de Vallehermose, Viceroy of the king of Spain in Mexico from 1771 to 1779. When he was twenty-four he had made his vows as a professed knight, the vows of poverty, chastity and obedience required of religious in the Catholic Church; he became an excellent administrator, incorruptible, conscientious, aware of the needs of the people, probably the best Viceroy Mexico ever had.[113] It is good to know that he gave much help to Blessed Junípero Serra, the Franciscan who between 1769 and 1784 established the Indian Missions on the Californian coast from San Diego to San Francisco.[114] It also became customary for officers of the French Navy to begin their training in the ships of the Order, men such as Tourville, de Grasse and Bailiff Pierre de Suffren, the splendidly aggressive admiral who fought against the British in India during the American War of Independence and who was a professed knight.

Prince de Conti and the Temple
In marked contrast to the life of such men was that of several of the Grand Priors of France in their official residence, "the Temple" in Paris,[115] a fortress, built by the Knights Templars, which had passed, after their suppression, to the Hospitallers. In the centre stood the grim tower in which Louis XVI and Marie Antoinette were to be imprisoned during their last months together on earth. This was not however the residence of the junior members of the royal family who were appointed Grand

[113] See Bernard E. Bobb, *The Viceregency of Antonio Maria Bucareli in New Spain 1771-1779* (Austin, Texas: University of Texas Press, 1962).
[114] See M.N.L. Couve de Murville, *The Man who Founded California: The Life of Blessed Junípero Serra* (San Francisco: Ignatius Press, 2000).
[115] Frederick W. Ryan, *The House of the Temple: A Study of Malta and its Knights in the French Revolution* (London: Burns Oates and Washbourne, 1930), pp.56-61.

Priors during the seventeenth and eighteenth centuries; because of the enormous income which was attached to this position, successive rulers of France were glad to impose members of the royal family on the Order, despite their total lack of any vocation to the religious state. In the *enclos du Temple*, the enclosure which surrounded the mediaeval castle of the Templars and covered nearly thirty acres, an elegant palace surrounded by extensive gardens was designed in 1665 by Giovanni Lorenzo Bernini, the great Italian architect of the Baroque. The *enclos* was a "peculiar" ecclesiastically and an exempt lordship civilly, outside the jurisdiction of the Paris police. Several Grand Priors had built town houses within it, which were rented out to private tenants and increased even more the income, derived from the responsions paid to the Grand Priory by the commanderies of France. What was left, after the various noble officials of the Priory had received their salaries, was sent off to Malta.

In 1670, Louis XIV decided to appoint as Grand Prior his cousin, Philippe de Vendôme, descended from an illegitimate son of Henri IV. He was only fifteen at the time and was not even in the Order. In spite of the indignant protests of Grand Master Nicolas Cotoner, the king obtained a brief from the Pope which dispensed from all the regulations of the Order. However, Philippe did have to become technically a religious so as to qualify for the appointment; this he did by taking the three vows, none of which he subsequently observed. He spent half of each year fighting in the interminable wars of Louis XIV (his brother was the Marshal de Vendôme, one of the King's generals) and the rest of the time in the Temple where he led a life of debauchery, lapsing into alcoholism. He was replaced in 1719 when the Duke of Orléans, Regent of France after the death of Louis XIV, appointed as Grand Prior one of his bastards, the Chevalier d'Orléans, aged sixteen, who became famous for the magnificent entertainments which he gave at the Temple.[116] And then in 1742 Louis François de Bourbon, Prince de Conti, a widower, descended from another junior branch of the royal family, became a notorious Grand Prior, bringing with him his equally notorious chaplain, the Abbé Prévost. Antoine François Prévost was the author of *Manon Lescaut*, a novel which had had a *succès de scandale*; it had been officially banned, was readily available and had been read by everyone. Not the least attraction of this affecting but scandalous tale was the fact that Prévost had written it in the unexpected setting of a Cluniac abbey when he was a monk. He had fled to England once his authorship was known, but returned to France after a few years and made his peace with the Church, though he was not required to return to the monastic life. He then approached the Prince de Conti and asked to become his chaplain. "How unfortunate!" said the Prince. "Don't you know that I never go to Mass?" "That suits me, Monseigneur," replied the Abbé. "I never say Mass."[117] He was appointed, and enjoyed living in the exempted territory of the Temple where he had "no ecclesiastical duties, his benefices providing a

---

[116] For Vendôme and Orléans see Claude Petiet, "Deux pittoresque Grands Prieurs de France", *Société de l'histoire et du Patrimoine de l'Ordre de Malte* (2002), pp.21-26; (2003), bulletin no.11, pp.28-32. I am grateful to M. Hugues Lépolard, Archivist of the French Association of the Order of Malta, for these references.

[117] Jacques Hillairet, *Évocation du Vieux Paris* (Paris: Éditions de Minuit, 1953), p.353.

comfortable house, a cook, a lackey and 'a good-looking housekeeper' ".[118]

Conti remained at the Temple until his death in 1776. Several literary *salons* met there, and he was a fashionable figure, entertaining lavishly; he was also a philanderer whose life was a public scandal. It was said that the Grand Prior requested a ring after each encounter with the ladies who were the objects of his amorous conquests. The rings were counted after his death and there were nearly four thousand of them; but it was also said that he had added to the number![119] Such was the society supported by pious donations contributed over the centuries for poor pilgrims and the defence of the Holy Land. Professor John McManners, the eminent historian of eighteenth century France, sums up the situation: "... a crusading Order devoted originally to driving the infidels from Jerusalem became the support of the life-style of French noble families and a major contribution to the efficiency of the French navy."[120] The corruption of the *Ancien Régime* called for a sea change, and this, unexpectedly, is exactly what happened.

In 1798 Napoleon Bonaparte, on his ill-fated expedition to Egypt, stopped at Malta with a fleet carrying some thirty-five thousand soldiers. He expelled the Grand Master and the Knights, leaving a French garrison on the island. It was a crushing blow for the Order, but with hindsight it is possible to see this as a condition of its extraordinary revival in the nineteenth century. Although the Grand Master, Ferdinand von Hompesch, has been

---

[118] John McManners, *Church and Society in Eighteenth Century France*, (Oxford: Oxford University Press, 1998), vol.1, p.663.

[119] Jacques Hillairet, *Évocation du Vieux Paris*, p. 353.

[120] John McManners, *Church and Society in Eighteenth Century France*, vol.1, p.488.

harshly condemned by some contemporaries and some historians for not resisting to the end, it is obvious now that he had made a realistic assessment of the situation. The Order had been deprived of even more of its revenues by the French Revolution, so that the defences were inadequate; repelling the French by force was not a possible option. Recently there has been a re-assessment of Hompesch, especially on the part of the Maltese who are grateful to him for not involving the population in needless destruction and loss of life.[121]

Reinvented

Once again the Knights were homeless. For a time it looked as if the Order would disappear altogether, but it was saved by two things: the Papacy and its aristocratic character. As a religious order of the Catholic Church, the Order is subject to the Pope; it was the Papacy that ensured that there was always a legitimate authority in the Order, in fact a Lieutenant appointed by the Pope after the abdication of Grand Master von Hompesch in 1799. Pius VII (1800-1823) was cautious in his support of the Knights because their survival seemed to be linked to the recovery of the island of Malta. This was a political issue between the Mediterranean powers in which the Pope did not wish to intervene. By the time of Gregory XVI (1831-1846) Malta had definitely been assigned to Great Britain. The Pope was therefore free to encourage Carlo Candida, the new Lieutenant whom he had appointed in 1834, to look in a new direction. The *Conventus* was brought to Rome and Candida began a "return to the roots" by emphasising the care of the sick. He asked the Pope for a

---

[121] See *Hompesch and Malta: A New Evaluation*, edited by Maurice Eminyan S.J. (Malta: Publishers Enterprises Group, 1999).

hospital where the novices could be introduced to this work and the Order took charge of the hospice of Cento Preti at the Ponte Sisto.[122] This was a development rich in possibilities for the future.

The other important element of continuity was the commitment of the Order to an aristocratic ideal. Blessed Gerard had brought those who were "first" in the World's eyes to serve those who were "last", i.e. the sick and the poor. In nineteenth century Europe, aristocrats were in a situation where their place in society was uncertain after the challenge of many revolutions. It was a comfort for Catholics from noble families to find in the Order a continuity which helped them to be in touch with their past. Local aristocratic groups provided a natural "parish" for recruitment, though sometimes these groups were described as "little more than an old gentlemen's club". In due course a new reality emerged, the National Associations, which, because of the very small number of professed knights, became the mainstay of the Order. National Associations made it possible for laymen and women to join the Order in the grade of Honour and Devotion without taking the three vows of religion. Such a grade is equivalent to what used to be called Third Orders in the Dominicans, Franciscans and Carmelites, that is, lay people who could be married and have professional occupations, but who were associated with the spirituality and the good works of a particular religious order. As H.A.J. Sire says in his extensive and perceptive history of the Order, the Knights of Honour and Devotion "became the means by which the Order

---

[122] H.J.A. Sire, *The Knights of Malta* (New Haven and London: Yale University Press, 1994), p.251.

recovered its social and political influence".[123] This was achieved without creating commanderies with endowments, or priories with communities of religious, neither of which would have been possible at the time. One could almost say that the Order reinvented itself in the nineteenth century while maintaining continuity with its religious reality.

Now a new phenomenon is emerging. It could be described as growth from the periphery to the centre. From the "Third Order" classes of the Order, religious vocations are coming forward to take the three vows of religion; as a result a Priory of the Order has been restored (that of England in 1993) and three Sub-Priories have been created (Germany 1961; Ireland 1972; Spain 1990). They will add a new dimension to the recovery of the Order's authentic traditions.

The expansion in numbers has also been a recent development. There are now eleven thousand members of the Order, one third of whom are in the United Sates of America. The range of hospital work, medical care and relief work undertaken by the Order is large and diverse; each National Association organises its own contribution in these fields, and Dame Rosita McHugh has produced in her book *The Knights of Malta: 900 Years of Care* a map showing the impressive spread of the Order's institutional presence throughout the world.[124] The British Association, for instance, has set up a Trust, in conjunction with the Venerable Order of St John of Jerusalem, to contract with local authorities, under the Community Care Act 1990, so

---

[123] *Ibid.*

[124] Rosita McHugh, *The Knights of Malta: 900 Years of Care* (Dublin: Irish Association, 1996), published at St John's House, 32 Clyde Road, Dublin 4.

as to provide residential care for the elderly: the Trust is currently managing fifty-four old people's homes with two thousand, two hundred residents. In the international field, one can mention ECOM, the Emergency Corps of the Order of Malta, created in 1998, which coordinates the work of Priories and National Associations of the Order in international disaster relief. Professor Riley-Smith recently wrote about ECOM: "Probably the most spectacular hospitaller and humanitarian achievement of the Order... is to be found in the aid convoys, mostly from Germany, France, Austria and Italy (but on a modest scale from Britain too) entering the war-torn areas of former Yugoslavia."[125]

In a world of increasing international contacts, the sovereign character of the Order had also found a new importance. It now exchanges diplomatic representations with eighty-eight countries and is a permanent observer at the United Nations. Like the Holy See, it has the possibility of addressing itself directly to Heads of State and of governments in defence of religious and humanitarian values. That is of no little importance in a world tempted to opt for a materialistic view of mankind and to ignore the spiritual dimensions of the problems that beset the human race.

The aristocratic character of the Order is one of its proudest traditions and is the object of much reflection in the Order today. As the pool of inherited nobility lessens in Europe, there is a search for *aristoi* who are aristocrats by their achievements (according to the motto of Trinity College, Cambridge: *Virtus Vera Nobilitas*). The many capable and devoted men and women who accede to the

[125] Jonathan Riley-Smith, *The Sovereign Military Order of Malta: A Short History*, p.15.

lower grades of the Order are needed in its higher grades as well; this is particularly evident in the Associations of North and South America. A personal ennoblement, on the lines of the life peerages of the English House of Lords, would continue the nobiliary tradition and use it to serve the needs of an expanding institution. Whatever solution is found, the vigour and effectiveness of the Order of Malta today is evident; its future, under God, is in the hands of its members.

The Most Reverend Maurice Couve de Murville is Archbishop Emeritus of Birmingham and Principal Chaplain of the British Association of the Sovereign Military Order of Malta. He was educated at Downside School, Trinity College, Cambridge and the Institut Catholique, Paris; he also obtained an M.Phil. from the University of London in 1994 and an honorary doctorate from Birmingham University in 1996. He was ordained priest in 1957, serving as a parish priest in Moulescoomb and as a chaplain first at the University of Sussex, then at Cambridge University. In 1982 he was ordained Archbishop of Birmingham where he remained until his "retirement" in 1999. He now lives in Sussex, where he continues to research and to write. He has published several books on Catholic history.

THE RISK OF ECUMENISM
LIVING WITH PARADOX

BISHOP BRUCE CAMERON

When Archbishop Mario Conti returned to Aberdeen in May 2002 to celebrate with his former diocese the Silver Jubilee of his Ordination as Bishop, his friends and colleagues from other Christian churches invited him to conclude that celebration with an Ecumenical Service in the "Mither Kirk" of the city – the Kirk of St Nicholas. The theme of that service was "The Ecumenical Journey" and it began with words spoken by Pope John Paul II on his visit to Scotland in 1982. In Bellahouston Park in Glasgow he said:

> I wish to address for a few moments that larger community of believers in Christ, who share with my Catholic brothers and sisters the privilege of being Scots, sons and daughters alike of this ancient nation. I know of the veneration in which you hold the Sacred Scriptures, accepting them for what they are, the word of God, and not of man. I have reserved until now and should like to read to you the remaining words from that passage of St Paul's Letter to the Ephesians: "There is one body, one Spirit, just as you were all called into one and the same hope when you were called. There is one Lord, one Faith, one baptism, and one God who is Father of all, over all, through all, and within

all."[126] This passage clearly reveals the will of God for mankind, a plan which human wills may oppose but cannot thwart. It is God's plan for all of us, "for there is no eternal city for us in this life but we look for one in the life to come."[127] We are only pilgrims on this earth, making our way towards that heavenly Kingdom promised to us as God's children. Beloved brethren in Christ, for the future, *can we not make that pilgrimage together hand-in-hand.*

These words, twenty years on, continue to present a challenge to all of us within the Christian churches; for though we have engaged in that "pilgrimage" through joint prayer, action and study in that time, the journey has only but begun.

A few years ago I spoke to an ecumenical gathering in a church in Aberdeen, sharing the platform with Roman Catholic and Church of Scotland speakers. I remarked that had this happened twenty years ago, the numbers attending would have been significantly greater, and in all probability our meeting would have been interrupted by Pastor Jack Glass and his supporters who opposed any "truck with Rome". Did, I wonder, the comparative serenity of our ecumenical meeting reflect progress? Or was it that, to the vast majority of folk in Scotland, it did not really matter, and did not impinge on their lives?

The "pilgrimage together hand-in-hand" of which Pope John Paul spoke is not simply a matter of our relationship with each other and to the communities of Scotland we seek to serve, but our relationship to the world. The real "risk of ecumenism" is to take it out of

---

[126] Ephesians 4: 5-6.
[127] Hebrews 13: 15.

the comparative cosiness of inter-church co-operation into that of mission in an increasingly secular and pluralistic society. However, I rush ahead of myself. Let me begin by reflecting further on that papal phrase from 1982: "pilgrimage together hand-in-hand".

The ecumenical pilgrimage
The concept of pilgrimage has its roots in the Bible – from the moment recorded in Genesis when "The Lord said to Abram 'Leave your own country, your kin, and your father's house, and go to a country I will show you.'"[128] The biblical understanding of pilgrimage is that while it is God-determined, the human response has in some ways to be "in the dark". There lies within the nature of pilgrimage an element of ignorance, and an acceptance of risk. The writer of the Letter to the Hebrews encapsulates this when he describes the faith of Abraham:

> By faith Abraham obeyed the call to leave his home for a land which he was to receive as a possession; he went away without knowing where he was to go.[129]

The modern pilgrimage can often be a shadow of that understanding, reflecting more the religious aim of the tourist industry, with all-risk insurance included! If we are to understand our ecumenical endeavours in terms of "pilgrimage" then the churches will require to rediscover the biblical experience and, like Abraham, to set out not knowing where we are going.

---

[128] Genesis 12:1.
[129] Hebrews 11:8.

The pilgrimage, said Pope John Paul II, is to be "together hand-in-hand". This mirrors the words spoken by the late Cardinal Basil Hume, a few years later in 1988, when he called on the churches in Great Britain and Ireland to move from "co-operation to commitment". This was at the time of a radical re-thinking of the "instruments of unity" in these islands, and saw the emergence of such bodies as ACTS (Action of Churches Together in Scotland) with, for the first time, the Roman Catholic Church being full members. That, in itself, was a tangible sign of progress. But "hand-in-hand" implies a greater degree of commitment than sitting on committees with each other, or sharing in social outreach, and making joint statements. It should mean entering into the pain and hurt that is part of our broken relationship as Christian brothers and sisters. Are we ready to go deeper into that area of pain? To share the hurt of history divided, of rights denied, or unshared sacrament? Yes, ecumenism is a risky business.

Over the years much has been achieved in Scotland in the ecumenical pilgrimage and we need to affirm that and rejoice in it. This has happened at different levels – in "action" through local initiatives between congregations; in "leadership" through growing co-operation and trust among those called to leadership in our churches; in "study" through various study groups that have grappled with some of the theological issues, sometimes finding greater consensus than many might have believed possible.

Yet, it is also during this time that all mainstream churches have seen significant decline in their membership and where the ecumenical agenda has moved on into an inter-faith agenda. There is said to be still a thirst for spirituality but the churches have been unable to engage effectively with this. There are those who believe that we should forget the attempts to bring about church unity and engage more effectively with the world, and the issues it faces. Unless we do, they argue, there will be no church to unite, at least in Britain, come the end of this century. Such voices have some validity, though when we engage in the world's issues how often do we find that the seeds of conflicts lie in religious division and disunity. The ecumenical pilgrimage needs to continue, not simply for the churches' sake, but for the world's sake.

> May they be perfectly one. Then the world will know that you sent me, and that you loved them as you loved me.[130]

How then do we move forward on our ecumenical pilgrimage? Maybe a Scottish Presbyterian theologian from the mid-twentieth century can give us a context in which we might understand better our "pilgrimage hand-in-hand".

Paradox – a way of understanding God
In 1948, Professor Donald Baillie, then a Professor of Systematic Theology at St Andrews University, wrote *God was in Christ*[131], which he described as "an essay on Incarnation and Atonement". One chapter is devoted to "The Paradox of the Incarnation".

"There can be no doubt," he states early in this chapter, "about the widespread recognition, in our time, of the presence of a paradoxical element in all religious thought and statement." God cannot be fully understood

---

[130] John 17:23.
[131] Donald Baillie, *God was in Christ* (London: Faber & Faber, 1948).

"in any human words or categories of our finite thought." "God, he says, "can be known only in a direct personal relationship." If then words and thought are inadequate to describe the mystery that is God, should we not just give up? No, says Baillie, "for we must theologise; and indeed the very act of worship, particularly corporate worship, involves the use of words and thoughts about God."

He then describes paradox as testifying "to the existence of a mystery beyond which human reason cannot penetrate" but which "nevertheless is actualised and lived in our religious experience." Baillie gives a helpful analogy: describing God in words, he says, is like drawing a map of the world on a flat surface like an atlas. There is bound to be a degree of error because the earth is not flat – and yet the map must be drawn for our understanding of earth. And so in an atlas you will have two "maps" – one consisting of two circles representing the two hemispheres, the other contained in an oblong picture. Both are needed, and taken together, they correct each other. Thus, argues Baillie, are the paradoxes of our Christian faith. For example, he speaks of the "paradox of grace" which involves holding together in tension, the belief that all goodness comes from God, and the belief that each human being has responsibility for choices in his or her life.

With this as his basis, Baillie goes on to describe what he sees as the central paradox – the paradox of the Incarnation.

> The whole problem of the Incarnation is contained in the old question which can be asked in so many ways: was Jesus divine because he lived a perfect life, or was He able to live a

perfect life because He was divine? To put it
another way, did the Incarnation depend on the
daily human choices made by Jesus, or did He
always choose right because He was God
Incarnate? It must, of course, be true that His
choices were genuine human choices, and that in
a sense everything depended on them. And yet as
soon as we have said that, we must inevitably turn
round and say something apparently opposite
remembering that in the last analysis such human
choice … is wholly dependent on divine
providence.

And so, concludes Baillie, by holding these two "truths"
in tension we can approach the mystery of Christ "which
will enable us to combine the transcendent claims with
the frankest recognition of the humanity of the historical
Jesus."

To apply Baillie's thinking to our ecumenical
pilgrimage is, I believe, to suggest that we need to
understand the unity that God wants for His church in
terms of paradox – of holding in tension what may seem
as two contradictory truths. In doing so we may well
discover new ways of continuing our ecumenical
pilgrimage, of entering into that deeper relationship with
each other and so engage more compassionately and
significantly with the issues that concern people most.

The remainder of this essay will focus on three
paradoxes which may help us to understand the nature
and challenge of our "pilgrimage together hand-in-hand".
First in considering the nature of the unity we seek I will
reflect on the paradox of "unity and diversity" arguing
that it is when we explore and are enriched by our
diversity that we discover the fullness of our unity in
Christ. Secondly, I will explore the process of church

unity reflected through the paradox of "organic and relational" arguing that we may need to step back a little from schemes for church union to develop a more relational approach to our ecumenical endeavour. Finally, I consider the purpose of our ecumenical endeavours in the paradox of "Church and Kingdom" reminding us that church unity is not in itself the ultimate goal, but rather a means of achieving what God wants His Church to be and do in the world.

Unity and Diversity

A concept of Christian unity that is reflected through diverse expressions of Christian discipleship is one that is at the heart of the New Testament – and in particular in the writings of St Paul.

> There are varieties of gifts, but the same Spirit.
> There are varieties of service, but the same Lord.
> There are varieties of activity, but in all of them and in everyone the same God is active.[132]

Paul moves on in this passage to describe the interdependence of the physical body: "If the whole were a single organ, there would not be a body at all; in fact, however, there are many different organs, but one body. The eye cannot say to the hand, 'I do not need you', or the head to the feet, 'I do not need you'."[133] He then relates this to the understanding of the church as the body of Christ: "Now you are Christ's body, and each of you a limb or organ of it."[134] This "unity in diversity" understanding of the church is further outlined in Romans

---

[132] 1 Corinthians 12:4-6.
[133] *Ibid.* 12:19-21.
[134] *Ibid.* 12:27.

12 and in Ephesians 4. The witness of other writers in the New Testament reflect how this is not simply confined to the different gifts or ministries that are needed for the "building up of the body of Christ" but also about how reconciliation is achieved between those of diverse traditions and beliefs. In Acts 15 we read of the debate at the Council of Jerusalem over different interpretations within the early church of the requirements for a new follower of Jesus. Were they required to fulfil Jewish beliefs and traditions before acceptance as a Christian? This, Luke reports, created "fierce dissension and controversy". In the end the Council resolved this dilemma by allowing a level of diversity to exist within the early church:

> It is the decision of the Holy Spirit, and our decision, to lay no further burden upon you beyond these essentials: you are to abstain from meat that has been offered to idols, from blood, from anything that has been strangled, and from fornication. If you keep yourselves free from these things you will be doing well. Farewell.[135]

The late Bishop John Robinson, best known for the controversy created by his book in the 1960s *Honest to God*, was a highly regarded New Testament scholar in his day. In a little known work, *The Body – a Study in Pauline Theology*, he interprets Paul's thinking in a way that can speak to our ecumenical endeavours. He writes

> Paul's argument is that the resurrection body of Christ can be articulated in diversity *without ceasing to be a unity*. All the members of a human body

---

[135] Acts 15:28-29.

170

form one body *despite* their number. So it is with the person of Christ.[136]

But, says Robinson, Paul is not arguing that there exists a diversity which has to find a way of being made into a unity. The unity already exists through our common faith in Christ.

> It is through faith that you are all sons of God in union with Christ Jesus. Baptised into union with him you have put on Christ like a garment.[137]

Christian Unity, for St Paul, is no longer to be understood in the exclusiveness of Old Testament theology, but in an inclusive, and therefore truly catholic way. What Pauline theology does not speak about, and which indeed would be alien to his thinking, is uniformity. To be moulded to the "mind of Christ" does not lie in some uniformity of belief and practice, but in the celebration of our baptismal union with Christ through the richness of an exclusive diversity.

What does that say to the churches in their ecumenical journey? There are, of course, those who might see it as an excuse that "anything goes" – let's not worry too much about our different beliefs, or Christian practice, and find a way of living tolerantly with each other. This "lowest common denominator" approach to church unity can devalue faith and tradition. It can lead to a sectarian approach to Christianity which accentuates division and creates a ghetto-like attitude, where Christian churches huddle behind the security of their own beliefs and prejudices. On the other hand, those who seek a unity

---

[136] John A.T. Robinson, *The Body – a Study in Pauline Theology* (London: SCM Press, 1952), p.60.
[137] Galatians 3:26-27.

within strictly defined doctrinal and behavioural patterns are in danger of wanting not Christian unity, but a uniformity and conformity that stifles any form of difference.

To search truly for that "unity in diversity" of which St Paul wrote, and to which the early church in its inclusive approach to mission reflected, involves us in risk and compromise, in listening and incorporating into our life new expressions and new beliefs of how we can become a Church that is enriched by diversity. It is within an understanding of what "unity in diversity" means that we would, I believe, be able to explore more creatively those pains and hurts of division referred to earlier – of history divided, of rights denied, of unshared sacrament. Within the contemporary church, as in Acts 15, there will be at times "fierce dissension and controversy". If we are to respond to and resolve that dissension the church must be ready to risk the paradox of believing in both its unity in Christ, and the richness of its diversity. The words of a modern hymn illustrate this:

> Summoned by the God who made us
> Rich in our diversity
> Gathered in the name of Jesus
> Richer still in unity.
> Let us bring the gifts that differ
> And in splendid varied ways
> Sing a new church into being
> One in faith and love and praise.[138]

Organic and Relational

But how are the churches endeavouring to achieve that unity? The main church ecumenical bodies over many

---

[138] Delores Dufrier O.S.B.

years have reiterated their conviction that the aim of all ecumenical study and action is to achieve the full and visible unity of the Christian church. The Lambeth conference of Anglican Bishops in 1998 strongly supported this in their reports and resolutions.

> This Conference reaffirms the Anglican Commitment to the full, visible unity of the church as the goal of the Ecumenical Movement.[139]

Later that year at the World Council of churches in Harare, a gathering of many church denominations throughout the world (including an observer delegation from the Roman Catholic Church led by Archbishop – then Bishop – Mario Conti) also reaffirmed this same goal.

> We are drawn by the vision of a church that will bring all people into communion with God and with one another professing one baptism, celebrating one Holy Communion and acknowledging a common ministry.

This is what we mean by organic union – not simply a federation of individual churches, but one where there would be a full integration of ministry, sacrament, doctrine and organisation.

And yet it is true to say that the past century, in which the modern ecumenical movement saw its birth, has also seen an increasing proliferation of churches. Many of these independent churches, statistics suggest, are ones where the most significant growth in numbers is

---

[139] Resolution IV.1a of the Lambeth Conference 1998.

evidenced. When I browse my own bookcase, I also at times despair at the number of reports, proposals, schemes for church unity that have fallen by the wayside, discarded by synods and assemblies of those who claim to be committed to the goal of "full, visible unity". The recent experience of those non-Roman Catholic churches in Scotland in the Scottish Church Initiative for Union (SCIFU) initiative does not reflect a great appetite for such a goal among the grass roots in our church congregations.

At the same time there have been very positive developments in other spheres of ecumenism. Agreements have been entered into between Anglican Churches in Britain and Ireland, and the Lutheran Church in Scandinavia and other parts of Europe. These "agreements" reflect a more relational approach to the ecumenical task where identity – be it Anglican, Lutheran, or Reformed Church – remains intact but a relationship of friendship and commitment is developed which may involve shared ministry and shared sacrament. The Lambeth Conference in 1998 seemed to recognise this when it said "One of the conclusions we draw from what we have heard of the present situation of the ecumenical movement is that friendship is not only a critical means for advancing on the path to unity, but is itself an essential part of the unity to which we are called."

I therefore wish to ask whether we need to open ourselves to the building up of a greater relational unity where the development of friendship and mutual respect and sharing can grow between our churches. Within that growing relationship there will be points where theological agreement can be affirmed, or pastoral practice changed to enable that relationship to deepen. Schemes for Union on the other hand seem to insist on a level of agreement which at present is beyond us, and often leads to frustration and despair. This is not to turn our backs on that ultimate goal of organic union, but to explore a more relational approach to it.

Church and Kingdom

"The Church of God a Kingdom is" begins the well-known hymn by L.C. Muirhead. Yet that reflects far more the vision of what might be than the reality of what is. St Mark's Gospel – the first Gospel to be written – sets out its purpose in the first chapter. "The time has arrived", proclaims John the Baptist. "The Kingdom of God is upon you";[140] and this furthermore is the "Gospel of God".[141] As we read through the Gospels, and reflect on the message of the Kingdom of God which Jesus proclaims, it seems far removed from the institutional organisation today which we call the church.

When Jesus refers to the "Kingdom of God" or the "Kingdom of Heaven" he speaks of justice for the oppressed, of a love that extends beyond the definitions of culture, race, or human division, of truth that is to be discovered not necessarily within the religious establishments of his time, but in the outcast and poor. Another well-known hymn encapsulates this vision:

> When comes the promised time
> That War will be no more
> Oppression, lust and crime
> Shall flee Thy face before.[142]

Through two thousand years of history the church has grown and developed. In some parts of the world it has

---

[140] Mark 1:15.
[141] *Ibid.* 1:14.
[142] Lewis Hensley, *Thy Kingdom Come, O Lord.*

become integrated with the state, and of necessity has required organisation. We see the beginnings of this in the Acts of the Apostles as Councils are called to meet (15) and ministries are developed to tackle the growing demands of mission (6). Like any human institution, it has its failings, and at times becomes corrupted by the power it holds. The Christian church, both past and present, is a picture of an institution that is both a channel of that essential message of the "Kingdom of God" yet is also a body of human failing and weakness.

The disunity of the church is an example of that truth. We need always to hold in front of us that the ultimate purpose of the ecumenical journey is to enable the church to be a more effective channel through which the "Kingdom Values" are communicated and lived out.

Today we see in the Western world a decline in membership of many institutions and the churches are part of that. Recent reports to the Assemblies and Synods of our churches can make depressing reading, and especially if all that they do is make us "tinker with the machine" so that it will run better, and the institution will survive. Sometimes we turn ecumenism into a form of "ecclesiastical joinery" and try to find an institutional way of becoming one. But, I would submit, is this not putting the cart before the horse, of making "institutional unity" our primary goal, rather than the Gospel prerogative of God's Kingdom"?

It is against this background that I find the joint Scottish Episcopal and Roman Catholic Churches Study Group report in 1997 of some significance and worthy of wider exploration. It offers a way in which the paradox of Church and Kingdom can be understood. The Study Group spent some five years exploring the nature of the Church; and their final report is entitled "A Contribution to the World-wide Ecumenical Debate on the Nature of the Church". It is a particular section on "Provisionality" which I believe has important points to offer to what should be part of our continuing ecumenical exploration.

> In this context we turned to the concept of provisionality, an idea which we discussed at length, an idea associated with Anglicanism but which, we suggest, has something to offer all traditions. Attached to provisionality, the following were important to us with regard to the Church:
>
> i)   change and development as unavoidably characteristic of its historical existence;
>
> ii) frailty and brokenness, the effects of the human fallibility of its members, their sinfulness and wilfulness.
>
> In both these senses the church which is visible in history can be recognised as truly the Church of Christ and at the same time as that reality which has yet to become what the church is called to be in God's design.
>
> The notion of provisionality was thought valuable for the following reasons:
>
> i)   it respects and recognises that we are in part shaped by history;
>
> ii) it recognises that whilst our faith is grounded in God's truth, our understanding of revelation is imperfect; we ever need the Spirit to lead us into the fullness of truth. Our understanding is also incomplete because our sinfulness

iii)

obstructs our assimilation of and obedience to the Word of God.

It also expresses the church's experience of God's gracious freedom to change and direct history. It keeps before the Church that it is founded and exists by God's grace and for His purposes, not by its own design and will. It also highlights the real creativity that the church possesses in responding to history.

It is therefore when we try to grasp the full meaning of how "the Church is founded and exists by God's grace and for His purposes, not by its own design and will", that we are challenged to encompass those "Kingdom Values" in the Gospel, and begin to grasp a vision of a Church that reflects the values of justice, truth, peace and unconditional love. The purpose of ecumenism therefore is not, in my view, to create some monolithic institution, but a Church that will reflect through diversity, in both organisation and relationship, those "Kingdom Values" which proclaim the Gospel of God.

My own experience of ecumenism over nearly forty years of ministry has convinced me that our "pilgrimage together hand-in-hand" is in the purposes of God, but that the journey has to move on to engage with the more difficult questions and issues that seem to divide us. We need to explore afresh the nature, the process, and the purpose of that unity to which we believe God has called us, and to live creatively with those paradoxes that are at the centre of that experience.

Bishop Bruce Cameron is the Episcopalian bishop for Aberdeen and Orkney and Primus of the Episcopalian Church in Scotland. He has held ministries in Glasgow, Edinburgh and

Perth and has worked as Youth chaplain, a University Chaplain and has been involved over many years in ecumenical ministry. He was elected as Bishop of Aberdeen and Orkney in 1992 and as Primus of Scotland in 2000. Since coming to Aberdeen he has worked with Archbishop Mario and others through the Regional Ecumenical Team in encouraging greater cooperation among churches. He and his wife were involved in the World Council of Churches Assembly in 1998, in Harare, to which Archbishop Mario was invited as a Catholic Church representative.

Church Architecture after the Second Vatican Council

Rev. Kenneth Nugent s.j.

There is a perception that the Second Vatican Council was the inspiration behind the development of what came to be known as modern church architecture. Equally, the Council itself was seen to be a sudden burgeoning of new life in the Church itself.

The Council articulated and validated much that had been spoken and written about from as far back as the 1920s, and this can be said of modern architecture too. New materials and building methods had a liberating influence on design constraints, and these went hand-in-hand with the social changes consequent upon the First World War, and the technological progress seen in the world of the media and travel industries.

Architecture has always resonated to social and religious changes, since it is a cultural medium which responds to the human need to articulate its aspirations. To that extent, there is a prophetic dimension to the arts in that the architect, artist, poet and musician responds to the movements of the age and speaks for it through the materials and techniques available, and under the inspiration of common and well-ordered regulation by due authority.

There is an interesting parallel in the sixteenth and seventeenth centuries, where there was an intense renewal of the Catholic church's teaching and practice following from the Council of Trent (1545-1563), which as a response to the influence of the Reformation, had something of the same reaction as the Second Vatican Council begun in 1962, which readdressed the nature and role of the church in a largely secular world.

As church buildings invariably echo the climate of the times in their design and execution, the Second Vatican Council heralded a new dawning with the promulgation of its first major text *The Pastoral Constitution on the Sacred Liturgy* of 1963.

By reasserting the pivotal role of the liturgy, the nature and practice of the Church's worship gave credibility to what had been a growing movement since early in the twentieth century. This was partly a development of ideas within the Church itself, and a consequence of the scope offered by new materials and forms of construction.

Just as the post-Reformation architecture was influenced by the Renaissance, with the discoveries of the New World and concepts of freedom afforded by learning and travel, so the churches after the Second Vatican Council began to demonstrate the spatial possibilities of the new architecture.

The parallel continues in the recognition that post-Reformation church architecture attempted to redress the shortcomings of the then traditional forms of design by reasserting the nature of the Church itself and facilitating the visibility and audibility of the liturgy to an increasingly more enquiring congregation. This found its sometimes dramatic manifestation in the baroque of the counter-Reformation, and in the eager participation of such architects of stature as Vignola, Michelangelo and Bernini, whose spatial concepts were further embellished by the rediscovery of the principles of perspective by Andrea Pozzo, which enabled a wider canvas to be created than that afforded by the structural confines of the building itself.

So too, the new buildings of the age of technology demonstrated that the spatial imagery of the late Renaissance could be realised in structural terms with the advent of steel, reinforced concrete and sophisticated developments in glass engineering.

The architects were there too: Le Corbusier, Breuer, Nervi and others, who gathered a host of acolytes, eager to learn from the masters and to make their own contribution to the new voice of the Church.

The Pastoral Constitution on the Sacred Liturgy, *Sacrosanctum Concilium* (1963), was not only the first major document of the Second Vatican Council, but was also the herald of a series of liturgical statements and instructions to follow over the years.

The primary purpose of the Council was to bring about the renewal of the Church, and through the Constitution on the Liturgy to set in train a radical reappraisal of the nature, teaching and practice of the Church in the modern world. This was to be initiated through a more profound understanding of the Church's liturgy as "the summit towards which the activity of the Church is directed ... the fount from which all her power flows."[143] "The liturgy, then, is rightly seen as an exercise of the priestly office of Jesus Christ. It involves the presentation of man's sanctification under the guise of signs perceptible to the senses and its accomplishment in ways appropriate to each of these signs. In it full public worship is performed by the Mystical Body of Jesus Christ, that is, by the Head and his members."[144]

---

[143] *Sacrosanctum Concilium* 10
[144] *Ibid.* 7

The promulgation of the Pastoral Constitution on the Sacred Liturgy in December 1963 set a seal on the beginning of the Church's radical review of its identity, role and mission in a world of changing values. It recognised how two world wars and an unprecedented development in science and technology had exercised a profound influence on human society. A secular society developed from the materialistic culture, and the influence of the Church had weakened in the face of a new morality.

At the same time, the Church sought to rediscover its identity and relevance in the face of all these challenges, and the ferment of the Second Vatican Council sparked off a reawakening beyond the confines of the Church itself. The worship of God engages all that we are, which includes both our faculties and perceptions. Our aesthetic sense is the perception of beauty and order, a reflection of the Creator. The renewal of the liturgy would be the source and inspiration of a new articulation of the role of the Church in all its aspects and ministries.

There had long been a call for a new expression of the Church in its liturgy and the Fathers of the Council recognised the importance of that fundamental statement of relationship between God and man which would embrace all that he is and seeks to be in collaboration with his Creator. That vital first document would set in train a whole series of documents: constitutions and instructions to embody the whole scope and intent of the Council.

The logistics of such an enterprise were daunting, and the cultural implications of major change would awaken both hopes and fears: that an "unchanging" Church could engage in such radical analysis brought unrest as well as high hopes. Above all there was no adequate precedent for such action. Reforming Councils, such as the Council of Trent of the sixteenth century, sought to redress the balance and arrest the damage already sustained; this new Council would take on board the issues of ecumenism and inter-faith relations as integral to the nature and mission of the whole Church.

How to express the liturgy in forms that spoke to the modern world and responded to its innermost needs was a major task, since the language had still to evolve, and consequent misunderstandings had to be addressed and resolved.

Theological and pastoral aspects of the liturgy were matters for the seminary, and scarcely touched the lives of the average parish congregation. It was vital that the priestly nature of the faithful should be reclaimed if they were to understand the mystical relationship of priest and people actively incorporated in partnership with the hierarchical priesthood; the passivity of the past did not afford them the quality of full participation. The windows of the Church which Pope John XXIII threw open to the wind of the Holy Spirit needed lubrication before they could begin to function in their proper role, admitting both light and air.

The Liturgical Movement which culminated in the Second Vatican Council had its seeds in the Catholic Church in France during the nineteenth century. Dom Prosper Guéranger refounded the Benedictine Abbey of Solesmes in 1832 as a monastery dedicated especially to the study and recovery of the authentic Gregorian Chant and the Church's liturgical heritage generally. The Liturgical Movement itself began to get under way in the opening years of the twentieth century with the issue in 1903 by Pope Pius X of a *motu proprio* on church music. Significantly, he saw in the active participation of the faithful in the liturgy the source of the renewal of the Christian spirit.

Perhaps the real inauguration of the movement came in 1909, when a Catholic conference was held at Malines in Belgium. The conference saw the liturgy as the fundamental means of the instruction of the people in the Christian faith and life. The outstanding leader in the conference was Dom Lambert Beauduin of Louvain. His book, *La Piété de L'Église*, published in 1914, contained ideas which became fundamental principles in the movement. He saw that a better understanding of the Incarnation and its meaning would lead to a deeper understanding and appreciation of the dignity of human life and all life.

In the years between the two world wars, the focus of leadership shifted from Belgium to Germany. The ideas of worship which the movement actively promulgated came under some criticism as being too radical a departure from the tradition of the Church. This was to be understood in the light of the Ultramontane theology of the early years of the twentieth century, and the fact that the earlier phase of the Liturgical Movement had been more immediately concerned with the pastoral needs of the Church, than with an apologetic for its position.

There then began the work of building a sound theology of worship, led by Abbot Ildefons Herwegen and Dom Odo Casel in the Rhineland Abbey of Maria Laach. *Ecclesia Orans*, first published in 1918, enjoyed wide circulation and was an important means of disseminating the new theology. It also served to open up liturgical theology as an important field of liturgical study; the names of Josef Jungman, Jean Daniélou and Louis Bouyer are outstanding in this period.

Study of the biblical basis of the liturgy made important contributions to biblical theology and served as a link between the Roman Catholic Church and the

Ecumenical Movement, and by the early years of the Second World War, the rediscovery of the role of the laity was emerging more clearly outside Europe through the studies in the United States at St John's Abbey in Minnesota, with its strong pastoral emphasis.

Parallel with these studies came developments in the field of liturgical music, art and architecture, and the publication in 1947 by Pope Pius XII of the encyclical *Mediator Dei* came as an endorsement of the Liturgical Movement, and an awakening which would find its clearest expression in the Constitution on the Sacred Liturgy of the Second Vatican Council and the subsequent instructions for putting it into effect.

At the same time, the movement for reforms in the liturgy was finding new resources in the fields of art and architecture. The Dominican publication *Art Sacré* maintained a high profile throughout the 1950s, and the *Liturgical Arts Quarterly* from Collegeville ensured a measure of coverage, and something of the spirit of renewal entered almost subconsciously into the expression of the Church through the arts.

Inevitably, there was considerable enthusiasm for innovative approaches which would embody liturgical requirements, but there was also a measure of resistance. This was largely due to an inadequate catechesis, and both clergy and laity were sometimes bewildered by the rate of change and apparent disregard for the traditions which were an integral part of their perception of faith.

In Britain, particularly in England, the Victorian influence on church architecture was pervasive, and the hand of Augustus Pugin and his sons was evident throughout the country. This had a bearing on the enactment of the liturgy itself, and it took the war years with all their devastation, and the new spring of the

Festival of Britain of 1951, to introduce new concepts of design and construction to these islands.

Le Corbusier, with his inspiring new church at Ronchamps, and Oscar Neirmeyer in a new approach to spatial architecture at Brasilia in the 1950s, began to arouse an interest in the potential of church design which rapidly gained ground as the liturgical reforms of the Second Vatican Council called for radical new thinking.

Meanwhile, the laity were largely unaware of the implications of the Council's progress into the latter half of the twentieth century, and were apprehensive when changes were introduced without an introductory catechesis.

The Council had ordained that there should be a liturgical commission in each country or region, with diocesan counterparts and specific divisions of pastoral rites, music and church art and architecture. Moreover, the Council decreed that Liturgy should be incorporated as a major course in the seminaries.

Parallel with this attempt to introduce a deeper understanding of the nature of Liturgy, with its sometimes ill-advised results, was the rise of the conservation movement, which was a reaction to hasty and inappropriate adaptations in the name of "re-ordering", and the unnecessary loss of features which were integral to the identity of the church building.

The 1950s and 1960s were years of architectural as well as liturgical ferment. In Britain, there was much rebuilding following the war years, and new towns and housing estates made their demands on planners and architects. Because they proclaimed a new way of life for many people, they called for a new approach to the idea of the church as the gathering place for a community in new surroundings. The Puginesque image of the church was no longer valid and was often alien to its environment since lifestyles and the scale of public buildings, as well as the development of post-conciliar liturgy, called for radical new thinking in church architecture.

The nature of the Catholic Church in Britain meant that there were few architects, artists or composers who were perceptive enough to discern the pastoral and ecumenical potential of the Council. In Germany, the United States and Ireland, there were clear signs of new thinking in the architectural empowering of the liturgy. In Britain, for many years, the only periodical to offer illustrated appraisals of new and re-ordered churches was *The Clergy Review*, later renamed *Priest and People*. Quarterly articles were published from the mid-sixties and for the following twenty years or so. Prior to that, the annual *Church Building Review* covered churches throughout England, offering a rather eclectic survey of new and altered buildings. The authorship was mainly that of the architects concerned, and lacked any real objectivity or appreciation of the criteria of good liturgical design.

The setting up of a department of Church Art and Architecture by the National Liturgy Commission of England and Wales in the late seventies enabled meetings and conferences to be convened, and a yet more informed level of briefing gradually produced work which was in keeping with mainstream design elsewhere. The New Churches Research Group brought in new thinking allied to an awareness of the ecumenical dimension of new liturgical development.

The work of J.A. Coia of Gillespie, Kidd and Coia in Scotland was perhaps the most productive of new architectural concepts and offered an environment for worship which developed as the principles of liturgical renewal became more clearly understood. Several churches of the late 1950s and through the sixties demonstrated a level of perception which greatly facilitated the acceptance of both new forms of church architecture and the practice of the Church's worship.

The mining village of Glenrothes in Fife became a new town in the early 1950s, and the church of St Paul, completed in 1957, was iconic in its simplicity and clarity of form. Acclaimed by *The Scotsman* as "the most significant piece of architecture north of the English Channel", it was a prophetic insight into the liberating influence of architecture on the environment of worship as liturgical innovations prepared the way for the wholesale renewal of the liturgy in the Second Vatican Council.

As the maestro, J.A. Coia gathered a group of young students and architects who began to explore the idea of the Church in the light of the evolving architecture of the post-war years. A significant series of churches followed throughout the sixties, and a number of awards, including the Royal Gold Medal for Architecture, established Coia as a major if sometimes controversial influence.

In England, Austin Winkley and Richard O'Mahony made their early mark with church designs informed by their liturgical awareness, and were instrumental in promoting a quality of church architecture which caught the imagination and demonstrated the influence which good design could have in furthering the principles and ideals for good liturgical practice.

The directory, *The Parish Church – Principles of Liturgical Design and Re-ordering*, published in 1984 by the Bishops' Conference of England and Wales, articulated the criteria for good liturgical practice in new churches and the approach to adapting existing churches to meet the requirements expressed by the Council.

At the same time, the conservation of buildings of architectural quality became a major issue where town centres as well as individual structures had been altered or demolished. It is true that some re-ordering of churches lacked both sensitivity and appreciation of the actual requirements of liturgical practice. Whether such controversies were concerned with authentic conservation, or were motivated by resistance to liturgical change as such, was debatable, and one can only regret the occasions when ill-informed adaptations or gratuitous removal of architectural features caused distress and a deeply felt sense of loss.

Now, after almost forty years since the promulgation of the Constitution on the Sacred Liturgy in 1963, achievements have been recognised and mistakes acknowledged; all of this in the context of a virtual renaissance where the Church was both inspiration and source of new vision through its own internal explorations.

Rearguard actions to maintain the status quo were inevitable and to some extent helped to clarify the issues and establish the authenticity of renewal rather than change for its own sake.

The Church's mission, codified by the Council, was not confined to liturgy alone, but extended to every aspect of its life. Not least among the benefits of the Council was the new climate of ecumenism which evolved in its train. The liturgy, not limited to the enactment of sacramental rites, but as the expression of a Christ-centred community of faith, caught the imagination of other Churches.

Liturgy, the worship of priest and people in active participation, constantly enlivened by the evolving pattern of the liturgical year, has enabled both Catholic and

Evangelical wings to find substantial recognition of each other's worth.

The faith and culture which has led to all that is good in post-conciliar church buildings has also awakened a new awareness of the commitment and skills of the past. If it is true that good architecture is the mirror of civilisation, then the Church's expression of itself in the aesthetics of culture is a perceptible expression of all that is truly human in its search for the divine.

Prior to joining the Jesuit Order in 1959, Kenneth Nugent had qualified at the then Glasgow School of Architecture, having served his pupillage with Gillespie, Kidd and Coia. Both the development of modern architecture in the post-war years, and the liturgical renewal brought about by the Second Vatican Council, as well as the widespread awareness of the importance of informed conservation led to his appointment to several national liturgical and heritage bodies. His work as a priest in city parishes in England and Scotland, and his collaboration with organisations in both the Church of Scotland and the Anglican Church, have helped to develop mutual understanding. Fr Nugent is now the Parish Priest in Kirkwall, Orkney.

PERENNIAL PROBLEMS OF SCOTTISH CATHOLICISM
MORALE, RESOURCES AND DIVISIONS 1820 – 2000

BERNARD ASPINWALL

My school history master, a Chindit in the Second World War, believed mankind's vital questions were easily answered but, infuriatingly, humans would change them. For almost two hundred years the Church in Scotland has faced a similar irritation. Each time she apparently solved problems, new crises emerged. In short, our problems are hardly unexpected. Original Sin does not change; its expression may.

Interpretations
Catholicism is popularly perceived as monolithic, deferential, advancing from rags to riches, from the margins to significance, from exclusion to inclusion.[145] Simplistic populist critics like Jimmie Reid see a bastion of sectarianism and so reinforce traditional Catholic self-perceptions as perennial victims of bigotry. Such views were perhaps valid in earlier generations but ignore endemic internal unease among faithful, clergy and laity. Amid tensions and disagreements, from 1790 the Church grew from 20,000 almost invisible souls to some 750,000

---

[145] The most scholarly illustrations are James E. Handley's magisterial *The Irish in Scotland, 1798-1943* (Cork, 1943) and *The Irish in Modern Scotland* (Cork, 1947)

at least nominal faithful. The rock of faith remained firm as debate ebbed and flowed over theological or liturgical emphases, political and social policies. In short, perennial crises are the norm. The question has been rephrased. What else is new?

Stages
Catholicism has moved through three stages: from dependency culture, through consolidation and emergence, to a more self-confident, upwardly mobile, socially differentiated body. It has invariably had a triple-layered division. Initially it comprised a traditional aristocratic and convert élite, staunch Highlanders and Islanders, masses of Irish-born harvesters and industrial workers. Their social, ethnic backgrounds and expression of Catholicism varied. A second phase had a socially conservative Unionist élite, a Liberal element and strong Home Rule mass. In more recent times, a meritocratic élite drawn from universities and professions has slowly differentiated itself from the traditional Labour core and a considerably poorer, less observant, excluded element. Conversions today are fewer and converts less influential.

Today a somewhat paranoid element hankers after old certainties: after the Second Vatican Council, their missed opportunities and startling social changes, they are confused about whom to oppose. Rather than face their own shortcomings, others mask their confusion in simplistic neo-Marxist notions of oppressor and oppressed to give attitudes some credibility even though we are all victims and manipulators. Like bigots they need scapegoats. Most of us travel in faith, hope and charity.

STAGE ONE
Preliminary Relocation

Catholicism moved from a quiet rural character into a rumbustious industrial Central Belt. Hard-pressed clergy struggled to maintain any influence upon mobile workers, whether seasonal agricultural labourers or victims of industrial depressions in a wildly fluctuating Victorian economy. Cultural battle lines were drawn: around local disturbances on St Patrick's Day or 12th July; a political identification of Catholicism with reactionary European régimes after the liberal revolutionary failures in 1848 or in opposition to Italian Unification. The Church had more than an image problem.

A celibate Church challenged the paternalist Victorian macho version of domesticity: the gentle self-sacrificing Mother of God versus the awesome Father. Today, in a consumerist age, portrayed as an irresponsible populating faith, she again defends the poor and dispossessed. To build credible theological, pastoral or institutional structures remains a massive challenge. To win friends and influence Scotland demands personnel, skills and financial resources, a process requiring time and stability. In recent times as earlier these have been in short supply. To build a permanent Catholic encampment when the campers often keep moving on remains a daunting task.

The Beginnings of Modern Scottish Catholicism
The arrival of the Famine Irish drastically disturbed the comfortable, genteel progress of the early nineteenth century: demands of a new urban industrial Church sharply challenged rural Highland dominance. Their numbers, poverty and needs almost overwhelmed available personnel and resources. Aristocrats, wealthy converts, Highlanders and Irish rallied to the faith for example in The St Margaret's Association (1848) but with differing agendas. By the 1860s, with those demands

seemingly met, an ethnic, political and organisational crisis emerged around the same elements. Factionalism abounded in Glasgow, Dundee, Edinburgh and smaller towns. That ultimately led Rome to impose Englishman Charles Eyre in 1868 on the unhappy, financially embarrassed, divided clergy and laity of the western District as a prelude to the restoration of the Scottish hierarchy in 1878.[146] The gradual elimination of inadequate clergy, the troublesome lay, Glasgow Free Press and shoring up faith through parochial missions, schools and other institutions followed.

The Organisational Revolutions: Districts to Dioceses

In 1827 two ecclesiastical districts, Highland and Lowland, gave way to three, Northern, Eastern and Western. The two archdioceses and four dioceses of 1878 added two more dioceses in 1948 to promote harmony, order and practice. The Church also managed two massive incorporations of faithful: 1840-80 and 1945-80. Those atypical boom eras saw more than four fifths of our present churches built. The first brought thousands of displaced Irish migrants into expanding institutional churches; their lives, spirituality and faith were revolutionised. In the second, after the Second World War, thousands of displaced inner city dwellers or seekers after suburbia were brought within well-organised new structures. New towns like Cumbernauld, Glenrothes, Irvine and Livingstone found networks for newcomers within churches. But then the immense promise but limited success of new industries, lifestyle changes and

---

[146] See my "Anyone for Glasgow? The Strange Nomination of the Rt. Rev. Charles Eyre in 1868", *Recusant History* 23 (1997) pp.589-601.

aftershock of the Second Vatican Council accentuated the perennial fissures with the Church.

The Background
The nineteenth century set the formative pattern of our modern condition. The 1851 Scottish Religious Census found one hundred and eighteen Roman Catholic chapels and churches providing almost 53,000 sittings. Almost one fifth were built before 1830, another fifth were of uncertain date, while just over half, fifty-one per cent, had been built after 1830. Just over a hundred chapels had Sunday morning Mass. Almost a third provided an afternoon service of some description but only twenty-six or twenty-two per cent had an evening service. Almost 44,000 Catholics attended Mass on 30 March 1851; 31,032 attended afternoon service and a further 14,813 the few evening services. The implications of this admittedly flawed survey are interesting. Devotional services were unusual. If the Irish-born population, 207,000 in 1851, was predominantly but not entirely Catholic, the returns suggest only a fifth to a third of all faithful attended Mass that day.[147]

In 1851 Catholic schools were also scrutinised. The thirty-two Church schools operated on only £1200 per annum. Their curriculum was weighted to the three "Rs": only four schools offered Mathematics, one Modern Languages, one Music. Although 5,673 pupils were enrolled, only 3,509 or slightly more than three fifths, attended on census day. Sixty Catholic Sunday Schools

---

[147] *Census of Great Britain: Religious Worship and Education Scotland, Report and Tables* (1854)

with 13,015 pupils fared somewhat better: 10,954 pupils or eight-four per cent attended.[148]

Before 1872 most children ended formal education by the age of ten: work in mines and mills was the norm. A mid-nineteenth century Jesuit found less than half of all Catholic children enrolled in school and only two-thirds of those usually attended. Their prospects in every sense were bleak. Their lives were frequently short: survival to school age was an achievement. Cholera, typhoid and numerous illnesses often proved fatal. Even in employment maiming or death was not unusual: the Blantyre mining disaster, October 1878, included dead barely out of school.[149] Their parents were equally prone to early death from infections, industrial injuries or, in the case of their mothers, in childbirth. Their limited lives and expectations we can only begin to imagine.

Fear and Apprehension

Imminent sense of death affected their spirituality. Basic knowledge for this life and for Judgement in the imminent hereafter was vital. Shortages of priests, nuns and teachers made for shortcuts. Modern counselling would have been impossible in terms of time, pressure of numbers, personnel and expense. Uncertainty, debate and angst gave way to authority, structures and discipline. Clear decisive moral guidance was vital. The priest, the educated man of stature in the community, had to give leadership. That notion neatly tied into a prevailing Catholic Ultramontane outlook which extolled clerical sacramental power, influence and status.

---

[148] *Ibid*
[149] See *Times,* 23-27, 29-31 October; 3, 5, 6, 9, 26 November 1878. The report followed on 5 March 1880.

Dependency

Until 1880 a dependency culture characterised the church: it relied on Lowland, Highland and Island proprietors, wealthy and aristocratic converts, goodwill of Protestants, priest from Ireland, Italy, the Low Countries and England. Only then could she minister to hundreds of thousands of displaced Irish, later Lithuanian, Italian and other incomers. Economic pressures gradually pushed native-born farming or fishing Catholics of the North into towns or overseas. Most had few possessions but their faith.

Poor, disenfranchised faithful then relied mainly on Banffshire clerical leadership; generous financial support from substantial patrons like the Constable Maxwells in Dumfries; Menzies of Pitfodels, great benefactor of Blairs and St Margaret's Convent in Edinburgh; the Lovats and others; converts like the third Marquess of Bute, reputedly the then richest man in the world; the son of textile wealth, Robert Monteith of Carstairs; Hope-Scott in the Borders; Oswald Hunter Blair in the Southwest; the Trotters and Douglas Dick in Fife and others; and the pennies of faithful not only in Scotland but from clerical begging tours through continental Europe, England and Ireland.[150]

Conservatism

Hardly surprisingly conservative social attitudes prevailed. Afraid of Protestant Orange outrage, anxious not to appear radical or revolutionary and understandably reluctant to bite patrons' hands that paid the bills,

---

[150] E.g. Bishop A. MacDonald, *Argyle and the Isles*, 24 September 1885, *Scottish Correspondence, Propaganda Fidei*, v 8 ff 772-81, Rome, stressed Catholic landlords kept the faithful; Lovat, 450 in Morar, Howard of Glossop, 750 in Moidart; another in Glenfinnan; Bute, 2 missioners and orphanage in Rothesay.

Scottish-born clergy and laity refused to rock the boat. They identified with embattled Pope Pius. To them agitating Irishmen, even demanding Catholic emancipation in 1829, supporting Chartism and revolution in Ireland, demanding more accountable ecclesiastics, more Irish power and greater lay participation in the 1860s were an embarrassment. Revolution and strikes, it seemed, invariably failed and the poor faithful ended worse off. To encourage such dreams was foolhardy, unchristian and counter- productive.

The Drive for Improvement

The implications are clear. A Church of limited financial resources and personnel must inculcate basic values, knowledge and skills but was unable to go beyond them. Minimal schooling soon ended as children, an economic resource for poor families, left at the earliest opportunity to work in mills, fields or to migrate elsewhere. Not surprisingly her children were poorer, less educated and had fewer opportunities than their Christian brethren.

An individual like Charles O'Neil (1828-1900), one of eleven children, was exceptional. Born in Inverary to hotelier parents from Sligo, he prospered in Dumbarton. A university graduate, an architect and active member of the early St Vincent de Paul Society, he subsequently emigrated to New Zealand in August 1863. There he became a prominent civil engineer, politician and Catholic social activist. He founded the first SVP conferences both there and later in Australia. A bachelor, he was vice-president of the Irish League and a staunch temperance advocate.[151] The three Donahoe brothers from Glasgow

---

[151] President of the Glasgow SVP Conference, he was also a captain in the 3rd Lancashire volunteers. Settling in Otago, he built the Clyde

went to America and later three different ways to California in 1849, one building the first ironclads for the Peruvian navy en route. They all became millionaires selling picks and shovels to prospectors, building the first railroads, railway engines and hotels in San Francisco. Their children married into European aristocracy. They even had a town named after them. But once again that success was outside Scotland.

Irrespective of bigotry, snobbery or ethnic jealousy, few Catholics were able to climb the social ladder until the advent of the teaching orders of men and women. With them and particularly after the Education Act of 1872 the limited number of Catholic schools massively expanded. In 1894-95, Sisters of Notre Dame from England began Glasgow Dowanhill training college to help the transformation. It gave women better opportunities, encouraged vocations both to religious orders and spinster lives dedicated to teaching. By 1900, a comprehensive if hard-pressed Catholic system was up and running. The 1918 Act would consolidate, improve and strengthen its position.

Values

That late nineteenth century spirituality reflected the dominant ethos: work, thrift and sobriety. These values would enable the faithful to become respectable: to prosper, acquire property, give generously and ultimately acquire the vote before 1918. Revolutionary criticism of the existing order discredited individual and Church.

River Bridge and designed the town of Milton, New Zealand, major railways and a tram system and served in the House of Representatives 1867-75. He was later a director of the Australian Northumbrian Bank.

Revolutions, invariably anti-Catholic, invariably failed: much pain and no gain. Prolonged strikes lost vital income and in some cases company homes. Principles were one thing, to punish your dependents another. Self-improvement begat social improvement. The buck stopped with the individual, not with others.

Outside Assistance

These developments emphasise dependence on the universal Church. From the earliest days, Glasgow attracted support from Catholic Lancashire lay benefactors.[152] Funds later came from Austria, France, Rome and all over Britain. English architects, the Pugins and Hansom (of cab fame) or decorative merchants like Goldie of Sheffield and Hardman of Birmingham, built the spiritual environment. Education drew disproportionately on the British Catholic Poor School Committee: almost half its funds were often allocated to Scotland. After 1872 English teachers served their vocation here in urban or remote schools. Numerous Scottish women teachers trained in England until 1894 and men even afterwards.[153]

Religious orders of women came from outside Scotland. The first, the Ursulines at St Margaret's, Edinburgh came from France. Belgian Franciscans arrived in 1847. In subsequent years more came from France, England and Ireland with members drawn from many countries. Throughout the nineteenth and early twentieth centuries Scotland was heavily dependent on Irish clergy although they never formed a majority of priests. Many

---

[152] Rev James M. Lawlor, "Benefactors of an Early Glasgow Mission, 1793 and 1707", *Innes Review*, 35 (1985), pp.22-32.
[153] See my "Catholic Teachers for Scotland", *Innes Review*, 45 (1994) pp.47-70.

remarkable influential priests came from England, the Low Countries, Germany, Italy and Lithuania. The Dutch Rev Peter Terken (1847-1914), for example, exercised Social Catholic teaching influence on Wheatley. Bishop James Lynch (1807-1896), the only Irish-born Scottish bishop before 1985, significantly served less than three years, 1866-69, in the Western District. In that way Highlander, Irish and wealthy convert were united. The Scottish Church was anxious to be seen as British and Ultramontane.

The Religious Orders
The Jesuits were brought from England by lay and clerical converts against the wishes of local bishops: in effect ecclesiastical leaders faced a *fait accompli*. Jesuits, often Oxford or Cambridge converts, from 1858-59 served even to death from cholera. Lancashire also provided numerous Jesuits for St Aloysius' School and other churches.[154] French and Irish Marists from 1856 further boosted educational opportunity for boys: their teaching careers and later entry into professions were stages in acceptance and respectability. They enabled sons of pawnbrokers and spirit merchants to move up socially and many to enter the priesthood.

Hostility
Popular prejudice created defensive, cohesive attitudes within Catholicism. Proselytism contributed, but an endless caravan of ex-priests like Rev Alessandro Gavazzi,

---

[154] See my "The Foundation of a British Identity within Scottish Catholicism, 1830-1914", in Robert Pope, ed., *Religion and National Identity: Wales and Scotland, c.1700-2000* (Cardiff 2002), pp.268-306 and James Handley, *St Mungo's Academy* (Glasgow 1958).

anti-Catholic orators like "Angel Gabriel" Orr and their kind merely confirmed existing perceptions. Neglect, ignorance, shifting residence with accompanying poverty amid a Victorian boom and bust economy played a part. In massive parishes in Glasgow or Edinburgh with 12,000 or more shifting faithful or in scattered rural groups, pastoral care could only be cursory at best.

Responses
Missions sought to stem leakage and reinvigorate failing commitment. Revivalism regenerated Catholic space in industrial society. These shock troops through colourful communal ceremonies, processions, hymns, medals and Confession revived Catholic sensitivities. Almost every parish experienced them. Packed every evening for two weeks with special children's services, separate addresses for men and women, rosary, sermons, special Masses and grand finales they proved immensely popular. If these rituals became routine they unquestionably succeeded in retaining numbers, improving attendance and cohesion.[155] Tight-knit ethnic and social networks reinforced clerical sanctions in close packed cities, towns and villages. A sense of Catholic identity in an uncompromisingly Protestant culture sharpened.

Loss and Gain
Leakage then is not a recent problem. Catholicism has always lost adherents. Popular myth made mixed

---

[155] Emmet Larkin, "The Devotional Revolution in Ireland", *American Historical Review,* 88 (1972) pp.625-52; T.G. McGrath, "The Tridentine Evolution of Modern Irish Catholicism, 1563-1962: A Re-Examination of the Devotional Revolution" Thesis, *Recusant History,* 20 (1991) pp.512-23; Mary Heiman, *Catholic Devotion in Victorian England* (Oxford 1995).

marriages the main culprit but they were always far higher than imagined. Episcopal condemnation indicated concern but more often reality was different. Male prejudice blinded us to the fact that leakage in mixed marriages was greater with Catholic husbands than Catholic wives: mothers brought children for baptism more readily than fathers.

To instil and maintain communal faith through a mixture of fear and exhortation, schools, devotional associations, parochial functions, concerts and clubs created further Catholic space for networks, potential marriages and families. To migratory workers they offered a ready-made community. In this vale of tears they alleviated distress, ended anonymity and isolation: tears had a higher purpose. Laity for example found mutual support through a slowly expanding St Vincent de Paul Society from 1846. It gave a role to them: support to unemployed, to needy children with clothing, shoes and school fees, and to penurious elderly. Such mechanisms reinforced "brand loyalty" and communal bonds. They sustained faithfulness among such minimally educated, poor faithful amid increasingly diverse attractions in a wider world. They gave a Catholic identity.

Temperance, Recreation and Advancement
To that end Catholics espoused temperance. In 1842 the Irish Franciscan Fr Theobald Mathew's crusade won Scottish Protestant and Catholic audiences. Many, particularly Irish, clergy backed parochial temperance endeavours. Archbishop Eyre demanded a branch of the League of the Cross in every parish. The implicit protection for women and families was repeated in his founder membership of The Scottish Society for the Prevention of Cruelty to Children.

That drive for uplifting pastimes, reading rooms and improving recreation coincided with brass bands, choirs, popular hymns and meticulous liturgies like those at Cumnock urged on by the Marquess of Bute. At the same time chapels were expanded, lavishly decorated and furnished with numerous statues, ornate side chapels and colourful German stained glass, often provided for and dedicated to the memory of parishioners. It was a statement for themselves and the local community. Pride and self-esteem naturally followed.

STAGE TWO

Growing numbers of Scottish-born clergy, building of chapels and schools, more permanent, rooted settlement and increasing political enfranchisement between 1867 and 1884 gradually gave rise to a more assertive outlook. Priestly and lay dedication formed a community. Innumerable parish missions by Passionists like renowned convert Rev Ignatius Spencer, by Jesuits, Redemptorists, Rosminians and seculars, from 1849, transformed folk religion to create Catholic space. Catholic marriages, births and families massively accelerated. Parish reading rooms, libraries, devotional, temperance organisations and choirs provided strong identity in a hostile world. Pilgrimages to Rome, Lourdes, Whithorn and Carfin developed. Recreational outings, like annual parochial trips as early as the 1850s, or football clubs like Rev Edward Hannan's temperance Edinburgh Hibernian or Brother Walfrid's Glasgow Celtic linked pastoral need and community. The foundations for more advanced education already mentioned were indicative of that shift. They promoted spiritual unity and stemmed "leakage". By the 1880s a strong communal base existed, a platform from which to move forward. Proud of achievements, organisational, financial and vocational, the community was no longer apologetic but an effective apologist.

Choices
Even the upwardly mobile followed different paths. Some Scottish Catholics for example went to the great Jesuit public school, Stonyhurst, only to follow divergent paths. Glasgow-born John Maguire went from there to Rome, became a priest and later a remarkable socially concerned archbishop of Glasgow until his health collapsed. Another Glaswegian John Conway (1854-1914) went from Stonyhurst to become a distinguished Dominican. Edinburgh-born Arthur Conan Doyle went from Stonyhurst to Edinburgh University medical school. The creator of Sherlock Holmes campaigned for Oscar Slater, homosexual traitor Roger Casement and Spiritualism. Schools did not guarantee Catholic outcomes.

The Architectural, Social and Organisational Framework.
Tighter financial control, bureaucracy and mass production of identikit Puginesque churches, particularly in the west, went some way to solve that crisis. Revolutionary changes confirmed clerical leadership. Recusant aristocrats or recent aristocratic converts might exercise restraint on exuberant Irish "democratising" laymen but in the wake of Vatican I assertive bishops eroded their patronage. Their economic decline as agriculture faced intense overseas competition in the late nineteenth century accelerated the end of their leadership. Their role, as influential aristocratic convert and papal confidant, Mgr. George Talbot (1816-86) said, was "to hunt, shoot and pray" – though some said merely to pay. The introduction of Canon Law into Scotland further emphasised that shift. The stringent ruling on mixed

marriages, *Ne Temere* (1908), though often challenged in practice, reinforced that clerical ascendancy.[156] By 1900 a subservient disciplined body was firmly under clerical control.

Cracks or Diversity?

Even then some clerical scandals persisted: a few succumbed to politics, drink or women.[157] Dissensions emerged again around vexed questions of Irish Home rule and socialism, atheist or otherwise. Catholic socialist John Wheatley was less than welcome in his home parish. In the late nineteenth and early twentieth century new migrants arrived: Italians, Poles, Lithuanians, Basques, Spaniards and Belgians placed new demands on the Church. Two World Wars brought refugees from Belgium, France, Poland, Ukraine and elsewhere. Catholic asylum seekers from Sri Lanka, Latin America or other disturbed areas followed in recent times. The nature of Scottish, Irish or even British Catholic identity slowly changed to become inclusive. Things were not what they seemed.

STAGE THREE

The apparent cohesion was fragmenting. Declining aristocratic economic power, political and religious influence saw greater Catholic concern for social justice.

---

[156] Throughout the period mixed marriages in the Ayrshire, Glasgow and Lothian parishes I have examined show a remarkable persistence between a fifth and four fifths. In modern times they are often 100 per cent.

[157] For example Rev Henry Murphy, Irvine and Muirkirk, outspoken supporter of Parnell and Davitt in the early 1880s, was suspended. He served briefly in America and spent almost twenty years vainly seeking reinstatement in Galloway diocese.

Sharp debates around distribution of property and wealth spawned by the Irish Land League, the Papal encyclical *Rerum Novarum* (1891) and further political enfranchisement (1884, 1918, 1928) placed Catholics as a whole in the social democratic camp. Anti-Modernist restrictions on intellectual inquiry pushed the faithful towards safer social activism. Democracy was the wave of the future. Add the sectarian twist of Catholic working classes, as in Patrick Macgill's *Children of the Dead End* and *The Rat Pit*, confronting Protestant and Unionist employers, the position was even more understandable. They rightly had severe reservations about atheistic socialism but pastoral concern, self-interested faithful and Papal initiatives united them. Élite Catholics were staunchly Unionist but by 1914 many laity were firmly in the Liberal camp like Professor John S. Phillimore or joining Labour, inspired by Wheatley and others. Frequent holy Communion from Pope St Pius X and the booming retreat movement from 1915 to the 1960s sought to contain that gradual fragmentation: in a sense that democratisation of spirituality united all classes and conditions in prayerful unity. Social justice did not mean class war.

Other developments
Neo-Gothic architecture marked a rejection of the more restrained faith of penal times, like in discreet Highland chapels of earlier days. To Augustus Welby Pugin, Gothic was the only Catholic architecture. Neo-gothic overwhelmed competition like Lord Lovat's Norman Eskadale (1826) or Gillespie Graham's Romanesque St Mary's Convent in Edinburgh (1835). Pugin and his son Peter Paul held sway, particularly in the dominant west. But after Archbishop Eyre's death, Glasgow and

elsewhere cast off the neo-Gothic straitjacket. Variations were already in train: English Jesuit Rev Richard Vaughan's Sacred Heart in Edinburgh (1860), William Burges' richly decorated St John's in Cumnock (1881-82) for the Marquess of Bute, or his Byzantine St Sophia in Galston shortly afterwards. St Aloysius' in Glasgow (1910) was even more radical. Early twentieth century designs of Reginald Fairlie and the prolific Jack Coia's post-war churches suggested an increasingly diverse, innovative Scottish Church. Architecturally and spiritually, adventurous outreach replaced idyllic immersion in past glories.

Infrastructure

Economically Catholicism arguably reached takeoff point around 1880. A more settled community had chapels, orphanages, primary and advanced schools: Glasgow and Edinburgh ran their own archdiocesan seminaries. Ireland, Blairs, Valladolid and Rome remained important but with the added advantage of cheapness, more priests trained locally for the Scottish mission. But Scotland remained dependent on Irish clergy until the 1970s. In the last generation, the seminaries were transferred from Drygrange to Gillis in Edinburgh for the Eastern Province and, for the Western Province, from Cardross to Chesters. Both were eventually amalgamated into Scotus College in Glasgow. Since then late vocations and eucharistic ministers have increased as youthful vocations markedly declined.

Influential Leadership and Broadening Horizons

Catholic professionals consolidated in the twentieth century. English converts, John Swinnerton Phillimore, Glasgow University's first Catholic professor since the

Reformation, and Rev Eric Hanson S.J., remarkable headmaster of St Aloysius', exercised immense influence in the early twentieth century. Improving education, upward mobility and better prospects particularly from St Aloysius' College were epitomised by the renowned brilliance of the Brogan family: Sir Denis W., Willie, Diarmid and Colum Brogan. In Edinburgh, convert Englishman Rev John Gray, friend of Oscar Wilde, resumed his literary and artistic pursuits. Convert Englishman Compton MacKenzie and George Scott-Moncrieff reinvigorated Scottish nationalism and Catholic identity. Eric Gill, G.K. Chesterton and Rev Professor John McQuillan contributed to the ill-fated distributist land colony near Biggar. Amid war and depression, innovation flourished.

That breakthrough was sustained in the interwar period by lively chaplaincies at the universities of Glasgow (1930) and Edinburgh (1931). In Glasgow, convert Rev Eric Brown until 1945 and after the Second Vatican Council, Rev Gerard Hughes S.J. and convert Highland Dominican Rev Anthony Ross, first Catholic rector of Edinburgh University, reflected vibrant, informed initiatives. Lay figures earlier like James Scanlan, medical student, H.L.I. officer, priest and later Archbishop of Glasgow, a host of professionals and clergy indicated the improved status and respectability of the community. The sharply observed early novels of A.J. Cronin or the converts Fionn MacColla's polemics and Bruce Marshall's humour were further proof. The welfare state, improved health, education and housing further transformed the Catholic condition. Their standard of living, expectations and outlook were altered beyond earlier dreams. By the late twentieth century Catholics shared similar social and political attitudes with comparable fellow citizens.

The Continuing Challenge of Success

Virulent Protestant attacks persisted in the interwar period but from 1945 the Church seemed triumphant as massive expansion in numbers, churches and schools followed. But the boom was merely a prelude to further crises around the Second Vatican Council, the heady Sixties and the disillusionment of the Seventies. Declining numbers, falling birthrates, fading vocations, amalgamating churches and financial crises followed. Cultural battles raged over the Catholic past, Irish, Scottish and otherwise; about music: guitar, disciplined choirs of old or James Macmillan.

The Third Age

The Pilgrim Church, the caravan of the faithful, had few traditional structures: competing blueprints and guides for the future abounded. The Second Vatican Council released considerable energies, hopes and expectations but the shock to some leaders, clergy and laity proved too much. Ill-prepared for change they lost confidence, direction and trust. The cacophonous market place of theological, liturgical and musical ideas overwhelmed them. Voguish zeal blurred established truths and brilliant new insights drowned in intransigent resistance. Trendy ideas seemed threadbare or questionable. Empowerment meant individual souls had to choose ways through the moral minefield. Your community was not the traditional version but where you found yourself. Common interest groups, whether professions, musical styles, interests, age or gender within wide-ranging subcultures, now defined you. It was an old problem restated. In short perennial crises are the norm. The question had been rephrased. What else was new?

Changes

Declining overt anti-Catholicism, ecumenism, urban redevelopment and affluence fractured old communities formed around the First Vatican Council. Neighbourhoods broke down in a real sense. Far from families, friends and jobs, their community became a dormitory. Jobs, golf clubs, football team or entertainment were elsewhere: parish devotional associations, dances, soirees, concerts suffered. Shifting diverse interests and erratic employment patterns further contributed. Isolation often followed in suburbia or in massive sprawling council estates. High-rise apartments did not readily become communities and the supermarket "sherry at 10 am" housewife was not unknown in desirable douce suburbs.

Variety

Some moved off enthusiastically to the new beat. Convert George Mackay Brown, however, retreated to an idyllic agrarian dream. Others found the outlook depressing. To them new forms of Mass and accompanying music were irritating. Colm Brogan for example proved an acerbic critic of innovations. Others like convert Hamish Fraser, former Communist fighter in the Spanish Civil War and militant trade unionist, moved sharply to the Right.[158] Hard core irreconcilables looked to Archbishop Lefebre, the Tridentine Mass and ultra-conservative tradition for solace. It was as if the goalposts were moved in the moment of triumph. Yet the old certainties of empire and industry, shipbuilding, coal and steel were also fast disappearing. Others among the clergy threw themselves

---

[158] See his *Fatal Star* (Glasgow 1950). Predictably Old Left selective amnesia omits him from lists of British fighters in the Spanish Civil War.

into outreach, serving in Africa, Central and Latin America. They were adapting to the rules of a new game. Liberation from sin and oppression went hand in hand.

Demography
The Church grew in tandem with steam railways. As they expanded into new areas so did chapels and faithful: as steam ended in 1968 so did significant growth. Together they reflected the rapid cohesion and later speedy fragmentation of chapel and society. Baptisms boomed from the 1850s. That was explicable by considerable numbers of migrants in child- bearing age groups: the elderly tended to stay behind. Children were a joy, an economic resource and a form of old age insurance: in the welfare state those notions largely disappeared. Earlier, few children survived to maturity. Mid-twentieth century parents expected their offspring to enjoy better health, better education, a longer life than their grandparents, even more than their great-grandparents. That trend continued through the 1950s but fewer births saw the population level out. The myth of large Catholic families died. Birth control had an impact. Women of education, careers and independent income were more assertive decision makers than an earlier generation: marriage was an option and often a delayed choice. In the twentieth century many young and recently wed had migrated south or overseas. Catholics shared Scottish industrial and population profiles: all were declining.

Vocations
The Church has always suffered from shortage of clergy, inadequate individuals and insensitive decisions. Vocations massively expanded through the early twentieth century until increased educational opportunities,

affluence and the sexual revolution eroded former confident leadership roles. Lay activism and new devotional styles changed the nature of their vocation. The supply of Irish clergy ceased. Numbers of clergy declined from the mid-1970s. Recruits dropped massively yet the proportion of (ageing) priests to faithful remained higher in 2000 than in 1900 or 1800. A similar development occurred in religious orders of women. From the 1970s they declined as older forms of service fell under state agencies or laity's and women's new roles. Many found new apostolates but the problem for both groups was they were ageing.

Levelling Off?
Marriages grew massively in the early nineteenth century from under 2000 a year and trebled to reach a peak of 7099 in 1970. In the last generation marriages have dropped almost seventy per cent to around 2000 a year. The same period saw great increases in Catholic divorces: since 1970 they have been around thirteen per cent plus annually of Scottish divorces. Mixed marriages undoubtedly increased but North Ayrshire and some Glasgow and Lothian parishes suggest mixed marriages were always far more common than imagined.[159] Lack of suitable local partners in the initial migrant settlement period, greater mobility through World Wars and transport in the twentieth century contributed to undermine *Ne Temere* (1908). That pattern evolved as ethnic marriages gave way to partners outwith the ethnic

[159] See my 'Baptisms, Marriages and Lithuanians: or Ghetto? What Ghetto? Some Reflections on modern Scottish Catholic historical assumptions', *Innes Review*, 51 (2000) pp.55-67.

group and then to ecumenical partners as Catholics moved upwards and outwards, socially and geographically. Assumptions about Catholic marriage were even less well founded in 2000 than a century before.

Quo Vadis?

Diversity of liturgy, practice and lifestyle has come of age. Quality not quantity dominates. Indifference, affluence and leakage have taken their toll. The last generation of inadequately prepared faithful and clergy failed to respond effectively: their spirituality, education, formation were wanting. We did not know our diverse roots, our assorted resources, our varied history and slipped into a confident triumphalist routine. Much damage has been repaired but the future remains as challenging as always.

We wish Archbishop Conti well as he faces enormous decisions. William Robertson, the Enlightened Scottish historian, saw how dynamic change invariably came from outside. The archbishop is well equipped as an "outsider", by his ethnic origins and his Scottish experience, to coax diverse groups in a similar direction. *"Caritas in omnibus"* loosely translated means "there's room for everyone on the bus." The Pilgrim Church moves on.

Bernard Aspinwall was educated by Jesuits and studied at Manchester and Indiana Universities. He has taught history at the Universities of Glasgow, Strathclyde, Eastern Kentucky, Miami and Notre Dame. He has also taught at the University of Constantine, Algeria and was a British Council lecturer in Poland. He has also taught in universities in Germany, Italy, France and Spain and has travelled extensively in Europe, USA, Central and South America. He is the author of several books and has published more than a hundred articles and essays in English, American, French, Belgian, Italian and Spanish journals and books and has contributed journalism to several

Catholic publications. He describes himself as prolific, well travelled and semi-retired!

THE PERMANENT DIACONATE IN THE DIOCESE OF ABERDEEN:
STOPGAP OR PROMISE AWAITING FULFILMENT

BISHOP JOHN JUKES OFM CONV.

Introduction

The Catholic Directory for Scotland of 1996 gives a list of fourteen Permanent Deacons in the Scottish Dioceses. The list is given by way of names and addresses after the list of Priests, Secular and Regular.[160] It is interesting to note that no figure for Permanent Deacons is included in the General Summary of Statistics for Scotland as at 1st October 1995.[161] The 2002 Edition of the same publication shows some shift in the returns concerning the Permanent Diaconate. The total number of Permanent Deacons is now included in the General Summary of Statistics for Scotland as at 1st October 2001.[162] The total is now twenty-seven. In 1996 the total of fourteen Permanent Deacons was comprised of seven from the Diocese of Dunkeld, five from Aberdeen, the remaining two in other dioceses. In 2002 The Diocese of Dunkeld had eleven while Aberdeen returned twelve. The remaining four (including members of religious orders) were in Edinburgh and Motherwell). Aberdeen therefore has become the lead diocese in Scotland for the presence

---

[160] *The Catholic Directory for Scotland 1996* (Glasgow: John Burns), p.429.
[161] *Ibid.* p.509.
[162] *Ibid* (2002), p.572.

of this Sacred Order in its particular configuration of permanence.

In offering our tribute to Bishop Mario Conti, Bishop of Aberdeen from 1977 to 2002, it seems appropriate to offer some considerations on the Permanent Diaconate. Bishop Conti has had the insight and courage to implement one of the most distinctive decisions of the Second Vatican Council. In so doing he has been responding to the needs of the People of God in the Diocese. It is not the intent of this article to examine or comment upon the decision to introduce and expand the Permanent Diaconate in the Diocese of Aberdeen nor upon the effectiveness of the service rendered to the diocese. I am too new to the Diocese and ill equipped to attempt such a task. Rather I offer in appreciation of Bishop Conti's initiative some thoughts that may be of help to his successor and the clergy and people of the Diocese in their understanding and appreciation of this Sacred Order with particular reference to the future of the Diocese of Aberdeen.

Some Elements in the Theology of Holy Orders with Particular Reference to Deacons
"Theology" for the purposes of this article we understand as an organised reflection upon revelation made known to us by God's loving providence in Jesus Christ Our Saviour and transmitted to us in the Tradition that comes from the Apostles and is contained in a special way in the Scriptures.[163] That organised reflection uses the experience of the life of the Church and of the history and circumstances of the human race and this creation to advance in understanding part at least of the mystery of

---

[163] *Dei Verbum* 7 & 8.

God's self revelation of Himself and His purpose for man. The work of the Catholic theologian is assisted in the search for truth by the teaching authority of the Church established especially in the College of Bishops whose necessary head is the Pope. That authority encourages research and reflection. It also offers protection against departure from the authentic understanding of the meaning of the Word of God contained in revelation.

The establishment and nature of the apostolic office in the Church were given detailed consideration in the documents of the Second Vatican Council.[164] It is clear from the New Testament that Jesus Christ selected twelve men to be His constant companions. These are called by the New Testament authors, Apostles. These men were entrusted with special tasks and powers which were to continue after Jesus had ascended to His Father. The constant tradition of the Church is that the Bishops of the Church are the successors to the Apostles in sustaining the apostolic office and as sharers in Christ's consecration and mission.[165] The narrative in the Acts of Apostles of the growth of the infant Church demonstrates how decisive was the role of the Apostles in promoting the mission entrusted to the Church by Jesus. It is also clear from a number of the New Testament writings that the Twelve as the Church grew were not able to sustain the duties given them by Christ by themselves.

The New Testament has no explicit mention of the organisation of the Sacrament of Holy Orders into the three degrees of Bishop, Priest and Deacon. Deacons are expressly mentioned in the Epistles of St Paul (Phil 1:1; 1 Tim 3:8-13). Indeed the post-Apostolic Fathers find in the

---

[164] Particularly in *Lumen Gentium* ; *Christus Dominus*; *Presbyterium Ordinis*.
[165] *Lumen Gentium* 28.

dispositions made by the Apostles in Jerusalem (Acts 6:1-6) establishing seven men to care for the distribution of material resources, the basis for the origin of the Sacred Order.[166] The presence of the ranks of Sacred Orders is clearly indicated in the Letters of St Ignatius of Antioch writing at the end of the first century or at the beginning of the second. The Order of Deacon is mentioned in six of his seven Letters. Each reference indicates that the deacons are seen as part of the sacred hierarchy at the heart of each Christian congregation and at that community's service.[167]

As the Church continued to spread and grow the functions of the deacons in the life of each local church became more varied. The deacon's function with reference to the order of Priests became more delineated. The deacon did not say Mass or forgive sins sacramentally. Areas of great material responsibility were imparted by bishops to deacons. They often became individuals of considerable power and importance in the local diocese. The difficulties experienced by Gregory the Great with his deacons have been studied in detail.

It is not easy to trace the causes for the gradual turning away from the employment of the deacons in the life of the Church. The Sacred Order became a stepping-stone to ordination to priesthood. The deacons then became largely liturgical functionaries, retaining duties of close service to the priest at the altar and some duties in the liturgical gathering of the people of God. In addition their duties related to the Blessed Eucharist meant that there

---

[166] *The Permanent Diaconate: Basic Norms for the Formation of Permanent Deacons* and *Directory for the Ministry and life of Permanent Deacons* (Vatican City, 1998).
[167] See text in English of Ignatius' letters in *Early Christian Writings*, (London: Penguin, 1987).

were occasions when Viaticum could be taken outside the church to those in need. The image of the diaconate as a transitional order on the path to priestly ordination predominated. The Council of Trent proposed that the diaconate as a permanent office should be restored. This prescription was not carried out[168]. The main preoccupation of Trent was to assert the sacramentality and relationship between the order of bishop and that of priest. Further developments in the Second Vatican Council on the Sacrament of Orders and the structures of the Church were to open the way for a fuller consideration of the diaconate and to its restoration in its permanent form in the Church.

The Hierarchical Church and Deacons

The teachings of the Second Vatican Council which help to illuminate the position of the diaconate in the Catholic Church include:

1. the College of Bishops as successors to the Apostles;
2. the nature of the diocese as a particular or local church;
3. the place and apostolate of the laity in the mission of the Church.

Each of these teachings needs to be understood in order to arrive at a vision of the part to be played by the deacon in the mission of the Diocese of Aberdeen as it awaits its new Bishop.

The First Vatican Council taught definitively on the position of the Roman Pontiff, the Pope, as Shepherd and

---

[168] *The Permanent Diaconate*, p.15.

teacher of all Christians and the sign of unity of faith and practice in the Church. The political turmoil of those times prevented the Council from completing its work with respect to the place of the Bishops and the Pope in the life of the Church. The Second Vatican Council embarked upon the task of completing this teaching of the First Vatican Council in its Apostolic Constitution *Lumen Gentium*. The Council teaches that the Bishops, always with the Pope as head, form a College which is the successor to the group of Apostles appointed by Jesus Christ. The task of the College, to which each individual bishop contributes in union with the Pope and the other bishops, is to sanctify, teach and rule the flock of Christ which is the Church. Accepting the duty laid on the Apostles by Christ and relying on the gifts He gave to them, the bishops are responsible through the ages for a role of leadership in carrying out the mission given by Jesus of preaching to all nations, baptising in the name of the Father and of the Son and of the Holy Spirit. That role of leadership and service of God's people is exercised in the context of the needs of the people on their path to holiness. Always faithful to the teaching of Jesus Christ and sustained by the Sacrament of Holy Orders given by Christ to the Apostles and which they transmitted to their successors the bishops, the Bishops of the Catholic Church have in their own times and circumstances to meet the needs of the people[169].

The process of responding to the needs of the people can be seen at work in the earliest days of the Church. Already in the Acts of the Apostles we note how the Apostles were exploring the duty laid on them by Christ and giving testimony of the grace given them by the Lord

---

[169] *Lumen Gentium* 22.

to proclaim His resurrection from the dead and His divinity and mission. To the infant Church of Jerusalem, in some confusion over the distribution of resources, the Apostles did not hesitate to appoint seven men to handle the matter (an appointment seen by many as an indication of the Order of Deacons, Acts 6:1-6). The Council indicates the delineation of Holy Orders into the threefold rank of Bishop, Priest and Deacon by stating in *Lumen Gentium* "Christ, whom the Father hallowed and sent into the world (Jn.10:36), has through his apostles, made their successors, namely the Bishops, sharers in his consecration and mission and these in their turn, duly entrusted in varying degrees various members of the Church with the office of their ministry. Thus the divinely instituted ecclesiastical ministry is exercised in different degrees by those who even from ancient times have been called bishops, priests and deacons"[170]. The Council in the same document goes on to explore the duties that are assigned to the Order of Priests and to the Order of Deacons, always remembering that the fullness of the ordained ministry is found in the order of Bishops.

There are no texts in the New Testament or in the writings of the Early Fathers that set out an organised rationale for the entrustment by the Bishops of some men with the particular functions that are proper to the order of Priests or of Deacons. From the New Testament, particularly from the Acts of the Apostles and the Epistles, there is evidence of the Apostles working confidently, under the guidance of the Holy Spirit, to meet the demands of the mission entrusted to them by Christ

---

[170] *Ibid.* 28.

to preach the Good News.[171] The Apostles and their successors the Bishops had to make decisions under the pressure of the needs of the faithful and the events and circumstances of living in this world as a pilgrim people. Those decisions could never depart from the remit and powers given them by Christ. Yet the decisions had to be tailored to the terrestrial realities they encountered. It is in this context that we are helped to understand more clearly the institution of the Order of Deacons.

The document *Lumen Gentium* describes the Sacred Order of Deacon as follows: "At a lower level of the hierarchy are found deacons, who receive the imposition of hands 'not unto the priesthood, but unto the ministry', for strengthened by sacramental grace they are dedicated to the People of God in conjunction with the bishop and his body of priests, in the service of the liturgy, of the word, and of works of charity". There then follows a detailed list of the various functions that may be performed by a deacon. After this list the Council observed that many of these functions were with difficulty fulfilled in the Latin Church and this gave occasion for the restoration of the diaconate as a permanent office in the Church. However it is to be noted that none of the functions listed require the particular grace that is obtained by ordination to the priesthood even if many of the same functions by Church discipline had been executed only by priests in the past centuries.

A great advance in understanding the role of the laity in the life of the pilgrim Church is found in the teaching of the Second Vatican Council especially in Chapter 4 of *Lumen Gentium*. That teaching was foreshadowed in the

---

[171] *Acts of the Apostles* 15:28: "It has seemed good to the Holy Spirit and us".

period after the conclusion of the War in 1945 when the worker movements in the Church began to make more profound their discoveries of the dignity of the Christian worker often faced with very difficult conditions in work or unemployment. They turned to the vision offered by Christ the worker of Nazareth living under the example of St Joseph the Worker. That vision was enshrined in seminal statements of the Council. The layperson is essentially an active contributor to the mission of the People of God on the path to holiness. "The apostolate of the laity is a sharing in the salvific mission of the Church. Through Baptism and Confirmation all are appointed to this apostolate by the Lord himself."[172] This enhanced vision of the laity whom as the Council further states "Christ intimately joins to his life and mission, He also gives a share in his priestly office, to offer spiritual worship for the glory of the Father and the salvation of man",[173] established the base for the possible re-allocation of a variety of duties which hitherto had been the prerogative of the clergy. Such a move has profound consequences for the Order of Deacons. It has been said that except when vested and performing his liturgical function, the deacon is indistinguishable in the view of the laity generally from the Catholic lay person acting from the base of the baptismal and confirmation consecration conveyed by those sacraments to that person.

These considerations give rise to the question as to what were the determining factors that led the bishops who succeeded to the Apostles to establish the divinely instituted hierarchy in the form of two ranks, priesthood and diaconate? Such a question if directed at the Order of

---

[172] *Lumen Gentium* 33.
[173] *Ibid.* 34.

Priests is relatively easy to resolve. In the case of priests the central factor is found in the provision of the Eucharist from which come the other gifts of the Lord which comprise the full pastoral care of the pilgrim people of God. Such care is primarily the responsibility of the bishops but it is clear that the bishops found that this duty could not be fulfilled by themselves as the Church spread and new communities were established. To ensure that the communities were not deprived of the gift of Christ Himself in the Eucharist and to execute the command "Do this in memory of Me", the Order of Priests was established to give full pastoral care.

The history of the tasks assigned to the deacons helps to underpin the teaching contained in the most recent document from the Holy See on the Ministry and life of Deacons. Here it is taught that the ministry of the deacon is characterised by three duties which give rise to a set of tasks to be performed in the service of the People of God. These are the duties of teaching, making holy and of ruling, thus mirroring, but in a lesser degree, the tasks laid upon bishops and priests in their own proper exercise of their sacred Orders. Teaching is shown by the call of the deacon to proclaim the Scriptures and instruct and exhort the people. Sanctifying or making holy is indicated by personal prayer and leading the community in prayer in the absence of the bishop or priest and in giving or assisting at the celebration of some of the sacraments and sacramentals. These actions have their focus in the Blessed Eucharist showing that the deacon is not a simple purveyor of forms of social service. Ruling is the work of service which may be expressed in organisation of the communities but above all by the promotion and encouragement of charitable service. It is this last which is said to be the ministry most characteristic of the deacon.[174] This latest teaching is rooted in the centuries long experience of the diaconal Order in the Church. Yet this office and service almost disappeared from the life of the Church. The diaconate was as a simple stage on the path to priesthood.

It is not easy to identify with certainty the reasons for the disappearance of the diaconate as a permanent feature in the life of the Church. We can speculate that the priesthood was seen as so essential for the life of the communities that the Bishops focussed upon that order. It might be that as the Church became more integrated and essential to the social order that only senior ecclesiastics would be trusted to handle secular affairs while ecclesiastical matters were left to junior rank clergy not including deacons.

These considerations of the past have significance for our understanding of the circumstances which led the Fathers of the Second Vatican Council to seek to introduce the diaconate as a permanent order in the life of the Church. I do not propose to investigate the motives of the Fathers in Council in promoting the reintroduction of the Permanent Diaconate. Rather I suggest that a fruitful direction for clearer understanding of the Permanent Diaconate is to review the insights of the Council of the nature of the Diocese and the duty of the diocesan bishop appointed to nourish each diocese. For the sake of brevity we will use the formulations taken from the documents of the Council as employed in the Latin Code of Canon Law.

"A diocese is a portion of the people of God, which is entrusted to a bishop to be nurtured by him, with the cooperation of the *presbyterium*, in such a way that,

---

[174] *The Permanent Diaconate* 9.

remaining close to its pastor and gathered by him through the Gospel and the Eucharist in the Holy Spirit, it constitutes a particular Church. In this Church, the one, holy, catholic and apostolic Church of Christ truly exists and functions".[175] The order of deacons is not in this description but is included in the text of *Lumen Gentium* (29) and by implication in *Sacrosanctum Concilium* (41), where the Bishop is shown as surrounded by his priests and his other ministers in celebration of the sacred mysteries.

Thus while the Permanent Diaconate by the will of the Council was to be restored, where the local bishop, with the approbation of his conference of bishops and the approval of the Holy See, so desired, the same Council had little to say on the function of the deacons in a diocese on parallel lines to the vision of the priests of the diocese forming a college of assistants to the bishop. The functions which can be assigned to deacons are listed in paragraph 29 of *Lumen Gentium*. These functions are neatly arranged in the *Basic Norms* (9) as the duties of teaching, making holy and ruling always in subordination to the bishop and any priests involved in a particular duty. The deacon however, as the *Basic Norms* remind us, is linked to the particular ecclesial body which has presented him for ordination and so acquires a constant bond of service to a discrete portion of the People of God. In considering the threefold functions or *munera* assigned to a deacon it is the function or duty of ruling expressed by dedication to works of charity and assistance and in the direction of communities or sectors of church life, especially as regards

---

[175] *Code of Canon Law* 1983: CIC 369 using the text of *Christus Dominus* 11.

charitable activities which are called in the *Basic Norms* "a ministry most characteristic of the deacon".[176]

The Permanent Diaconate and the Diocese of Aberdeen

Among the Scottish Dioceses only Dunkeld and Aberdeen have a significant number of permanent deacons. Aberdeen in fact has a slightly higher proportion of deacons to priests than Dunkeld. The Catholic Directory for Scotland indicates that Aberdeen is divided into forty-two parishes and is served by thirty priests of the diocese, a number of whom are retired or working outside the diocese. There are thirteen priests belonging to religious communities in the diocese but a number of these are not dedicated to parochial duties. There are other diocesan clergy on loan to Aberdeen who form a valuable help to staffing some parishes. However there is a short fall in that there are not enough priests to provide a resident priest having the care of each parish listed in the Directory. Two parishes have permanent deacons listed as having care of parishes. Some religious who are not priests give valuable help to a number of parishes. The Directory indicates that Aberdeen has five students in major seminaries.

A number of issues will face the new Bishop in Aberdeen as he reviews the duty laid on him by his Episcopal ordination and canonical mission given him by the Holy Father. Only those matters which are likely to affect the permanent deacons of the diocese and their present and future apostolate will be considered here. The new Bishop of Aberdeen will have to take note that there are not enough priests in the Diocese to provide resident pastors as required by the law of the Church. A Diocesan

---

[176] *Permanent Diaconate, Basic Norms* 9.

Bishop has the power, after due consultation, to establish new parishes or to amalgamate existing parishes (CIC 515 § 2). He can also, in the circumstances of a shortage of priests, appoint to assist with the pastoral care of a parish a deacon or lay persons, but a priest must be nominated with the power and faculties of a parish priest to direct the pastoral care (CIC 517 § 2).

It is clear that the permanent deacons in Aberdeen offer a valuable and in some places essential element in the ministerial response to the needs of the people of God. The carrying out of duties of preaching, praying for the people, administering Baptism, distributing the Eucharist, assisting at weddings and presiding at funerals and burials and in the administration of sacramentals provides a great relief for the priests who would otherwise, unless laity were appointed, have to do these services. In addition there are some works of diocesan administration that are conveniently done by the deacons. A new Bishop may well feel that these services should simply be continued since the arrangements in the past could operate into the future having been tested by experience.

However it is right to ask whether this approach to the deployment of deacons shuts off other areas of the apostolate that might serve to assist the diocese to develop a thrust of evangelisation not as yet explored. These areas are preaching the full Gospel to those who have not yet received it and the development of works of charity. The history of the diaconal order in the first centuries of the Christian era bear testimony of the significance of the work of the Order of Deacons in these two areas. Both in the New Testament writings and in those of the early Fathers the deacons are the associates of the Bishop in these tasks.

It is true that as the centuries developed matters of material administration came to assume great importance in the organisation of the local church. Under the influence of freedom from active persecution and becoming an essential part of the fabric of civil society the material dimension of the church organisation placed significant demands on the leader of the local church, the bishop, which were met by the deacons. This is well illustrated by the deacons in the service of the Roman Church estates under Pope Gregory the Great. However the duties of material administration are obviously subject to the need to deal with secular persons and affairs. Such a reality could readily lead to the employment of laity rather than the ordained and hence lead to a perception that the deacons were surplus to requirement.

In our own times the material administration of Church goods, while remaining under the care of the Bishop of the diocese, are best handled by employed, suitably qualified professionals. Such a practice is often required by the civil law concerning charities. Should then the deacons be seen as useful stopgaps in the absence of ordained priests? Such an approach is inadequate in the light of the teaching of the Second Vatican Council and the series of documents issued by the Pastors of the Church in the last forty years. So the appointment of deacons at the parish level simply to supply, as far as they are able in the absence of a priest, those sacramental services that the faithful need, should not obstruct the wider vision of the possibility of their assistance to the Bishop in the field of preaching the Gospel to the unconverted and the work of promoting practical works of charity both within and without the Catholic Community. While neither of these fields of action for the sake of the Kingdom is the exclusive preserve of any individual Catholic since they flow from the original gift given in baptism, it will be of help to a new Bishop to examine the actual situation in the Diocese of Aberdeen in these areas. By such an examination he will be able to gain an indication as to the manner in which the permanent deacons could be deployed in the diocese.

I am not equipped to anticipate in any way the direction such reflection by the new bishop should go. From my own very limited knowledge of Aberdeen I note the following elements which might be brought into consideration. The style of Christianity among our fellow Christians seems often to include a suspicion or rejection of episcopacy and priesthood. It may be that a Catholic deacon would appear to be less threatening to deeply and long-held views when he talks about the Faith and the Catholic Church. In our society despite the availability of resources in medicine and care that is much greater than in the past, many individuals feel isolated and neglected. It may be that the deacons are well placed to initiate and encourage the attention and training of parish communities to provide a service of assistance and hope for those who feel neglected in our communities.

Archbishop Mario leaves behind him in Aberdeen a significant body of Permanent Deacons with much potential for the life of the Diocese of Aberdeen. His successor will have much to thank him for in this and many other respects. May the Holy Spirit guide the new Bishop of Aberdeen with the insights needed for the development of the Catholic Church of Aberdeen.

RESTORATION OF THE PERMANENT DIACONATE IN SCOTLAND

DEACON JOHN FUTERS

In November 1982, after much deliberation and consultation with bishops where the diaconate was already established, the Scottish Hierarchy submitted an application to Rome for permission for the restoration of the Permanent Diaconate in Scotland. Responsibility for taking measures to bring this about fell to Bishop Mario Conti, as coordinator.

In September 1983, after assessment of applicants and their wives, two suitable applicants commenced their studies. This was made possible with the assistance of the Diocese of Lancaster, where a formation programme already existed, and where Bishop Foley was happy to accept these first two Scottish applicants for training for the Diocese of Aberdeen.

After three years, towards the end of which the diocese of Motherwell had already accepted and ordained its first permanent deacon, the two Aberdeen students were ordained: the first on 22nd June, 1986, was appointed to serve at St Mary's, Inverness; and the second on 13th July, 1986, to serve at St Mary's Cathedral, Aberdeen.

In 1988, Bishop Conti decided that, as others had expressed an interest, a course for diaconal students should be set up for the training of future Scottish applicants. A programme was drawn up based on that of the Lancaster Diocese, but with some modification and hoping for improvement. Lecturers were recruited, with some difficulty, to cover the range of subjects and, after careful assessment, five applicants were accepted and they commenced their studies, using the largely vacant premises of Blairs College, in February 1989.

In 1990, the Diocese of Dunkeld added its first batch of four students who, together with one new student from Aberdeen, brought the number up to ten at the beginning of study year three in February 1991. The first intake of Aberdeen students completed their studies prior to ordination in 1992 and by this time there was an annual intake of students from the two dioceses. In 1996, the diocese of Motherwell joined in, sending two students.

Due to the deterioration of the premises at Blairs College, it was necessary to find an alternative venue for the course and it was arranged for it to relocate to St Mary's, Kinnoull, from February 1997. It remained there for two years, before moving again to St Francis', Dundee, the former Friary, where there was overnight accommodation. By this time, some difficulties were being experienced, particularly with regard to the availability of suitable lecturers, due to increased demands on the time of a falling number of priests.

A comparison of the Aberdeen syllabus with the *Basic Norms for the Formation of Permanent Deacons*, issued by the Vatican in 1998, highlighted the need for some improvement. It was apparent that there should be a considerable increase in the number of hours spent in lectures and seminars, and that arrangements should be made to provide these without the need to call on busy parish priests for help.

When, in the year 2000, it became clear that the Bishops of Argyll and the Isles and of Paisley were preparing for the restoration of the diaconate in their dioceses, Bishop Conti saw this as an opportune time for a review of the formation structure. With the cooperation of the Ogilvie Institute in Aberdeen and Maryvale

Institute in Birmingham, a new structure was established, combining distance learning with residential weekends and an annual study week, which would include pastoral assignments. A parish placement plan is included in each year's programme. This four-year programme leads to a Higher Education Diploma in Applied Theology, validated by the Open University. Candidates are ordained after four years' formation, but may choose to continue their studies for two years after ordination in order to graduate with a BA in Applied Theology, designed and offered by Maryvale Institute in collaboration with the Ogilvie Institute. Deacon Tony Schmitz has been appointed as Director of Studies for the national formation programme for Scotland. Thus Bishop Conti was able to take up his new appointment as Archbishop of Glasgow in the sure knowledge that his twenty years of dedication to the process had left a firm foundation for the future of the Permanent Diaconate in Scotland.

The Right Reverend John Jukes OFM Conv. is Titular Bishop of Strathearn and Auxiliary Bishop Emeritus of Southwark. He entered the Franciscan Order in 1946 and studied at the Pontifical Faculty of St Bonaventure in Rome, being ordained priest in 1952. He served as a parish priest in Manchester and Waterloo and for ten years was Vice-president and Lecturer in Canon Law at the Franciscan Study Centre in Canterbury. He has been Chairman of several bodies and has published numerous articles in theological reviews and in Canon Law publications. In November 2000 he "retired" to Huntly in Aberdeenshire, where he has been parish priest ever since.

The Rev. John R. Futers was ordained Permanent Deacon for the Diocese of Aberdeen in 1986. He currently serves at Portlethan, near Aberdeen.

THE ICONOGRAPHY OF THE WESTERN RITE
INTRODUCING ICONS INTO CATHOLIC CHURCHES

SISTER PETRA CLARE

Historical Overview: when did the icons disappear?

If we had gone into a church or cathedral in the Europe of the Holy Roman Empire, we would have found not only richly carved screens and elaborate stone façades and statuary of a very high artistic quality, but we would also have found the walls brightly painted from floor to ceiling with images witnessing to the experience of the One, Holy, Catholic and Apostolic Church, to which the entire western world belonged. "At the time of Charlemagne's coronation, in AD 800, Rome was the only city with wall painting extending back almost continuously to the time of Constantine and beyond."[177] Carolingian Europe consciously bases its cycle of imagery on the fifth/sixth century mosaics in Rome. Even the elaborate Celtic scrollwork of the Celtic schools in the eighth century bears marked similarities to Byzantine gilded and enamelled work, translated into a different medium, supporting the claim that there was a lively cultural interchange between Ireland and Byzantium.[178]

Particularly important is Romanesque iconography. If we examine British manuscripts from the time of the Norman Conquest, we find not only that the illustrations

---

[177] Dodwell, *Painting in Europe* (London: Penguin, 1971), pp. 10-11.
[178] The Book of Kells, for example, belongs to the early ninth century, the early Carolingian period.

are similar to icons in content, but that the technique is merely a translation of standard iconographic method into watercolour on vellum. The English "dampfold" depiction of garments was an adaptation of Byzantine models. By the twelfth century, Byzantine influence in England was at its height. Many English nobles were in Sicily at this time, and English craftsmen were able to work first-hand from Byzantine models. Three artists of the Winchester Bible had Sicilian connections, as did artists of the Westminster Psalter. The two mediaeval frescoes of the *Lamentation over the Dead Christ* in Winchester Cathedral (the later of which was carefully remounted to reveal the earlier one) can immediately be identified as to subject matter, style and method by anyone familiar with the icon. Frescoes both in Cefalu and Barcelona show influence by English artists trained in Sicily. The twelfth century St Cuthbert at Durham was originally part of a full Romanesque wall-painting cycle.[179] Manuscript images such as the *Death of the Virgin* (AD 1010) in the Staatsbibliothek, Munich, and the Gothic stained glass *Virgin with Apostles* in Le Mans Cathedral (AD 1150) retain the vigour of the common tradition. The mosaic cycle of San Marco in Venice, begun in the second half of the eleventh century, is an iconographic bridge between East and West, which has been studied in depth by Otto Demus.[180] The artistic traditions remain closely related until the emergence of western iconoclasm as a characteristic of the Reformation.

---

[179] Notes from a lecture by Peter Murphy at a conference to commemorate the 1200th anniversary of Nicaea II, hosted by the Society of St John Chrysostom, 24th October 1987.
[180] Otto Demus, *The Mosaic Decoration of San Marco, Venice* (Dumbarton Oaks: University of Chicago Press, 1988).

However, Charlemagne's opposition to the Seventh Ecumenical Council prevented the theological basis of iconography being fully developed in the Western Empire: in AD 794, as King of the Franks, he called a council of Frankish bishops at Frankfurt, condemning the Second Council of Nicaea. Although this was prompted by a mistranslation and led to a papal rebuke from Pope Hadrian I, and Charles professed a nominal neutrality, he was deeply opposed to the Council, and this stifled theological debate on icons.[181] The resulting weakness of the theology of images in Charlemagne's Europe paved the way for the iconoclasm of the Reformers.[182] However, until the mutual excommunications of 1054, the whole eastern and western Church was one Church, despite local disagreements, and the real bitterness between east and west did not develop until after the looting of the churches of Constantinople in 1204 by the Venetians during the Fourth Crusade.[183]

---

[181] T. Hodgkin, *Italy and her Invaders* (Oxford: Clarendon Press, 1899).

[182] It may be argued that western iconoclasm had its roots in eastern iconoclasm because at the Triumph of Orthodoxy the Eastern Empire pushed its heretics over the border, where their ideas developed through various western sects.

[183] T. Ware, *The Orthodox Church* (London: Penguin, 1963), p.69: "What shocked the Greeks more than anything was the wanton and systematic sacrilege of the Crusaders....the Byzantines watched the Crusaders tear to pieces the altar and icon screen in the Church of Holy Wisdom and set prostitutes on the Patriarch's throne."
Alexander Schmemann, *Historical Road of Eastern Orthodoxy* (New York: SVSP, 1977), p.252, comments: "The worst part lies in the fact that through the centuries we find hardly any sign of suffering from it, any longing for re-unification, any awareness of the abnormality, sin and horror of this schism in Christendom. There was almost a satisfaction with the separation, and a desire to discover darker and darker aspects in the opposite camp." The temporary re-union of the Council of Florence 1438-9, and more recent controversy over the

Both the Eastern and Western Empires had two distinct but overlapping iconographic traditions. The most important images were the theological cycles within the churches, linked with the liturgical events taking place within. The other tradition developed via manuscripts and books of hours, and the imagery reflected more personal issues, sometimes including political lampoons or local pastoral scenes, and sometimes a woman is complimented by depicting the Virgin Mary with similar features, something taken up by Renaissance canvas painters such as Da Vinci. When the liturgical images were whitewashed over by the Reformers, the emphasis was placed more and more on personal devotional images: canvases of the Mother of God dressed as a society woman of the day became popular (Parmagianino, *The Madonna with the Long Neck*), or St George as a tiny figure in the corner of a forested landscape (Altdorfer). Guild account books in archives in the Netherlands and parish records during the Catholic Revival under Mary Tudor in England show the move to transportable canvas for religious images.[184] In the following centuries, the religious images of Western Europe increasingly reflect the social ambivalence of the times towards images, inclining to secular taste and popular devotions, as distinct from the highly liturgical and theological image cycles of the pre-Reformation Church.

Uniate churches of the Ukraine only served to re-open the wounds of bitterness among many Orthodox Christians. The current controversies over whether western Catholics should write icons are rooted in the attitudes fostered by the schism.

[184] David Freedberg, "The structure of Byzantine and European Iconoclasm", *Iconoclasm, Papers for the Ninth Spring Symposium of Byzantine Studies*, (Centre for Byzantine Studies, University of Birmingham, 1975), pp.165-177.

As the images returned to the whitewashed churches of Western Europe in the nineteenth and twentieth centuries, what returned was largely either statues related to popular devotions, e.g. Sacred Heart, St Anthony, Our Lady of Lourdes, or a self-conscious updating of the Gospel to "look modern" or to reflect what the artist personally felt about Jesus. Often their quality and position in the church reflect the taste and preferences of successive incumbents, rather than any seriously thought out schema. It is with some justification, therefore, that Orthodox Christians observe that we have lost the fundamentals of liturgical art, and point to their own unbroken tradition. Overlaid as they are with the elaboration of Imperial Russia or the faded Byzantine splendour of Greece, the wall paintings and icons of the eastern Church are still unmistakably the liturgical descendants of the same tradition as San Marco, Ravenna and the great Roman basilicas. It is this ancient tradition of the theological and liturgical image which, in the spirit of the Second Vatican Council, we are called upon to renew.

In calling for the renewal of a theological and liturgical iconography in churches, it is important to emphasise that this does not mean brushing aside the social tradition of religious art which has developed in post-Reformation Europe. I would suggest that the dual model of earlier centuries be retained. The icon is essentially a theological and canonical art: like priests and religious and conciliar documents, we trust it to convey the teaching and liturgy of the Church, and it is therefore appropriate for the decorative and devotional schema of the church building. The other tradition, deriving from the manuscript commentary and observed natural facts, is more akin to the hidden but powerful life of the secular institutes — it is

240

an art which places the Church in the world and derives its validity from this. The one art is apophatic and ascending, placed where earth reaches up to heaven; the other is cataphatic and descending, placed where heaven reaches down to earth. Like the angels ascending and descending on Jacob's ladder, they both have their place.

Theological infrastructure of icons: Duodecimum Saeculum and all that.

The icon is a theological art. It grew out of the same influences which shaped the Church from its birth to the sixth century, finding its definitive form after the Council of Chalcedon. The methods grew out of the mingling of four great cultures: Rome, Egypt, Classical Greece and Hellenic Judaism. Mural cycles of Moses, such as at the synagogue at Duras Europas, were gradually transposed into the life of Christ, via Pauline exegesis. Crossing the Red Sea became the icon of the Baptism. Depictions of Melchisedech and the sacrifice of Abel developed along with the Roman Canon of the Mass. The wall paintings of Rome relate stylistically to those of Antioch, whereas the Hellenic Egyptian sarcophagi of Fayum provide the basis of the "beyond this world" gaze of the icon and use the same layered pigments that we use today. The Jewish, Greek and native Egyptian mix of Alexandria produced both a significant theological school and the groundwork for the earliest surviving icons at Sinai.

Witness to the definition "true God and true man" became the crux of iconography, and in the three centuries following Chalcedon the icon became the banner of Chalcedonian orthodoxy: many martyrs, particularly Eastern Empire monks and clergy, died in defence of the Council as witnessed by the icon. As a material object, the icon "portrait" gave concrete evidence of the humanity of Jesus Christ, as a human being who was born and who died; as a theological statement in line and colour, it gave witness to the transcendence of his Godhead. If one considers the role of art, it has always been called upon to witness to aspects of nature and of the human character which transcend the world – whether it is the light of Turner's *Fighting Temeraire*, of Monet's umbrellas in the rain or of Rothko's infinite spaces of colour.

It was in the Council in Trullo (the Quintisext, AD 692), the Eastern Church working party in Constantinople, after Chalcedon, that the core theology of the icon was worked out – to avoid confusing Christ with a pagan deity, pre-Christian or prophetic symbols were largely suppressed in favour of images of the Incarnation: "Having welcomed these ancient figures and shadows as symbols of the truth transmitted to the Church, today we prefer grace and truth themselves, as the fulfilment of the Law, Therefore ... We decree that henceforth Christ our God be represented in his human form ... We understand this to be the elevation of the humility of God the Word, and we are led to remembering his life in the flesh ... ."[185]

Ouspensky explains: "The truth has to be revealed not only in word but also in image: it has to be *shown*. Therein lies the most radical refusal of abstractions[186]... The truth has its own image, for it is not an idea or an abstract formula: it is a person ... And it has an image. This is why the Church not only *speaks* of the truth, but also *shows* the truth: the image of Jesus Christ".[187] This is also why

---

[185] Rhalles and Potles, *Syntagma*, vol.2 (Athens, 1852), p. 492, quoted in Ouspensky, *Theology of the Icon*, vol.1 (New York: SVSP, 1978), p. 92.
[186] As an end in themselves.
[187] Ouspensky, *ibid*. p.94.

Orthodox iconography has consistently rejected attempts to depict Jesus in modern dress, because this turns him from a historical person to a symbolic person, promoting unconsciously the idea that Jesus is just another mythical character or only a good man. "The historic traits of Jesus, his portrait, are a witness to his coming in the flesh",[188] therefore the icon has always depicted Christ with the features of the *Icon Made without Hands*, an image miraculously imprinted on cloth, with a pedigree indicating first century origin. This image underlies the historic features of Christ, as portrayed from the sixth century encaustic portrait on Sinai to Rubens' depiction of the crucified Christ in the seventeenth century.

The canon also indicates the way in which the icon must be painted – we must depict *the elevation of the humility of God the Word*. We must represent the humanity "in such a way that, when looking at the image, we contemplate also his Divine glory".[189] The specific techniques developed over the next thirteen hundred years following the Council, and still developing today, express a profound creative tension between accepting the limitation of the material image and pointing to a divine reality which, of its nature, cannot be depicted. It is in this context that the iconographer is defined as a contemplative theologian. It is in expressing the supernatural paradox of the Incarnation that the iconographers have developed a physical method of painting which combines precise linear depiction with vast abstract spaces. It has also led to a method in which God, the ground of our being, is expressed by the background of the icon having spatial rules which make it as dynamic a

---

[188] Ouspensky, *ibid*. p.96.
[189] Ouspensky, *ibid*. p.96.

part of the image as the depiction of the saint upon the foreground.

This dynamic abstract interaction of background and foreground virtually disappears in the Renaissance[190] and reappears in the abstractions of the modern school. The interesting thing is that, as the "divinity" ceased to be depicted in favour of the "humanity" in art, so did philosophy and theology take on an increasingly humanist character. From an iconographer's point of view, the reduction of perspectives to one materialistic viewpoint, i.e. that of the natural world with a vanishing point, tended to focus the soul exclusively on the realities of this world, as distinct from the deliberate aim of iconographers to use multiple perspectives combined with the dynamics of the flat surface to *transcend while in this world the perspectives of this world.*

In today's art, the human and abstract tend to be mutually exclusive (neo-realist versus abstractionist), and humanism and atheism are dominant characteristics of the culture. In spiritual art of the "New Age" school there tends to be a fuzziness of depiction which expresses a hazy syncretist theology. In mainstream religious art in the Catholic Church there is still a tendency to sentimental statuary which *by its artistic method*, as distinct from its subject (the saint displayed), suggests a faith not engaged with theological reality. Our images tend to express our spiritual temperature, and the renewal of the icon in this millennium, actively engaging with conciliar theology of the Church and, in particular, expressing the teaching of the Second Vatican Council, is overdue and a matter of urgency for the church in the modern world.

---

[190] Compare Raphael's *Transfiguration* with the well-known Novgorod *Ascension*, or the same by Theophanes the Greek.

Pope John Paul II has shown his keen knowledge of this real gap in the Church's ministry in the latter to the Bishops, *Duodecimum Saeculum*, in December 1987,[191] on the twelve hundredth anniversary of the Seventh Ecumenical Council, the Second Council of Nicaea, convened in AD 787. This Council confirmed the icon as an authentic and necessary witness of the Christian faith, after nearly three centuries of controversy with iconoclastic groups, themselves often influenced by Jewish or Moslem[192] worship, following the Council of Chalcedon in AD 451. The Council concluded after a heated debate, which called on the writings of a galaxy of Church Fathers: "We preserve all the traditions of the Church... *One of these traditions is the making of iconographic representations — being in accordance with the narrative of the proclamation of the Gospel — for the purpose of ascertaining the Incarnation of God the Word, which was real, not imaginary, and for being of an equal benefit to us as the Gospel narrative. For those which point mutually to each other undoubtedly mutually signify each other.*"[193]

The most important text cited by the Council was undoubtedly *"the honour given to the image passes to the prototype"*, lifted from St Basil of Caesarea's treatise *On the Holy Spirit*.[194] This text defined that honour given to an

[191] Printed in *L'Osservatore Romano,* English edition, 15th February 1988.
[192] Mohammed conquered Mecca in 630, the same year that Heraclitus returned the Cross of Christ, which had been captured by the Persians, to Jerusalem.
[193] Daniel J. Sahas, *Icon and Logos: translation of the Horos of the seventh session of Nicaea II* (University of Toronto, 1986), p.178. The seventh session also summarises the artistic and theological roots of the iconography in the previous Christian centuries. My italics.
[194] St Basil the Great, *On the Holy Spirit*, (translation, New York: SVSP, 1980), p.72. The treatise was written in the closing years of the fourth

icon of Christ, the Mother of God, or the saints, was distinct from that given to idols. The icon is more like the motherboard of a computer – it has no value in itself but takes its value from being a vehicle of communication: the icon is a means, sanctified by the Church, by which the individual focuses his prayer, and the honour given to the icon passes to its real object: Our Lord, the Mother of God or the saints, really present in heaven and willing to have an effective relationship with us.

After an extensive consideration of the theology of the Council, the Holy Father concludes:

> Over the past several decades we have observed a resurgence of interest in the theology and spirituality of Oriental icons, a sign of the growing need for a spiritual language of authentically Christian art. In this regard I can only invite my brethren of the episcopate to "maintain firmly the practice of proposing to the faithful the veneration of sacred images in the churches"[195] and to do everything so that more works of truly ecclesial quality may be produced ... .

> The rediscovery of the Christian icon will also help in raising the awareness of the urgency of reacting against the depersonalising and at times degrading effects of the many images that condition our lives in advertisements and the media, for it is an image that turns towards us the look of another invisible

century, in defence of the doctrine of the Trinity defined at the first council of Nicaea, AD 325.

[195] *Sacrosanctum Concilium*, pp.122-124, quoted by Pope John Paul II in *Duodecimum Saeculum 1989*, printed in *L'Osservatore Romano*, English Edition, 15th February 1988.

one and gives us access to the reality of the
spiritual and eschatological world ... .

In recalling the pertinence of the teaching of the
Seventh Ecumenical Council, it seems we are sent
back to our primordial task of evangelisation. The
growing secularisation of society shows that it is
becoming largely estranged from spiritual values,
from the mystery of our salvation in Jesus Christ,
from the reality of the world to come ... The
language of beauty placed at the service of faith is
capable of reaching people's hearts and making
them know from within the One we dare to
represent in images.[196]

Model of a Catholic church interior AD 2022 – a guided tour.
I would like to take you for a virtual tour of a large church,
set a little bit into the future, a modern Catholic church,
decorated with new icons and designs from the Twenty-
first century, according to the classical theological schema.
We will shape our buildings on that most unpromising of
designs which led to one priest describing his church as "a
consecrated warehouse". We will assume this priest has a
sound building and has been able to afford to strip the
plaster back and re-plaster in lime in order to have a full
schema of murals. If this has not been possible, then he will
have used large marine plywood panels set into the walls,
combined with artist's quality emulsion paint (more
expensive, but longer lasting and much richer and stronger
in colour resonance).

As well as the large permanent icons, incorporated into
the walls, he and a colleague have commissioned some

---

[196] Pope John Paul II, *Duodecimum Saeculum 1989*, printed *in*
L'Osservatore Romano, English edition, 15th February 1988.

moveable panel icons, which can be brought into the church for feast days, for the Lent Stations of the Cross and for RCIA Rites, and one or two icons for special devotions (such as the Divine Mercy). As this is quite an expensive schema, we can assume he started the project for the millennium and it is now nearing completion.

When we come through the door we realise that the entire interior of the church is painted from floor to ceiling. Some of the paintings are icons of the saints or the life of Christ: these are set in big abstract coloured areas of wall, treated like the big areas of marble and decorative mosaic we would have seen in an early Christian basilica. The priest who is showing us round has chosen large areas of colour in soft abstract layers which seem to make the walls glow with an inner light. His close friend, from the same seminary, has used similar full wall painting in his church, but it is smaller and darker, so he has used a light panelled effect more in the style of Mondrian. Both realise that it is important to surround the worshipping congregation with colours and forms which lift the heart – "Lift up your hearts" … "We lift them up to the Lord". The artist has tried to make an environment which will make present a similar experience to that of the envoys of Vladimir of Kiev when they came into Sancta Sophia and "did not know whether they were in heaven or on earth. They only knew that God dwells there among men. They could never forget that beauty."[197]

We come first to the baptistery, at the back of the church. Here we see by the font a nearly life-size icon of the Baptism of the Lord. This not only reminds us of our entry into the Church by baptism, but it is also a focus of

---

[197] Francis House, *The Russian Phoenix* (London: SPCK, 1988), p.6.

prayer for church unity among the congregation; as we now accept converts without baptising them again, in most cases, this is also our most potent signal that we accept that Christ has begun a good work in those outside the Roman Church. The rest of the baptistery is painted in abstract colour resonances in sea greens and blues, in a similar way to Rothko's vast colour canvases; these are interspersed with decorative panels with highly decorative abstract fish themes, including a Jonah and the Whale. These are painted in the manner of Kandinsky's later work, on brighter blue panels, and are a source of endless fascination for the children. The "Kandinsky fishes" and molecule-like objects floating in space remind them of computer clip art, while the adults are reminded of Celtic decorations. Among the fishes are texts about "fishers of men", and the baptised being "like fishes".

The priest explains that his friend's baptistery is, in contrast, completely bare, except for the baptism icon, but he has a series of RCIA icons which are used as a focus of prayer during RCIA classes, and by the wider congregation when they have novenas for those preparing for the rites, including children preparing for baptism and confirmation. These icons are designed to show, around the most important theme, e.g. baptism, both the Scripture readings of the rite and the most important liturgical events, forming a guide to each rite.

When you turn round to go out of church, you find, on the opposite wall to the baptism, a large icon of the Anastasis (Resurrection), known in the Western Church as "the Harrowing of Hell". It is right by the big stone holy water stoup, and lots of candles and flowers are placed by it on Easter night at the blessing of the waters. The children are shown Adam and Eve being lifted out of hell by their hands, but they are a bit more fascinated by the nuts and bolts flying from the gates of hell at the bottom. Their parents have done a Bible study with them by the icon in Holy Week, which has helped them to understand what the picture is trying to teach them about being saved by Jesus. They have shown them the prophets waiting to be saved with Adam and Eve: "Look, there is David, Jesus' many times many great-granddad, and Isaiah whose book we read in Advent, and John the Baptist who baptised Him". On Holy Saturday, the whole congregation has gathered by the icon for the Office of Readings and has found that the icon exactly illustrates the "reading from an ancient homily for Holy Saturday" from the office of the day.

As you walk up the nave you find yourself between rows of life-size icons of standing saints, interspersed by blocks of luminous colour; it is like being escorted up to the altar in procession. You are reminded of St Paul saying: "seeing we are encompassed about with so great a crowd of witnesses...looking up to Jesus, the author and finisher of our faith",[198] (who is depicted in glory above the altar at the far end of the church). To your surprise, you notice the saints are not just haphazardly jumbled around. Through your head flow the words of a litany you have heard recently – how did it go? ... Lord have mercy, Holy Mary, Holy Angels, Saint John the Baptist, Saint Joseph, Apostles, martyrs, Church Fathers, various saints ... Ah! The saints follow the order of the Litany as they progress up to Jesus, and you discover that the holy men and women are at the back of the church – you pass St Anthony of Padua and the married couple canonised at the turn of the century. Your church, being in Scotland, also has an icon of St Rose of Lima, because she reputedly was able to stop the mosquitoes biting, and they even joined her to sing their

---

[198] Hebrews 12:1-2.

prayers! At the back of the church is also an icon of the recently canonised Mother Teresa of Calcutta, holding a scrawny Indian child. As you move further up the church you find the icons of the Doctors of the Church: these are two large, life-size square icons on each side of the nave. One is of the women doctors – St Catherine of Siena, St Teresa of Avila and St Thérèse of Lisieux; opposite these are three male doctors of the Church. The new icon of the philosopher martyr, Edith Stein, holding a book with one of her writings in it, is opposite St John Ogilvie, the Reformation martyr. As you come to a stop in front of the sanctuary, you see on the side walls the Apostles walking towards Christ in an attitude of veneration, as if they are going to receive Holy Communion. Above them is a truly splendid Christ in Majesty, surrounded with cherubim and seraphim (which you can hardly see, because they are just sketched lightly on red and blue, because they represent the invisible angels around God's throne: "Gloria, in excelsis Deo, et in terra pax hominibus bona voluntatis. Laudamus te. Glorificamus te … ."

When the children were being introduced to the four Gospel books, they were taken right up to the icon and shown the four strange beasties poking out their heads on each side of the icon and told about the visions of Ezekiel and St John on Patmos, and how to remember which Gospel is which – St John is an eagle because his thought is so penetrating and uplifting. The wall around the icon of Christ is a blaze of bas-relief gold which reflects the light into the sanctuary – you recall how the medieval sanctuary was always the most highly decorated part of the church, showing that it is the holiest part of the church – the altar where bread and wine are made God for us. Gradually your eyes recognise that the colours among the gold patterns are not just decorative, but the formulae of molecules and

251

patterns of sub-atomic particles – the wall is an abstract of the beginning of creation focussed on the incarnate Christ in his gold-rayed robe in the centre. What a glory of light …"lumen de lumine … light from light, God from God". You recall that in the icon gold is used only to signify the presence of God. When gold is in the background and gold is rayed on the clothes, indeed it represents the incarnate God from the pre-incarnate God.

The friend of the priest who is showing us round has a different icon here – it does not have much gold, only very light, bright, luminous colours, and it shows the Holy Trinity appearing at Mamre as three angels, with Abraham and Sarah bringing up gifts; the children love it because they are sure that the old married couple are just like Mr and Mrs Graham coming up in the offertory procession. The priest has used the icon in numerous homilies and children's liturgies to explain the mystery his church is dedicated to – the Holy Trinity. He also chose the Mondrian-type wall schema because of this dedication; although most of the squares are white, the other squares form a kind of dialogue of three colours – red, blue and yellow – the trinity of colours which make light and form. It is as if the walls of the church themselves become windows, and the windows themselves are large flat sheets of coloured glass through which the drab grey roofs surrounding his city church take on a mysterious light of their own: as if he was encouraging his poorer congregation – come, life is not so grey, there is the joy of the Spirit if you look deep enough into the dullness to find the light.

Back in our own church, the children have stopped investigating the icons of the altar area and are looking at our two freestanding wooden icons each side of the altar for personal devotion.[199] One is of Our Lady with the Child Christ, and the other is of the Sacred Heart. They are both on rich gold backgrounds and have big loving eyes; the eyes of icons are tremendous – they seem to embrace you with loving compassion and at the same time look beyond you into vast depths of infinity. These eyes inspire hope that there is infinite love beyond the deep suffering you have experienced, and you stop to say a prayer for Aunt Millie, who recently died. These icons are placed each side of the altar, as they would be in an eastern church, and are always surrounded by women who have come in from shopping to light a candle and say the rosary, and men stopping off on their way back from work.

Before we go into the two side chapels, we look up above the rows of standing saints, interspersed with panels of rich abstract colour, which form a wide ribbon of colour around the bottom half of the church, and discover that painted above the saints on the white plaster wall is a set of roundels of the life of Christ. The priest explains that, just as the Stations of the Cross were originally a way of the parish following the way of pilgrimage in Jerusalem at home – a kind of virtual pilgrimage – , the festal set came about so that the parish could follow the stations of the Holy Land pilgrimage at home. He shows us the Birth of the Virgin with her loving parents, and her Annunciation, the cave at Bethlehem, the Presentation in the Temple, the Miracle at Cana in Galilee, the Mount of Transfiguration, the Raising of Lazarus, the Crucifixion, the Appearance to Thomas, the Ascension, Pentecost and the Assumption of Our Lady. He explains that these icons are chosen because

---

[199] Freestanding icons specifically for personal devotion are distinct from the liturgical cycles on the walls.

they help us to meditate on the mystery of God in the flesh as a preparation for the Eucharist.

His friend, who cannot afford such a grand cycle in his church and who, anyway, wants the feast day icons available for the parishioners to venerate, is building up a set of icons which he keeps in the vestry and displays on a special stand at each big feast or season, so that the icons change at the same time as the vestments and are made a focus of special prayers, such as the Pentecost novena, when the Ascension icon is displayed, and May, when the icon of the mother of God is displayed.

The priest is asked where the icons of the Stations of the Cross are. He explains that they come out into the main church during Lents, so that they can be a special focus of prayer then, but that during the year they are kept in the side chapel of the Passion, where he now takes us. The chapel is emulsioned in deep purple and blue abstract panels and hung with the Stations. One of the party expresses surprise because the icons start with the Entry into Jerusalem and include the foot-washing and the Last Supper. The priest explains that he had discussed it with the parish, and they wanted Stations which would take them through the entire liturgy of Holy Week and could be a focus of prayer during this time, when more of the congregation come to the Divine Office.

He then leads us into the adjoining small chapel of the Resurrection, which contains the Blessed Sacrament and is set up for private prayer. Here the walls are light-toned emulsion, with a faux white/cream/beige granite effect, and a big icon of the Spice-bearers at the empty tomb behind the Blessed Sacrament, which is on a big plinth of natural uncut stone, with just the top and bottom sawn off to allow it to stand. The effect is freeing and radiant.

After a little time in front of the Sacrament, he leads us into the final chapel – where the children have their liturgy. This chapel has a big icon of the child Jesus teaching in the Temple and is a golden room – rich abstract of gold-toned emulsion paint, but the rays on Christ's garments are real gold leaf, to show that he is really God.

I should add that these side chapels are nothing very elaborate – just a screened off area of his "consecrated warehouse", with the walls formed by big plasterboard sections; nevertheless the combined effect of the emulsioned abstract design walls and the large icons on plywood actually help to break up what would otherwise be a forbiddingly large space, not conducive to personal prayer.

We come outside into the daylight, full of the glimpse we have seen of a world beyond this world. We will go back by ourselves to pray quietly later.

Sister Petra Clare is from a farming family in Shropshire, born of a Welsh Methodist father and an Anglican mother. She gained an Honours Diploma in Art and Design and went on to study the icon. In 1973, she entered Anglican religious life, converted to Catholicism in 1985 and became a Consecrated Virgin a year later at Prinknash Abbey where she lived a semi-solitary life in the grounds. In 1992 she received permission to make Benedictine formation at St Cecilia's Abbey, Ryde, with a view to forming a monastic skete. In 1995, she was invited by the then Bishop Mario Conti to start the foundation at the old presbytery at Marydale in Cannich, where she continues to write and to teach icons.

THE BISHOP AS PASTOR

BISHOP MAURICE TAYLOR

Hello. I am Fiona. I am well. How are you?

It will be really nice to see you again and I suppose you are wondering why you are going to see me. We are making our confirmation – but we have one problem. We haven't got a bishop and we were wondering if you could possibly confirm us. I really hope you can come because we really need you.

Yours sincerely and the peace of Christ be with you.

From Fiona your friend xxxxx

P.S. Come at 7 p.m.

Sometimes I have invited children, when preparing for the sacraments, to write to me. The letter quoted was one sent to me some years ago and I enjoyed receiving it because it is amusing and because it is written in a very down-to-earth way, without a sign of the awe with which bishops are sometimes regarded.

What is the popular conception of a bishop? It used to be of a rather remote and somewhat forbidding figure who appeared in a parish once every few years to do confirmations but who, otherwise, was little known by "ordinary" people. Inaccessible, even unapproachable.

In my own years as bishop, that remoteness has largely gone, I hope. Even so, some people are still surprised when they phone the diocesan office and discover that it is I who am at the end of the line. When occasionally someone phones and asks hesitantly if it is possible to speak to the bishop's secretary, it gives me some perverse pleasure to say who I am and to ask if I will do.

The Second Vatican Council speaks of bishops as those who "have been appointed by the Holy See and are successors of the apostles as pastors of souls.... Bishops have been made true and authentic teachers of the faith, pontiffs and shepherds". "The order of bishops", the Council continues, "is the successor to the college of the apostles in teaching authority and pastoral role"*(Decree on the Bishops' Pastoral Office in the Church,* nos. 2 and 4).

The Code of Canon Law (canon 375 §1) states: "By divine institution, bishops succeed the apostles through the Holy Spirit who is given to them. They are consecrated pastors in the Church to be the teachers of doctrine, the priests of sacred worship and the ministers of governance."

The *Catechism of the Catholic Church* repeats this teaching, citing the various authoritative documents and situating a bishop's ministry within the long and living tradition of the Church.

It is evident that the pastoral ministry is an essential for bishops, that a bishop must be a shepherd (i.e. pastor). And even if sometimes the documents seem to divide a bishop's duties into different categories such as teacher, pontiff and shepherd, really everything that a bishop does should be seen as part of his pastoral ministry. I hope that that is not an unjustifiable extension of the term "pastoral ministry".

Visiting a primary school in Galloway diocese, I once asked a class if any of them would like to be priests. A few male hands went up. When I asked if any would like to be bishops, practically everyone, girls as well as boys, put their hands up! Had that any wider significance? I suspect not. But I have also been asked "How did you become a bishop?" Well, to satisfy such curiosity, here's how.

One day in 1981 I answered the phone in Our Lady of Lourdes presbytery in East Kilbride where I was parish priest. The foreign voice at the other end identified himself as the Apostolic Delegate and said he wanted to see me. When I said that I was very busy the following week and would the week after be time enough, he said "No, not next week. This week – and don't tell anyone about this." So I made a surreptitious journey to London and was met at Heathrow by the Delegate's secretary and driven to the Apostolic Delegation (my first ever visit). I was put in a room by myself but in a few minutes Archbishop Bruno Heim appeared, looked me up and down, and said that the Holy See wanted to appoint me as bishop of Galloway. "Do you accept?"

This was the climax of a process that had been going on without my knowledge. My predecessor in Galloway, Bishop Joseph McGee, had submitted his resignation, the Delegate had sought the names of possible "candidates" (a strange word, when you are unaware of what is going on), had received detailed information about some of them and had then sent to the Holy See three names (along with details and his own recommendation). The Roman Congregation for Bishops, having sought the

Pope's agreement, informed Archbishop Heim of its choice.

The criteria used for selecting one person from among the "candidates" are not difficult to imagine and, in most cases, the choice is a good one. But, like every newly appointed bishop, I had no previous experience. Nowadays the Vatican runs a short course which recently appointed bishops can attend but I really think that more could and should be done, especially about "being a bishop in Scotland" and not just "being a bishop". True enough, you learn by experience but perhaps a few of the mistakes and omissions of inexperience would be avoided if there were some kind of training offered and accepted, locally as well as in Rome.

So what does a bishop *do*? Does his life consist in confirmations, meetings, visits to Rome, and signing documents? Priests get annoyed if someone suggests that they must have an easy time because they work only one day a week. Bishops can be suspected of something similar; or, on the other hand, of being so extremely busy that they have to turn down every invitation that may come. People look at the "Bishops' Engagements" column in the Catholic newspapers and marvel how busy we are. But if you look a little calmly at his published engagements and calculate the amount of time they will take up, you would have to conclude that a bishop must have a fairly relaxed life. So there has to be more – and there is!

However, rather than attempting to give a detailed list of a bishop's activities, I suggest we look at the matter from the point of view of the various ways in which a bishop is in relationship with others and how these relationships have to be fostered.

The bishop has to sustain the whole diocese as the local church; he has to maintain contact with each priest in the diocese (and each priest has his own needs, gifts and commitments). The bishop has to keep in touch with the various religious congregations and their members resident in the diocese. He has to be available to the people of the diocese, not only when an individual or a group asks to meet him, but in constant and manifold contact with people in the different parishes.

Despite that catalogue of duties I have never liked to be called "the boss" because that is not what I want to be nor the relationship that I see myself having with the priests and laity of the diocese.

In addition to the bishop's work in the diocese, he also has to be in close and frequent contact with the other Scottish bishops (as a member of the Bishops' Conference of Scotland). Clearly he is also in relationship with the Holy Father (and his officials in the Roman Curia) and indeed with his brother bishops throughout the world because, in union with the Pope and in various ways, each bishop shares in the responsibility of caring for the worldwide Church. Every bishop has these relationships external to the particular diocesan church which he leads. In addition it is not uncommon for a bishop to have specific responsibilities in some area of service outside the diocese – which entails travel to meetings abroad and a great deal of unseen work at home. In my own case this has been as a member of the Episcopal Board, and latterly chairman, of the International Commission on English in the Liturgy.

I have spoken of a bishop's life and work as being a series of relationships, and that is true. But the relationships exist because the Church is a community or, rather, a community of communities. You cannot be a

Catholic, or a Christian for that matter, and be a loner! Jesus didn't establish a Church of individuals acting as individuals but of disciples in close relationship to one another. In recent times moreover we have begun to speak not only of community as an essential of the Church, but of *communion*. Communion adds something special to community, something that we are only slowly realising but which is all to do with the mutual relationship that Christ has with us, both as individuals and as the Church. It is that reality of divine love which engenders unity, a love and unity which God shares with us through Jesus Christ (divine and human) and the Holy Spirit who loves and inspires. So the "Communion of Saints" is not only those who are already in heaven or waiting next door but also, as we used to call it, the Church Militant on earth (although the bellicose-sounding adjective is not frequently used nowadays!).

The Vatican issued a booklet a few years ago on the priesthood. It was for and about priests but the title is equally applicable to bishops: *Teacher of the Word, Minister of the Sacraments, Leader of the Community*. I hope that, as a bishop, I can group my pastoral ministry and responsibilities under the same three heads.

Teacher of the Word

The teaching ministry of a bishop (and indeed of any disciple of Jesus) can be described as sharing the Good News with faith, conviction and enthusiasm. In many ways, this is a bishop's primary duty.

> Outstanding among the foremost functions of bishops is the preaching of the Gospel. Bishops are heralds of the faith – they bring new disciples to Christ. They are authentic teachers,

teachers authorised by Christ. (Second Vatican
Council, *Dogmatic Constitution on the Church,
Lumen Gentium,* 25)

The diocesan bishop is bound to teach and
illustrate to the faithful the truths of faith which
are to be believed and applied to behaviour.
(Code of Canon Law, canon 386§1)

Teaching is certainly a constant, daily responsibility but
to be effective it is fairly obvious that a bishop has to be
aware of those whom he hopes to teach and to make his
message capable of being "heard" in the full sense of the
word.

It is sometimes said that bishops could be better
communicators if they were to avoid theological language
and speak in a way that "ordinary people" can understand.
I recognise the problem in myself. It is the difficulty of
putting fairly profound theological ideas into words which
people can follow – and, at the same time, avoiding the
danger of inaccuracies. Happy the bishop who has such a
gift!

Different bishops have different ways of teaching the
faith, proclaiming the Good News, evangelising,
witnessing (whichever word or phrase you want to use). In
my own years as bishop I have tried to spend each
weekend systematically visiting every parish in the diocese
(there are forty-seven in Galloway), preaching the homily
at each Mass. I visit each Catholic primary school
annually, going from class to class; visits to secondary
schools are more difficult to arrange (and I would have
liked to have been oftener in them).

In the diocese we also have *The Galloway Newsletter,*
which offers me an opportunity, each month, to include

something about the practice of the faith (in a fairly wide sense). A twice-yearly diocesan pastoral council and occasional letters or other written communications to the people of the diocese are other vehicles of evangelisation. Personally I have no great enthusiasm for writing and issuing pastoral letters "to be read at all Masses ... ." But of course I am happy to transmit to the people of Galloway whatever messages, letters etc. are issued by, or on behalf of, the Bishops' Conference of Scotland.

The bishop has of course to be committed to ecumenism, to promoting Christian unity and fostering good relations among Christians of different traditions. This duty will, from time to time, engage him in sharing his Catholic faith in order to clarify, to correct misunderstandings, to state the Church's teaching and thus, in a gentle and non-proselytising manner, to exercise his office of teacher. So often ignorance of the Church's doctrine, rather than outright rejection of it, causes the obstacles to good ecumenical relations and development.

Occasionally I get letters asking for an explanation of some aspect of Catholic teaching. Of course I am happy to oblige as well as I can although requests from someone doing a school project to "tell me what the Catholic Church teaches" or seeking a full explanation of the Trinity can be a little difficult.

Sometimes I try to reflect on how "teaching" (whether by bishop, priest, parent, teacher, another etc.) is received nowadays. It seems to me that there is some interest in hearing more about the Scriptures (since in the sacred books there is so much more than meets the eye) and the Church's history. There is some limited interest in the Church's social teaching, little interest in what is called dogmatic or systematic theology (the doctrines of the Church) since we are not in an age in which controversy or even discussion on such matters flourishes, an acceptance of the old moral certainties but a silent reluctance (even refusal?) to follow the Church's teaching on certain more contemporary (and very important) moral issues. Perhaps that summary is not only judgmental but also too pessimistic. If it is, I shall be delighted.

Minister of the Sacraments
Celebrating the liturgy is probably the area of a bishop's pastoral ministry with which people are most familiar. There is the famous statement in *Sacrosanctum Concilium*, the Second Vatican Council's *Constitution on the Liturgy*, (no. 41) that the local Church is most truly such when the bishop presides at the celebration of the Eucharist, with the priests concelebrating and with the participation of deacons, other ministers and the faithful.

That particular situation occurs best in my experience at the annual Mass of Chrism with the presence and participation of the great majority of the priests and of people from every parish in the diocese. The occasion is not merely the Mass at which the bishop consecrates the chrism and blesses the oil of catechumens and the oil of the sick for use in the diocese during the succeeding twelve months. It is also a celebration of the ministerial priesthood of Christ in which bishop and priests participate through their sacred ordination.

In 1994 I was recovering from eye surgery that saved the sight of my one "good" eye (having gone blind in my left eye in 1993) but I was as yet hardly able to see and was feeling distinctly weak. That Holy Week, the late Cardinal Winning was kind enough to offer to preside at the Mass of Chrism but I felt fit enough to concelebrate. He blessed the oils but encouraged me to lead that part of the rite at which the priests rededicate themselves, the laity promise them their support and the bishop asks everyone to pray for him. I had difficulty reading the text but I shall never forget the emotion of that moment. It brought home to me the importance, the intimacy and the beautiful reality of those relationships in which the bishop stands and of which I wrote earlier.

There are innumerable times I have felt so privileged to celebrate the Church's liturgy and to be the chief liturgist of the diocese – the parish Masses each weekend, school Masses, special occasion Masses, Confirmations and first Holy Communions, funeral Masses … . Two liturgical celebrations have been really special and dear to me: the Easter Vigil and Ordinations.

Year by year I have found the Easter Vigil ever more impressive and challenging. The climax of the Sacred Triduum at which the Church commemorates and relives its Saviour's paschal mystery of death and resurrection, the Easter Vigil is so rich in content that we can never exhaust, nor tire of, its significance. This is probably not the place to go into more detail but let me make two points. First, one often hears grown-ups talking about young people, especially those who cease going to Mass, and how "there ought to be a ceremony of dedication (or something similar) for teenagers". I believe that it is not only teenagers who need such an opportunity but every one of us – and that we already have the required opportunity (recognised by so few) – the Easter Vigil and especially that moment when we renew our baptismal promises. Could not the awareness of this fact (I hope it's a fact) attract more people and give them reason to attend and appreciate the greatest liturgy of the year? Second, although we can renew our baptismal promises at Mass on Easter Sunday morning, I feel that that is a poor substitute because the whole context found in the Easter Vigil, the atmosphere, the drama of the blessing of the baptismal water and the initiation of new members, is missing.

The other very special liturgy for me is, of course, an Ordination. To be empowered to transmit the Sacrament of Holy Orders, to be in the unbroken line of apostolic succession since the time of Jesus himself, to be God's instrument whereby the ministerial priesthood of Christ is continued into the next generation – this has always been for me a breathtaking, almost unnerving, experience. Need I say more? Only that I thank God to have been allowed to be one link in an unbroken chain that enables the Church to continue its life, its mission and its work. God does indeed make use of weak, unworthy, human instruments.

Leader of the Community

Especially nowadays words like jurisdiction, authority and power need to be used sparingly and sensitively. They are too easily associated with the misuse or abuse of power, with tyranny and unjust oppression. Besides, Jesus used his gifts and his mission in order to serve others, to set them free, to unite, to reconcile, to encourage. So a gentle phrase such as "leader of the community" is one which I like for a bishop or for a priest, each in his own role.

So how does a bishop carry out the ministry of leadership in the diocesan community? In hundreds of ways, mainly humdrum, some more public. Leaving aside his work as teacher and his work as chief liturgist, the bishop has daily opportunities to exercise leadership. He has to encourage, to affirm, perhaps occasionally to correct, to try to be an example of Christ-like goodness (how conscious I am of my failures in this respect). The bishop has to be approachable and accessible to any and all, to lead and work with people as they are and not as he would like them to be, to be a man of ideas and vision, to be able to inspire others with that vision; and, at the same time, to listen to others' proposals, suggestions, criticisms and to be willing to work collaboratively, in close and friendly co-operation with others.

As I was writing the foregoing lines, I was aware how far, in my own case, the reality falls short of what it should be. But people are usually very understanding and tolerant; and God will have to be as well.

The word "bishop" derives from the Greek *Episkopos,* which means an overseer. To have kindly oversight of all the people of the diocese and to enable them to be what they should be and do what they ought is the bishop's work and privilege. "Oversight" in English has two meanings. I thank God for what I have managed in one sense of the word and ask pardon for what, through oversight in its other sense, I did not do. Or, to put that in slightly different terms, a bishop has to oversee rather than to overlook.

However, as already noted, in 1993 I lost the sight in my left eye and that has taught me the value of being able, or forced, to turn a blind eye now and again!

Leadership, service, oversight – the bishop has to take care of everyone in the diocese. Let's not overlook the fact that that includes himself. I have always wanted to be seen and regarded as a normal human being with some good qualities and skills but also with the inevitable weaknesses and frailties that are to be found in us all. Leaving aside the moral aspects, we have to recognise that a bishop doesn't have superhuman physical strength or endurance or stamina. He needs rest, relaxation, recreation like any other human being. He needs to take care of himself. I think it is easy, for others and also for a bishop himself, to forget this. The temptation is to be a workaholic and to allow oneself to be always on duty and on call. I know – from my own personal experience! And it's not merely a matter of being a slave to duty. There is a strong element of job satisfaction involved, because being a bishop is indeed a very fulfilling role in life and it's not difficult to convince oneself of being needed, even indispensable! So, you people out there, help us not to take ourselves so seriously that we begin to feel that way!

I want to be a normal human being; I want to be myself and to be seen and known as such. I don't want to wear a mask, making myself out to be what I am not. For that I need human contact, frankness, openness and, at times, correction!

So, at the end of all this, am I happy to be a bishop? Yes, undoubtedly. And why?   First of all – and I hope this does not sound too pious or predictable – because I truly believe that I have been given a task to carry out that is according to God's will and for the benefit of people. To be certain of that reassures me constantly and makes me deeply grateful. And it ought to, and does, ensure a high degree of job satisfaction. There are other reasons to be happy and contented, apart from the many individual events and encounters that can be so affirming. To be a bishop is to be someone who has been given great responsibility – and that is welcome. Even more, it is to be someone who is trusted – by one's superiors and fellow-bishops, by the priests, religious and laity and, we can truly say, by Jesus Christ in whose priesthood and ministry we participate.   I have had the privilege of knowing so many people, of being given glimpses of their amazing goodness, of being admitted into friendship and trust. For all this, I praise God.

Don't conclude that a bishop's life is heaven on earth. There are crosses to bear. A fairly obvious one is the loss of the close contacts that I enjoyed when I was a parish priest. As one's "parish" becomes a diocese, one inevitably loses much of the daily intimacy. It can sometimes be quite lonely as a bishop, not only because confidentiality can be restricting but also because people can understandably presume that you must be busy and they don't want to intrude! There have also, of course, been crosses that have caused more acute pain or anxiety.

One of these has been the worry of scarcities – the decreasing number of priests, the dearth of seminary applicants, falling numbers of practising Catholics, shortage of money to carry out necessary maintenance and repairs and to pay for much-needed pastoral projects (ongoing education in the faith, post-graduate courses, youth, social care, employment of pastoral assistants of many kinds). To an extent, such hopes have had to remain unfulfilled. And that has been a disappointment.

Another matter which I dislike - I have always found the business of asking priests to transfer from one parish to another to be difficult and unpleasant. I am aware that it can so easily be seen as an exercise of power, that the proposal is viewed as unwelcome by the priest and by the parishioners he is leaving, that it does demand sacrifice, renunciation, letting go and all the attendant emotional strain and upset etc. Believe me, I have never relished having to embark on the process.

It says something about me, I think, that I don't like criticism, whether justified or not. And when, as has sometimes happened, such criticism gets into the press – well it's not pleasant but one has to try to accept it and let God be the judge. So there are hardships or crosses in being a bishop – some brought on by one's own folly and errors, some not – but it would be foolish to imagine that anyone's life is, or should be, always tranquil and trouble-free. And, without a doubt, the balance between fulfilment and grief is clearly and heavily in credit.

As I come to the end of this essay and to the end of my term as a diocesan bishop, I should like to express a view on the Church and to make a heartfelt plea.

The Church is God's; it is founded by Jesus and sustained by the Spirit to enable our Saviour to be present and active in the world. So it is not going to fail. But the Church is also human and needs always to be open to change and to growth. In our own time, the Second Vatican Council was a God-given, Spirit-driven means for change and growth, unexpected, surprising, disturbing for many, but undeniable. Some of the riches that came to the Church through the Council have been acknowledged, "unpacked" and gratefully accepted.

But the Council's graces are not yet fully realised. We are in the midst of a long, sometimes painful, process — some of us ahead of others, but none yet having reached the end of our journey of discovery.

Let's not be afraid or faint-hearted. Don't let us turn back, as the Israelites wanted to go back to the security of slavery in Egypt. Let's not be "restorationists" in that sense. That is not Christ's plan for us. Our Lord brought us the gift of being free, as God's adopted children; free, above all, from fear. "*Duc in altum*" John Paul echoes Christ's words to the Apostles. Do not be afraid, don't turn back, launch into the deep where Jesus wants us to be. It is only there that we can fulfil his plan of bringing his life to the world and the world to him.

Bishop Maurice Taylor was born in Hamilton in 1926. He was educated in Hamilton, Glasgow and Motherwell before studying at the Pontifical Gregorian University in Rome, where he was ordained priest in July 1950 for the Diocese of

Motherwell. He subsequently gained a Doctorate in Theology in Rome. As well as working as a parish priest in parishes in the Diocese of Motherwell, he taught at St Peter's College in Cardross and was Rector of the Royal Scots College in Valladolid, Spain from 1965 – 1974. In 1981, he was ordained Bishop of Galloway. He is Vice-president of the Catholic Institute for International Affairs and Chairman of the International Commission on English in the Liturgy.